Robi Engler

Animation Cinema Workshop
from motion to emotion

Author
Robi Engler

Publisher
**John Libbey
Publishing Ltd.
3 Leicester Road
New Barnet, Herts
EN5 5EW
United Kingdom
www.johnlibbey.com**

**© 2015
Animagination
John Libbey Publishing Ltd.**

**Animagination
70, Chemin de la Rueyre
CH-1008 Jouxtens-Mézery
Switzerland
animagination@bluewin.ch**

ISBN: 9780 86196 720 9

Distributed Worldwide by
**Indiana University Press
Herman B Wells Library - 350
1320 E. 10th St.
Bloomington
IN 47405, USA
www.iupress.indiana.edu**

Printed in China by
1010 Printing International Ltd

An Eye for the Dragon

Robi Engler

Born in St-Gall, Switzerland on November 18th in the Year of the Dragon. Robi Engler graduated from the School of Fine Arts, did an apprenticeship as a graphic artist and worked at various advertising agencies in London and Paris. He then studied animated film making at the Ecole Nationale Supérieur des Arts Decoratifs in Paris with Professor Jean-Pierre Deseuzes.

In 1975, Robi Engler founded the Animagination Company and established himself as an independent animation filmmaker in Lausanne, Switzerland. He directed a great number of animated films for Swiss-French Television, as well as advertising spots, scientific and educational films for TV and cinema.

He is scriptwriter and director of animated films and television serials and made the first Swiss feature-length animation film. He is a Guest Professor at various art schools and training centres in Beijing, Berlin, Calcutta, Fleurville, Katmandu, Lausanne, Lisbon, Lugano, Lusaka, Lyon, Nimbo, Saxon, Singapore, Tainan, Taipei, Vientiane .

Abstract of Filmography

The Study of Animal Biology *3 min*
Metamorphosis *3 min*
If I were... If I had...*8 x 5 min*
Poursuit *5 min*
Open wide your eyes *26 x 5 min*
Highway *10 min*
Alice-Patch & Crack *8 x 5 min*
Zoé *13 x 5 min*

Denty / Blendi *13 x 5 min*
The Volbecs *26 x 5 min*
The Z'animals *52 x 2 min 30*
English with Victor *Language course*
Tramway 12 *8 min*
Globi and the Stolen Shadows *80 min*
Traces *13 x 26 min*
Twindows *6 min 30*
Tao *7 min 30, work in progress*

Robi Engler

Animation Cinema Workshop Film_Video_Digital

from motion to emotion

Preface by Sir Peter Ustinov

Postface by Nicole Salomon

John Libbey Publishing Ltd.

This page is for your own drawings.

Content

Thanks

This book would not have been written without the great interest in animation from students all over the world and in particular from

Atelier AAA, Annecy, France
Beijing Film Academy BFA, Beijing, China
Centre de Recontre et d'Animation CRA, Renens, Switzerland
Cepta Television, Singapore, Republic of Singapore
Chitrabani Media Research Centre, Calcutta, India
College of Science and Technology Ningbo University, Ningbo, China
Deutsche Film und Fernsehakademie DFFB, Berlin, Germany
Ecole Cantonale d'Art de Lausanne ECAL, Lausanne, Switzerland
Ecole Emile-Cohl, Lyon, France
Ecole professionnelle des arts contemporains EPAC, Saxon, Switzerland
La Distylerie, Fleurville, France
Qingdao University of Science and Technology QUST, Quindao, China
Radio Televisao Portuguesa RTP, Lisbon, Portugal
Tainan National University of the Arts TNNUA, Tainan, Taiwan
Taipei National University of the Arts TNUA, Taipei, Taiwan
Television Training Center TTC, Berlin, Germany
Television Training Center, Katmandu, Nepal
Television Training Center, Vientiane, Laos
Zambian Institute for Mass Communication, Lusaka, Zambia

Special Thanks

for the opportunity to teach at TNNUA

Yu Wei-Cheng
Film Director and Professor
Tainan National University of the Arts

for their contribution to this book

Ionel Luca
Animator and Professor
Cereleum School of Art
Lausanne, Switzerland

Samuel Chen
The maker of portable Tracing Boards
Mascot Technology Inc
Tainan, Taiwan

I was not happy at school.

*I was afraid of several things -
the words, the figures, the facts.*

*Once the school left me behind,
I made peace with the words and they
became my friends.*

*As for the figures, I discovered the
pocket calculator.*

*As for the facts, I became aware that
nobody did know them all.*

I was never afraid of the pictures.

*I would have learned a lot more if
Mr. Engler would have been
alive at the time -
with many fewer spelling errors!*

Je n'étais pas heureux à l'école

J'avais peur de plusieurs choses —

Les mots, les chiffres, les faits

Une fois que j'ai laissé l'école derrière moi, je me suis
réconcilié avec les mots, qui sont devenus mes amis.

Pour les chiffres, j'ai découvert l'ordinateur de poche.

Quant aux faits, je me suis rendu compte que personne ne
les connait en tout cas

Je n'ai
~~J'avais~~ jamais eu peur de l'image

ERREUR

J'aurais appris beaucoup plus si M. Engler avait été
déjà en vie à cette époque — avec beaucoup moins
de fautes d'orthographe !

ENGLER

USTINOV (13 ANS)

This page is for your own drawings.

Introduction

Keep animating !

Animated Cinema is a never ending procedure of learning. There is only one way to learn, it's by doing. You have no choice: Keep animating !

Spring 2015   Robi Engler

Animation: The Total Art

With the arrival of digital electronics, the evolution of animation techniques has turned into a revolution. During the first ten years of digital technologies, more technical changes have emerged in animation than in the hundred years of traditional filmmaking. Since the history of animated films has always been conditioned by technical inventions, the near future will hold some nice surprises.

However, this book is more about what has not changed in animation: the classic animation techniques, the content of films, and how to turn them into creative and appealing movies. Most of the basic principles, the language of animation, the picture composition, as well as the creation of the soundtrack are not necessarily affected by new technologies. It is a challenging and permanent task for every animator not only to follow the mainstream technical evolution, but also to invent new ways to catch the public's attention.

I like to look at animation as a total art, the perfect synthesis of many forms of art: pictorial fine arts for animation techniques, music and sound effects for time and rhythm, dance for movement and space, theatre for acting, and literature for narrative structures of the film's content. Making animated films therefore means collaboration with artists from all these fields. The animator is a kind of go-between, situated at the crossroads between these fields. And, I am happy and proud to work with artists from all these fields.

Spring 2013   Robi Engler

Most Important: The Content

The least that you can say is that the technical evolution of film animation, and particularly so in the field of computer assisted animation, has not stopped since the first edition of this book in 1981.

Animation is by definition a moving trade. Hard disk and digital video tapes are the new supporting media. Just as film stock and video tapes are used to record images, the animator uses this support medium to capture and store the created images and sounds.

However, the basic principles of animation, the thinking and creation of the content, and how to transmit it to the audience, remains the same. If too much energy is occupied by the technical challenges of the new images, the filmmaker tends to forget the most important thing: the interest of the audience in animated films is not the technical support but its **content.**

Spring 1993   Robi Engler

Animation Fever: Catch It!

Animation is to me not so much a profession as a disease - a disease which infects almost all professional animators. Since nobody is really germ-proof, you might as well get infected. The first sign that you have animation fever is when you forget all about real time. As your infection grows, you may find yourself getting up in the middle of the night with the compulsion to jot down an idea you have just dreamed about, convinced that you are about to produce a masterpiece of animation. So there you are, hopelessly ill, and you will probably never want to become quite normal again. To spread the germ of animation fever is the principal purpose of every animation workshop.

This manual is a résumé of my experience made while working with many future animators. It is intended to help you with your own work and to make it easier to to pass your knowledge on to others.

Spring 1981   Robi Engler

Animation as a Tool...

Animation is a tool in the head and hands of the animator. Just as a knife is a tool that can be used to sculpt wood, to cut bread, to chop vegetables or to kill somebody, animation can be used for a variety of tasks.

Animation as an Entertaining Tool

This is the origin of animated filmmaking. All the early animators from Emile Cohl to Tex Avery were entertainers, performers and actors. It's a really big challenge for an animator to entertain audiences, to make them laugh and cry.

Animation as an Informational Tool

We got so used to the advertising spots on TV that we don't even remark on them anymore. Making advertising spots that the audience will notice is big challenge and great fun for every animator. Besides, you can make a lot of money, but it can also be very stressful, because there are airtime deadlines to be respected.

Animation as a Creative Tool

Artists from various artistic backgrounds -- painting, sculpture, dance, music -- have been tempted to use animation as a creative tool. Their desire to make static images move, to blow life into lifeless things, is as old as mankind; animation makes that dream come true.

Animation as a Teaching / Educational Tool

Animation is particularly effective when used as a teaching tool. The saying *A picture is worth a thousand words* is particularly true when it comes to explain complicated scientific procedures or teach languages. Educational animation is sometimes labeled as an edutainment media.

Animation as a Learning Tool

There is a saying: *Tell me and I will forget, show me and I will remember, let me do it and I will understand.* This holds true for participants of animation workshops, to develop their skills and competencies. In animation workshops, participants surely learn to animate, but the principal goal of those films is not so much the result but the making of it. The participants have to master the subject before they can make the film and will learn to express themselves in a creative and non-verbal way.

Animation as a Social Tool

Creating an animated film can help people who are disabled or having trouble overcoming a particularly difficult situation in their lives, to bounce back and stand again on their own feet. By working in a team, working with perseverance and learning to never give up is a way to be proud of what you do and who you are. Animation for Social re-insertion!

Animation as a Window... as a Mirror...

Animation as a Window

In commissioned films, the cinema is often used as a window or a door to a world unknown to the audience. An informational film will make things clear and understandable. Like a telescope, a magnifying glass, or a microscope, it can bring things nearer to the viewer, show phenomena that would otherwise be invisible to the human eye. Like a map, animation can show complicated situations as a whole and put loose things in relation one to another.

For most human beings, the first time they dive into the deep sea or take a trip to outer space will be with the help of documentary films. Today's 3-D movies let you swim among fishes and sea monsters. They also can scare you to death by taking you up in the air, over cliffs and breathtaking abysses.

Animation as a Mirror

Very different are animated films that act as mirrors. They also take you on a trip, but it's a trip into inner space. Animation as a mirror reveals the hidden face of the one who animates. Like a painter shows his feelings and emotions in a self-portrait, the animator, by the means of animation as a creative tool lets the audience come into his or her inner world.

It's common knowledge that the eyes are the windows to the human soul. Indeed, by *looking into the mirror* the animator will discover his inner landscape. Imaginary landscapes are necessarily mind-scapes. Ways of thinking, state of mind, spiritual attitudes and approaches, mind-benders and revelations, mind-readers and mind-setters, and keys to the door to inner imaginary worlds.

Everyone has experienced their own mindscapes, either in dreams, adventurous phantasms, hallucinations, fantasy, extreme euphoric happiness, or deprecating sadness. To give form and to communicate these emotions to other humans is the *raison d'être* of every artist, and particularly the task of the animation artist.

This page is for your own drawings.

0100_Basic Equipment_Material

This chapter is about how to use cameras and computers as recording devices for handmade artwork, rather than creating images and sounds with a computer program.

It is commonly thought that animation is a highly technical business. This chapter doesn't prove otherwise, but will assure you that even fairly complicated technical equipment can be understood and handled by non-technicians. There is no need to be especially technically-minded to load a camera, to change a light bulb, or to format a hard disk.

If there is anything too complicated to understand, do not hesitate to ask a technician. You'll find that technicians are often just as interested in animation as you, and you'll get to know the skills behind which is the right *button to push*. Animation is basically teamwork, but it is most important that you understand the functioning and handling of the equipment you work with.

Basically there are three supporting kinds of media used to record, store, and distribute images and sounds: Film, Video and Digital.

01_Film
Mechanical, optical, recording to film. Chemical processing. Screening with film projector or editing table.

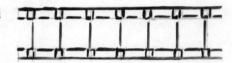

02_Video
Optical, magnetic recording to videotape. Immediate playback on a video monitor or TV set.

03_Digital
Digital recording to a computer hard disk or to digital videotape. Immediate playback on a computer screen or projector.

This manual is not intended to make you a perfect technician. However, you should know how to maintain your equipment at a basic level and not waste your energy, time and money with unnecessary trips to a repair shop.

Preventive maintenance is the most important; it means spotting potential trouble before it becomes a problem. Cleaning is the most effective maintenance procedure. Every instruction manual that comes with the equipment has ample instructions on how to clean and maintain it.

Besides cleaning you should develop some basic skills - to change a fuse, repair a cable - and know when you should call the repair shop.

There is no hierarchy to distinguish between the different supporting media of recording. None of the media are more valuable than the others, nor is any one easier or harder to handle. Everybody can handle a film camera just as well as computer program.

The important thing is to know the different possibilities of each support medium, to explore its advantages, and make the best use of it.

The choice of production format is conditioned by the distribution of the film. For the animator the technical side of the format is less important than you might think. Whether you press the button of a 35mm camera or of a computer device, from an animation point of view, it doesn't make any difference. The important thing is not the technical equipment, but what's behind it: **the Animator!**

Approximate conversation table

5 mm	/ 0.5 cm	= ¼ inch
10 mm	/ 1 cm	= ½ inch
25 mm	/ 2.5 cm	= 1 inch
50 mm	/ 5 cm	= 2 inches
100 mm	/ 10 cm	= 4 inches
200 mm	/ 20 cm	= 8 inches

0101_Recording on Film

Mechanical, Optical, and Chemical Procedures

Film production formats and equipment (35mm, 16mm and Super-8mm) are standardized the world over. The exchange of a film is therefore easy, but it is increasingly difficult to find film projectors and especially people who can properly operate them!

Tremendous progress in the quality of film stocks and film equipment, and the growing costs of these same items, has produced a tendency to use smaller formats. This means that people who traditionally worked with 35mm moved to 16mm, and 16mm producers tended to move to Super-8 equipment.

Motion Picture Films

Films for movie cameras are available in various formats, in colour or black-and-white, and in negative or reversal. Film formats range from the extinct 8mm to the ultra-panavision of 70mm. The formats that are interesting for today's filmmaker are Super 8mm, 16mm and 35mm.

Super-8 film uses 8mm stock in cassette form. Super-8 film is available in black-and-white or colour. Colour film prices usually include processing by the manufacturer. All super-8 film is reversal stock. Prints and enlargements can be made from the original. One edge is perforated and a magnetic sound track can be added on the opposite edge. *Super-8 Aspect Ratio 1:1.45*

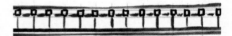

16mm film is available in black-and-white or colour, negative or reversal, and single- or double-perforated. Prints, enlargements or reductions can be made from either negative or reversal stock. A magnetic or optical sound track is added on the opposite side to the perforation on the single perforated film.
Standard 16mm Aspect Ratio 1:1.33
Super 16mm Aspect Ratio 1:1.85

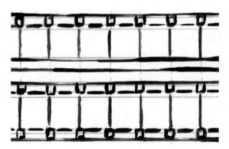

35mm film is available only in negative, and either black-and-white or colour. Prints or reductions can be made from the original. It has four perforations per frame on both edges. *35mm Standard Film Aspect Ratio 1:1.30*
For sound films part of the picture is masked off on one side to receive the optical sound track. *35mm Academy Aspect Ratio 1:1.33*
Wide screen uses the same width as academy but top and bottom are cut off to obtain a larger picture. *Wide Screen Aspect Ratio 1:1.85, 1:1.75 or 1:1.66.*

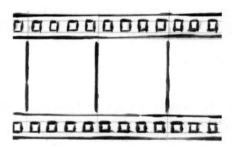

Recording: Film Camera

For animation any type of movie camera with a single frame release system will do. However, it is very helpful if the camera is equipped with the following:
01_Close-up lens, able to focus on a field of 8 x 10 cm
02_Zoom lens
03_Frame counter
04_Reflex viewfinder, to permit precise viewing of the artwork
05_Forward and reverse movement of film

For more professional purposes, you can use a camera with a shuttle movement and registration system to keep the film in multiple exposures at an exact position, or a variable opening shutter with a scale for fade-ins and fade-outs as well as dissolves.

The function of a film camera is to record onto light sensitive film stock the light and movement that comes through the lens. In cinema, just like in photography, the image is the result of the successful mix of optics and chemistry. The incoming light falls onto the fresh film emulsion. Millions of silver grains on the emulsion undergo a transformation according to the amount of light they receive. This procedure is called exposure. The result of this exposition, the film image, can only be seen after chemical processing in the film laboratory.

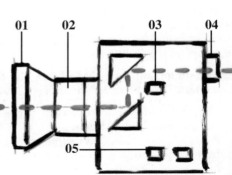

Rotating Shutter

The primordial condition for a successful recording is the steady position of the film stock during the exposure. The invention of the intermittent mechanics and film perforation made it possible to maintain the film in a fixed position during the time the rotating shutter is open and the film is exposed. The same mechanism advances the film to the next frame while the shutter is closed. In professional cameras the shutter speed and the speed of the film in the camera are variable and can be operated either frame by frame or at standard sound film speed of 24 or 25 frames per second. High-speed cameras can record up to 400 frames per second.

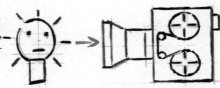

Open 1/4 *Closed*

1/2 *Closed* Closed

Exposure

Exposure is influenced by six different elements, some of which are given, some of which can be adapted.

01_Film Speed / Sensitivity

The film speed is a given element and indicated in either ASA or DIN on the film stock.

02_Processing

Labs process the film under standard conditions according to film speed/sensitivity, unless you ask for *extras*, such as double sensitivity, and so on.

03_Camera Exposure Time

The camera speed for single frame exposure is measured in fractions of a second: 1/2, 1/5, 1/10, 1/40 are the most common and they can be chosen on professional cameras.

04_Light Source

The light source, measured in foot-candles, can easily be adapted by adding more lights or taking them away.

05_Shutter Opening

Shutter opening is measured in degrees, from 0° to 180° and can be adjusted on professional cameras.

06_Lens Aperture

The lens aperture measured in f-stops is probably the easiest to adapt; however, the lens is at its best when using a medium f-stop. For example, with a lens ranging from 1.8 to 22.5, an aperture of 6 to 8 is a good f-stop.

Screening: Film Projector

The functioning of a cinema projector is exactly the reverse of the camera; the projector throws the image created in the camera onto a screen. The same type of intermittent mechanics used in the camera maintains the film in a steady position while a rotating shutter is opened and the picture is projected. The intermittent mechanics will also move the film forward to the next picture while the shutter is closed. The speed of a sound projector, however, is not variable but calibrated at 24 or 25 frames per second.

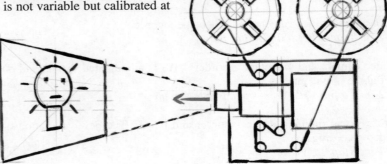

The full process of film recording and projection goes as follows:

Light penetrates into the camera lens and transforms the small silver grains of the film emulsion. The image on the film becomes visible and durable through chemical processing. Then, the projector recreates the picture and the movement by projecting the film frame by frame onto a screen at a constant and given speed.

0102_Recording on Video Tape

Mechanical, Optical, and Magnetic Procedures

Unlike film production formats and equipment, video systems are not standardized worldwide. Though the size of the video tapes, and the cameras and players are the same, the way they record and play back is still different from country to country. Basically, there are three different systems in use: PAL, NTSC and SECAM.

Although there are more and more multiple playback systems available on the market, the changing of videotapes remains a headache for the traveling filmmaker.

The film animation techniques proposed in this book can be recorded on video if you have a device for single-frame video recording. Recording frame by frame straight to tape will always be a problem. Most camcorders equipped with a *single-frame release* still produce about 4 to 6 frames on the tape. Analogue frame by frame recording is definitely outdated since the arrival of digital video systems linked to a computer. Analogue video systems are, however, still used to store and distribute picture and sound.

To buy and own video equipment is a frustrating situation because the best piece of video equipment today is most probably outdated next year. Every video equipment manufacturer is planning to introduce new equipment all the time. The problem is that to avoid panic among future customers, the manufacturer keeps the information about new models top secret; so it is hard to find out about a particular model after the production has been discontinued.

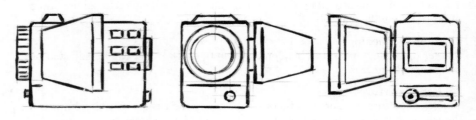

Video Formats

This list of available video equipment and tape formats cannot remain valid for too long. This is what you can actually expect to find on the market:

Professional video camera and videotape recorder.
1/2-inch tape: Beta-SP, Digital Beta

Video camera and videotape recorder. VHS is an outdated format and only used for home movie purposes.
1/2-inch tape: VHS, domestic cassette system

Professional digital video camcorder and player. The new generation of digital video recording.
1/4-inch tape: DVCAM

Digital Video Camcorder. The new generation for semi-professional and domestic purposes.
1/4-inch tape: Mini DV

Camera HD DV (High Definition Digital Video).
The new generation for professional usage.
DVD or Hard disk

Recording: Video Camera

Even though the recording of light onto magnetic tape is an outdated technique, it is still interesting to know how it works.

The function of a video camera is to change the incoming light into an electrical signal. This electrical signal is called a video signal. The part of the camera that changes light into a video signal is the cathode ray tube. Strong light striking the tube produces a strong video signal, dim light produces a weaker video signal, and no light causes no electrical reaction.

Another function of the cathode ray tube and the whole camera is to read or scan the incoming picture. Just as your eyes must read every line of this page in order to understand the entire page, the camera scans the same number of lines each time it reads the entire surface of the picture.

The camera must scan 625 lines in order to see all the light striking the surface of the tube. When the camera has completed the scanning of 625 lines from top to bottom, it has scanned a full frame. In PAL system where the 625 line system is used there are 25 full frames in every second.

To avoid a flickering image, the camera must scan the entire surface of the tube picture twice in order to produce a full frame. On the first trip the camera covers 312.5 lines. To cover the remaining 312.5 lines, the camera returns to the top of the picture and scans the remaining lines by filling in the spaces left between the first series of scanned lines. Each time the camera scans the picture, it produces half a frame, called a field. Since a field is half a frame, there are 50 fields (25 frames) in every second.

Format: 4 x 3 resolution 720 x 576
Rendering Options: Lower field first

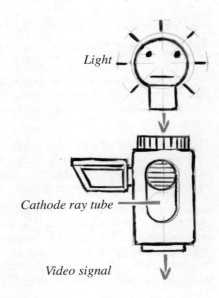

Light

Cathode ray tube

Video signal

2- 4- 6- 8- 10
Lower field

1- 3- 5- 7- 9
Upper field

1- 2- 3- 4- 5- 6- 7- 8- 10
Full field

Video Tape Recorder (VTR)

The function of a VTR is to record and store the video signal. When a VTR receives a video signal from a camera, it converts that electrical signal to magnetism. This magnetism is transferred onto videotape during the recording process. The process of changing magnetism from the tape back into a video signal is called playback.

Videotape is made of a thin strip of polyester plastic, coated on one side by a film of iron oxide particles. When there is nothing recorded the particles are magnetically neutral. When the tape is passed over an electromagnet or a head with an alternating video current, the particles on the tape become magnetically oriented. This orientation process is called recording.

Video playback is based on the fact that magnetism can produce an electrical current. When a recorded videotape is passed over the recording head, the magnetically oriented oxide particles on the tape produces an alternating current in the head. This reproduced current can be sent through the electronics of the VTR to a monitor or a projector where it appears (almost) exactly the same way the camera had originally seen it.

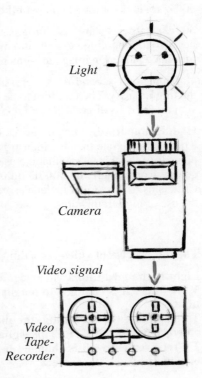

Light

Camera

Video signal

Video Tape-Recorder

Screening_Monitor_Video projector and TV Receiver

The function of a video monitor, a video projector, or a TV receiver is just the reverse of the camera: it changes video signals into light.

A video monitor and a TV receiver differ only in the way they receive the video signal. A monitor will accept a direct video signal such as the one generated in a Video-Tape Recorder. TV receivers accept a broadcast or radio frequency (RF) signal.

The image sensor of a monitor is in a way the inverse of a camera sensor. When the video signal from a camera (or VTR) is fed into the image sensor, the amount of light produced on the screen is proportional to the amount of light that was striking the camera image sensor. The original picture is therefore recreated.

Another job of the monitor and the projector is to *write* the picture, which is *read* by the camera and then display or project it onto a screen. The monitor and projector recreate the camera picture by using a scanner, similar to the one in the camera, to display the video signal on the screen, line by line, one field at a time. It scans each line horizontally in the same manner as the camera. The monitor and the projector *show* what the camera *sees*.

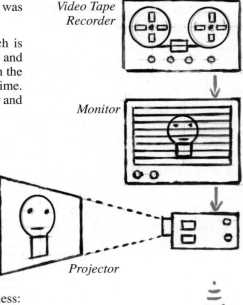

Video Tape Recorder

Monitor

Projector

Frames-per-Seconds

There are three main frame rate standards in the TV and movie-making business: 24p, 25p, and 30p. However, there are many variations on these as well as newer emerging standards.

24 frames-per-second is a progressive format and became the de facto standard for sound motion pictures and the production of hand made animation films.

25 frames-per-second is a progressive format and runs 25 progressive frames per second. This frame rate derives from the PAL television standard of 50i (or 50 interlaced fields per second). Film and Television companies use this rate in 50 Hz regions for direct compatibility with television field and frame rates.

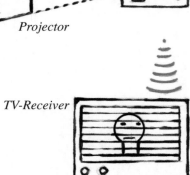

TV-Receiver

30 frames-per-second is a progressive format and produces video at 30 frames per second. Shooting video in 30p mode gives no interlace artifacts but can introduce judder on image movement and on some camera pans.

48 frames-per-second is a progressive format and is currently being trialed in the film industry. The first film to be filmed at 48 FPS was *The Hobbit*, a decision made by its director *Peter Jackson*.

High Frame Rate, often abbreviated to **HFR,** is a motion picture format where a higher frame rate than the industry standard 24 frames per second is used. Proponents of the format say that the use of a higher frame rate improves the image quality – particularly that of 3D films – by reducing strobing and motion blur. Criticisms of the format include assertions that the "cinematic look" is lost with the use of high frame rates.

The full process of video recording and playback goes as follows:

Light is changed into a video signal in the camera. This signal is sent to the VTR where it is changed to magnetism. The magnetism is stored on a video tape.
To play back the recording, the magnetism on the tape is reconverted to a video signal in the VTR. This signal is sent to a monitor, video projector, or TV receiver where it is changed back into a representation of the light that originally struck the camera.

0103_Recording on Hard Disk

Digital, Electronic Procedure

With the arrival of digital electronics, video has become a handy medium for animation. Digital electronics store data as numerical quantities, rather than physical quantities as in analogue video. Because numerical data is individually distinct, the digital medium is better suited to record the single images required for animation.

The machines able to record and play back digital information are called computers or camcorders. In the late 1970s personal computers became popular. In the beginning, these computers were merely used for writing and calculating. As technology progressed, personal computers became more powerful and could soon handle images and sound. They are now used for graphic design, layouts, sound creation and, of course, animation.

The recent development of digital video has greatly aided the production of animation on computers.

Digital recording offers several advantages and only a few disadvantages. The main argument in favour of digital recording is that there is no waiting for the film to be processed before you can see the animation, and also its flexibility for manipulating sound and visuals.

Compared with film, working digitally means accepting a change in image quality. The digital image of a computer screen is harsher and more contrasted than the soft but sharply projected image of a film.

To buy and own a computer and digital video equipment is an even more frustrating experience than buying an analogue video camera because the best equipment you can buy today will be outdated tomorrow. The computer is the heart of all digital recording. Even as computer hardware and programs are fast evolving, the general principles are likely to remain constant.

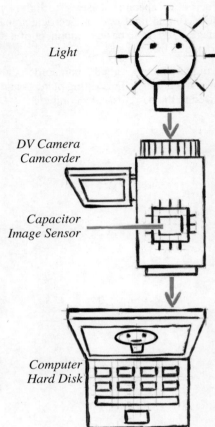

Light

DV Camera
Camcorder

Capacitor
Image Sensor

Computer
Hard Disk

Recording: Computer Programs

Computers offer the ability to work with individual frames. Digital images can be manipulated in the computer. So, there is no loss of quality no matter how many times the images are copied.

Most computers can be used to install animation programs. The minimum requirements should be at least a 20 GB hard drive. It is very helpful if your computer comes with a CD/DVD ROM drive, Firewire/USB ports, and audio in and out ports for a microphone and speakers.

This manual suggests using computers as a recording device to digitise handmade artwork rather than creating images and sound with 3-D program.

Before you start entering images in the computer, the recording program has to be set to the parameters according to the final screening format. Check with the lab for the distribution format.

Recording Images

Contrary to the analogue video camera, a digital camera doesn't use a cathode ray tube but a capacitor sensitive to light. The capacitor, or image sensor, transfers the incoming light into an electrical signal which is digitised to become a digital image. This is the basic component of a digital camera, the equivalent to the film stock of a film camera.

A digital camera, called a camcorder, can record and save digital images on the internal hard disk. For editing pictures and sounds, these images can then be transferred to the hard disk of a computer.

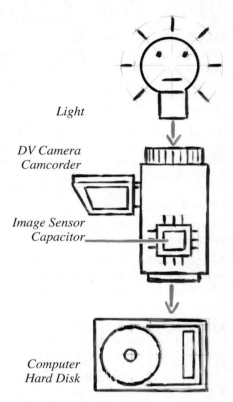

Light

DV Camera
Camcorder

Image Sensor
Capacitor

Computer
Hard Disk

There are several techniques to bring digital images into a computer:

A **DV Camcorder** or a **Digital Photography Camera** can be used to capture drawings or stop-motion animation frame by frame into computer program. The camcorder connects to the computer by a cable and can be controlled by the computer program. The camcorder will also serve to record finished animations to video tape.
Program examples: Adobe Premiere, iMovie

DV Camera

Computer
Hard Disk

The **Drawing Tablet** is a flat plastic board connected to the computer. A plastic pen is used to make hand-drawn animation and enter them directly into the computer.
Program example: Macromedia Flash

Drawing
Tablet

A **Scanner** can be used to digitise flat artwork made outside the computer. The scanner captures artwork like drawings, paintings, collages or cut-outs. For pegbar animation you may use a pegbar pasted to the scanner or a scanner with automatic paper feed and peghole registration. The scanned images are transferred into drawing and editing program.
Program examples: Adobe Photoshop, Adobe Illustrator, Adobe Painter, iMovie

Scanner

Recording Sound

Before you start entering music and sound effects into the computer, the recording program has to be set to the parameters according to the final distribution format:

DV-PAL Standard Audio Settings
Rate: 48000, 48 kHz,
Format: 16-Stereo
Compressor: Uncompressed

DV-NTSC Standard Audio Settings
Rate: 48000, 48 kHz
Format: 16-Stereo
Compressor: Uncompressed

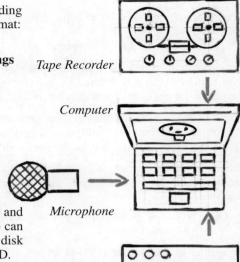

Tape Recorder

Computer

Microphone

Keyboard

A **Microphone** is used to record audio straight into the computer's sound and music program. A portable audio **Tape Recorder** (MP3 recorder, Mini-disc) can be used to record sound away from the computer and put it onto the hard disk afterward. Prerecorded audio can also be captured directly from a CD or DVD. *Program examples: Digidesign, ProTools, Adobe Premiere, iMovie, Final Cut Pro, etc.*

With a **Keyboard Sound Synthesizer** you can create your own music. It is used to play and control a synthesizer program that can simulate and digitize the sound of musical instruments.

Playback_Image and sound

To screen the images captured by the camera a monitor or digital projector is used. The image sensor of the monitor or a projector is in a way just the opposite of the image sensor of the camera. When the digitised images arrive in the screening facility the light which was initially captured by the camera will be retransformed into light on the screen or on the projected image.

The function of a screening facility is therefore to *write* the picture which was *read* by the camera. Monitor-screen and digital projector recreate the recorded pictures, pixel by pixel. The monitor or the projector *show* what the camera has *seen*.

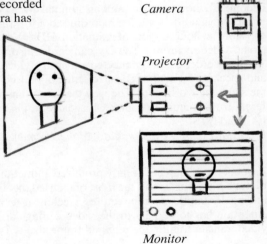

Camera

Projector

Monitor

Editing, Storing and Distributing Digital Animation

The computer can be used to edit the recorded animation and to add music and sound effects.
Program examples: Adobe Premiere, Adobe AfterEffects, Final Cut Pro.

The animation recorded and edited in the computer can be output to different media for storage and distribution. Digital storage means that copies are identical to the original, so copies do not degrade in terms of the quality of the images.

There are several possibilities to show your animation. Decide on the final screening format at the beginning of the working process. This saves you time and money when it comes to showing the finished work to an audience.

Computer Hard Disk Drive

You can play the animation straight from your computer **Hard Disk Drive** and show it on the computer screen. This is the fastest way to show it to a few people at a time.

A handy way to store and carry your animation is to copy it to a **Memory Stick** or to a **USB Flash Drive.**

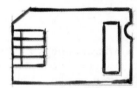
Memory Stick

Recording to a **CD-R** or **DVD-R** allows you to make copies and play them on other computers or players able to read those formats (for example, home DVD players). One CD-Rom can store about 700 MB compared to a DVD which can store 4.7 GB. You need special program to record animation on CDs.
Program example for output: Roxio Toast Titanium.

USB Flash Drive

DVD (Digital Versatile Disk) is a real alternative to videotape and will sooner or later replace videotape altogether. Today a DVD-Rom can store about 5 GB of information. You need a special program to convert animation files into a format suitable for DVDs. The size of DVDs and their drives are the same the world over. The way they record and playback is however still different from zone to zone.
Program examples for output: DVD Studio Pro, Apple iDVD.

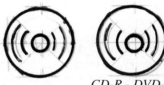
CD-R - DVD-R
DVD Digital Versatile Disk

Another support for digital images and sound is the **Internet** or **World Wide Web.** The Web is a worldwide medium for communication and it is more and more used not only for e-mail and chats but also to view and distribute animation.
Examples: YouTube, Facebook, Twitter

Although DVD is taking over fast, **videotape** is still a popular support for distributing media. Although analogue video is an outdated media, digital video has become the new standard among filmmakers. DV tape is the recording medium and DV camcorders are the recording tool for digital video. A **mini-DV cassette** can store an hour or more of animation. HD-DV is the preferred format for professional video recording. The DV camcorder also acts as a player for digital video. The camcorder can be connected either to a video monitor or to a video projector and speakers for sound. The size of the digital videotapes and the camcorders are the same the world over. The way they record and playback is, however, still different from country to country. Basically you have to face two different systems: PAL and NTSC.
Program examples for output: Adobe Premiere, Adobe AfterEffects, Final Cut Pro.

www.Internet / World Wide Web

Last but not least, the digitally produced animation can be **transferred to motion picture film**. This is still the most often used medium for theatrical release. Transferring digital files to film requires a technical service and can be quite expensive. Attention has to be paid to the video settings at the beginning of the work: for video transfer to film, the required frame size is 1440 x 1152 pixels.

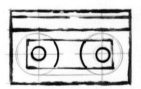
Mini DV Cassette

The full process of a digital recording to hard disk and playback is this:

Images are recorded by an image sensor or capacitor which converts the light into digital images. These images can be stored as a picture file on the hard disk of the camera.
These computer data files can be transferred to the hard disk of a computer, a CD-DVD disk, a DV cassette, a website, or to film stock in order to be stored and distributed.
To play back the recordings, a screening device will convert the numerical date into light and recreate on a monitor or by a digital projector the original image and sound.

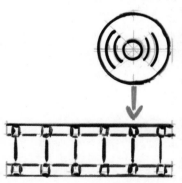
Transfer to motion picture film

0104_Light Sources

Animation is traditionally exposed using artificial light. Daylight can be very interesting for experimental filmmaking, but for traditional animation films, daylight is not stable enough. It is not steady in its intensity, angle, or colour temperature.

There are two possible light sources for the animation stand:

Top Light: All the light falls upon the artwork from above, either from a refracting surface or straight from a light source.

Bottom Light: All the light shines from beneath, either from a refracting surface or straight from a light box through opal glass.

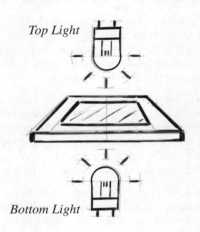

Top Light

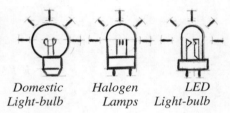

Bottom Light

Domestic light bulbs are an outdated technology. However they still can be used, either four 60 watt bulbs or two 100 watt ones. Although in theory these lights don't have the right colour temperature for artificial light film, in practice they are suited for animation since you can correct the *colour temperature* in the camera or by using blue light-bulbs or a blue colour correction filter.

Halogen 12-volt lights are very handy. The light will not heat your artwork and the colour temperature is close to daylight.

Actually there is a wide choice of **LED** *Light Emitting Diode* light bulbs available. A LED lamp is a solid-state lamp that uses light-emitting diodes as the source of light. LED lamps offer long service life, high energy efficiency and are considered as the technology of the future. They are perfect for animation.

| *Domestic* | *Halogen* | *LED* |
| *Light-bulb* | *Lamps* | *Light-bulb* |

The **Colour Temperature** is a standardization of light sources. The colour degree of the light is measured in relation to the temperature of a heated *black body*, in this case a piece of charcoal. When the piece of charcoal is heated to sheer white, its colour has the quality of daylight.
The colour temperature is expressed in degrees Kelvin; daylight measures 3200 degrees Kelvin *(Lord William Thomson Kelvin, 1824-1904)*.

3200 degrees Kelvin

In animation the shooting area used must be evenly lighted. Check this with the exposure meter and shoot a gray cardboard of the required field size. The lights can be wired to individual switches or controlled by a dimmer. The dimmer permits you to adjust the desired light force and eventually to save light bulbs, but it's unsuitable for dissolves and fades on colour film because the colours will turn into a brownish gray.

No other light should fall on the animation table during shooting. Switch off all neon or fluorescent lights and other light sources in the room. During the daytime, cover the windows with black curtains.

Your light units should be permanently attached to the animation stand so that when you have tested for exposure they won't move.

To avoid reflection, the lights should be at an angle of **30°** to **45°** in relation to the shooting area.

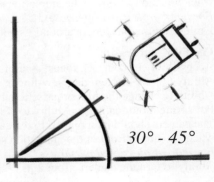

30° - 45°

0105_Stand for Plane-View Animation

No matter whether you are working with film or Digital Video equipment, animation stands are basically the same. DV equipment happens to be lighter than film equipment, so the structure can be lighter too. Animation stands are categorised according to animation techniques and grouped into *Plane-view Animation* and *Stop-motion Animation* stands.

In plane-view animation, the camera looks down at the artwork at an angle of 90°. Camera, artwork and lights must be in a fixed relationship with each other. This necessitates an animation stand comprising a carriage for the camera, columns to hold the carriage, supports for lights, and a tabletop to lay out your artwork. The camera should be mounted to the carriage so that the artwork is right-side-up when you are in front of the animation stand and looking through the viewfinder.

You can protect your film from reflections by painting your animation stand in matte black and by mounting a Reflection Guard Board to your camera. A black cardboard with a hole in it just large enough for the lens to shoot through will do the job.

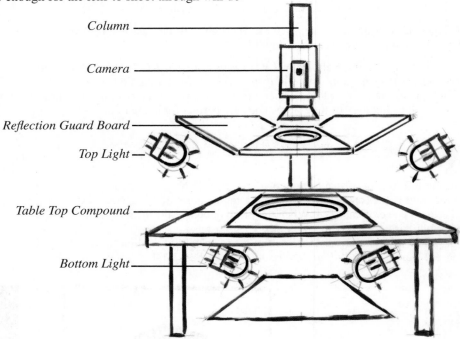

Column

Camera

Reflection Guard Board

Top Light

Table Top Compound

Bottom Light

Carriage for the Camera

Special attention must be given to the way your camera is mounted on the animation stand. The camera support must be a steady, solid "cradle". The camera must fit like a hand in a glove, so that when you remove the camera it can be put back in exactly the same position. When designing the carriage the following points should be considered:

For DV cameras
Accessibility of controls: focus, aperture, fade lever, touch screen, etc.
Ability to look through the eye piece or see the picture on the LCD screen.
Ability to change the cassette without removing the camera.
The camera should be mounted to the carriage so that the artwork is right-side-up when you are in front of the animation stand.
For more professional purposes:
Ability to turn the camera around its optical axis.

For Film cameras
Accessibility of controls: focus, aperture, fade lever, etc.
Ability to look through the view-finder.
Ability to change the film or cassette without removing the camera.
For spring motor cameras: Ability to wind up the camera motor
The camera should be mounted to the carriage so that the artwork is right-side-up when you are in front of the animation stand.
For more professional purposes:
Ability to turn the camera around its optical axis.

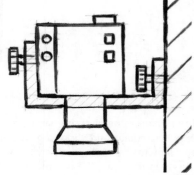

Camera Carriage

Columns to Hold the Carriage

If your camera has a good zoom, you don't need any columns at all. The focal length of a zoom lens is variable and capable of simulating the effect of the camera's movement toward or away from the subject. The carriage can then be fixed above your animation table, but within the given limits of the zoom lens.

A tripod makes a sturdy camera stand.

A photo enlarger makes a good support for a not-so-heavy camera.

An X-ray stand has two marvelous columns and usually a smooth gliding carriage on counter weights.

Rails from mechanical toy sets or an angle iron may also do the job.

Photo enlarger

Supports for Lights

If your lights are simply two office lamps, you can attach them directly to the table or, even better, to the wall behind, in order not to restrict movements on the table.

If you undertake your own construction, remember that the distance and the angle of the lights must be adjustable. Pieces of water pipe and fittings are good materials to use to construct light brackets. The lamp itself can be fixed to the brackets with clamps.

Lamps are evenly spaced on either side of the table. The light is directed to the opposite side of the working surface. Thus, the field size is cross lighted.

For bottom lighting the lamps are fixed under the animation table in order to hit a an opal glass to diffuse the light spots.

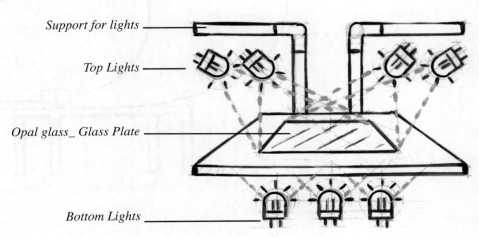

Support for lights

Top Lights

Opal glass_ Glass Plate

Bottom Lights

The Animation Table

A sturdy wooden table is a good base for an animation table. In the optical axis of the camera, a rectangular or round opening is cut into the table top and two rails mounted alongside. The east-west compound table top will travel on these rails. The rails of the north-south compound table top have to be mounted on top of the east-west compound table top. This system permits you to make moves in all directions. The opening in the table should be at least the size of a standard cel of 25 x 30 cm or, better still, about 50 x 60 cm. The compound plates can be made out of sheets of glass in order to use the total surface for back-lighted work.

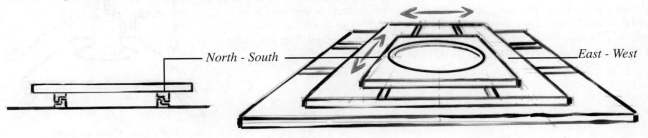

North - South

East - West

0106_Stand for Stop-Motion Animation

In stop-motion animation, the camera is facing the objects on the set horizontally or at a low up or down looking angle. The lights are in a fixed relationship with the tabletop set. Curved paper attached to the wall and the table can form a *cyclorama,* or a smooth cove, to create the illusion of depth.

Tabletop and Set

A long heavy wooden table makes the best set for convenient shooting. The background can be in a circular form to avoid shadows in the angles. A curved surface placed at the foot of this cyclorama can mask the hard edge at the floor level.

A paper can be taped to the wall and the table to form a smooth cove to create a specific stand for animated objects. Its horizontal working surface curves up into its vertical backing without a joint.

The middle ground, where the action takes place, must be open in order to move the objects around freely. Focus is on the middle ground, and the focus line should be indicated, out of frame, on the animation table. The foreground is important to give the impression of depth of field. It can either be attached to the table or mounted on separate tripods.

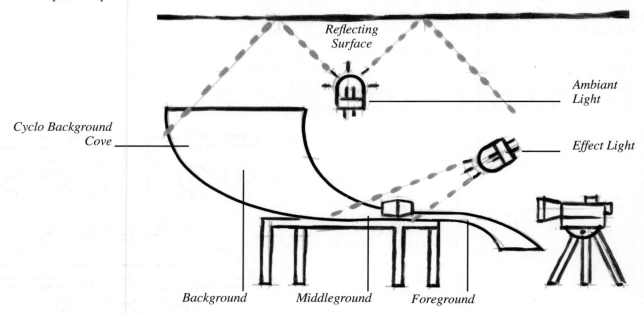

Camera Support

The simplest way is to mount the camera to a tripod that can be adjusted for height and equipped with a head for pans and tilts. The tripod should be put on spider-legs and taped to the floor. A zoom lens can simulate the effect of the camera's movement toward and away from the subject. The camera is aimed at the animation set at an angle of 30 to 60 degrees, or horizontally for more dramatic effect.

If you want your camera to travel backwards and forwards, you have to build a rail system, similar to the traveling device for plane-view animation. A tripod head to hold the camera is screwed onto the traveling device. This allows the camera to tilt and pan. The rails can be either fixed to the ground or to the ceiling. The advantage of the latter is that your camera can travel over the subjects

Travelling Camera Device

Lights

Lighting the stop-motion set is a creative issue. Avoid too many light sources. Remember how many lights we have outside during daytime: **only one – the sun!** This only light creates an infinite number of ambiances by changing its position, intensity, acting as a reflecting light, as back- or front-light, and so on. Use lights for a stage setting. No other parasite lights should fall on the animation table. Switch off all neon lights and other light sources in the room. During the daytime cover the windows with a black curtain.

There are two different light sources:

Ambient light from above. This overhead light provides an even and general light with nearly no shadows, like daylight on a foggy day. If the light source is strong enough, you may use it as indirect light, rebouncing from a white surface above.

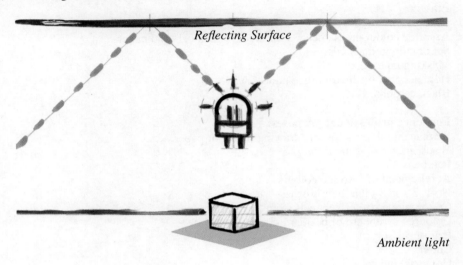

Reflecting Surface

Ambient light

Effects light comes from the side and creates an atmosphere with light and shadows. A spotlight can be used to highlight the scene and to throw the subject into relief. A slide projector can easily be used as a spotlight.

Different masks, cut-outs of black drawing paper, can be used in the slide projector for special lighting effects. Coloured gelatine filters attached to the lights can be used to create different atmospheres.

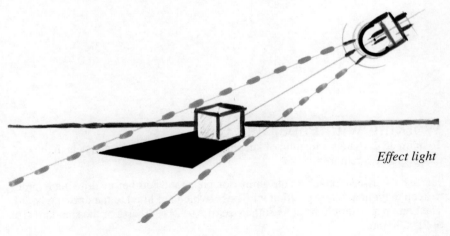

Effect light

0107_Tools for Pegbar Animation

Animation is not so much a question of materials as of time. Yet, for every workshop there should be enough materials on hand. Every artist has his or her favourite tools. The participants of a workshop may use their own materials if they desire. For the rest, keep these simple but reliable materials in stock:

Basic Tools

Bond paper, A4 60 gsm
Acetate cels, (thickness 0.07 – 0.10 mm), size 50 x 60 cm,
which can be cut to the following sizes:
25 x 30, 50 x 30 or 25 x 60 cm.
Soft pencils, no 2b
Erasers
Ruler
Assorted colour grease pencils for colouring on cels and paper
Set of coloured pencils
Masking tape
Hole puncher (ordinary office puncher)
Black cardboard

For more professional purposes:

Permanent ink pens for line drawing on cel or paper
Black ink for drafting films
Felt pens
Acrylic paint of assorted colours
No 1, 3 and 8 sable-hair brushes
Cotton gloves (to protect cels from fingerprints)
Coloured cardboard of postcard thickness
Pair of scissors
Cutter
Universal quick-drying glue
Pastel colours
Eyelets and an eyelet puncher
Black plastic seal paper
Double-sided adhesive tape
Drawing pins

Working with Paper and Cels

To animate drawings a method of keeping the different papers and cels in the correct position is required.

The usual way is to punch all the animation paper and cels before drawing in order to keep them in a steady position with pegs, which are fitted to the drawing board. The bond paper should be at least the size of A4 (21 x 30 cm) or the standard size of 25 x 30 cm.

The weight of the paper should be about 60 g/m2 in order to be able to see through the paper. Use paper with no watermarks.

Cels usually come with a thin paper in between. Don't remove this paper for punching or drawing. Keep dust and fingerprints off the cels. Use cotton gloves with three fingers cut off for cel manipulation. Remove sticky things with a few drops of rectified benzine (Lighter fuel). For standard sized cels of 25 x 30 cm, the best thickness is from 0.07 mm to 0.10 mm.

Puncher

Most convenient and least expensive for hole punching is an ordinary office hole puncher that makes two holes about 8 cm apart. Don't punch more than 4 cels or 8 sheets of bond paper at one time. Lubricate the puncher with dental wax once in a while.

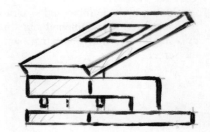

Pegs

The pegs can be improvised from all sorts of materials: round pins from electric plugs, or shafts of screws after cutting off the heads and smoothing with a file. You can also ask a mechanic to turn a few pegs out of a brass bar, according to the illustration.

Whatever you use, the important thing is that the pegs fit the holes that your puncher makes: not too large to distort the perforation, not too small that the paper or cels could move around.

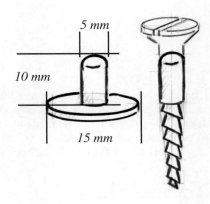

Pegbar

A professional pegbar with three pegs, one round and two square, requires a special puncher, unless you buy the pre-punchend paper stock.

The pegs are mounted on a wooden ruler or a piece of cardboard to make a pegbar.

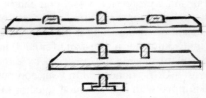

3 Pegs Professional Pegbar
Office Puncher Pegbar

Traveling Pegbar

This pegbar fitted into a glider makes a traveling pegbar, which can be most useful for moving backgrounds or pan-cels.

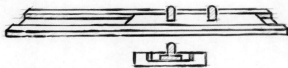

Drawing Board: Animation Board

Pegs should be be fitted to the drawing board so that paper and cels can be held in a steady position for drawing. The drawing board itself can be made out of sturdy cardboard or plywood (4-5 mm thick). Transparent material (acrylic glass) is the best because it can be used, if necessary, with a light source underneath. A handy size for a drawing board is about 30 x 40 cm.

The drawing board, pegs and traveling pegbar make an animation board which will have a double role: a drawing board and an improvised compound table-top board on your animation stand for shooting.

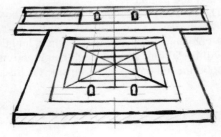

Field guide

Now, you are sitting in front of the drawing board. You are ready to put pen to paper. Just before you start, you should decide where you will make your drawings.

The field guide is here to indicate the screen size. Working for cinema, television or computer the format of the sceen will however not be the same. In standard video the screen proportions are **5:4.** In HD video the screen proportions are **16:9.**

Make a choice of the screen size corresponding to your work and copy the field guides from the next pages on a piece of paper or a cel. Punch this paper or cel and put the field guides over the pegs on the Animation Board.

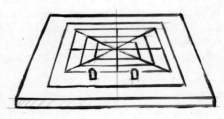

Field Mask

According to the number and size of fields, you can cut out a series of field masks in black cardboard. Punched and slipped over the artwork, they show you on the drawing board what your camera will actually be filming and what will appear on the screen.

Light Box

The light box is a useful instrument for paper and cel animation. An opal glass, or acrylic glass, is lighted from below either by domestic light bulbs or two neon lights. The box itself can be made of 15 mm plywood.
A convenient size is a box of 700 mm in length and 560 mm in width. The front height should be 50 mm and the back height 160 mm.

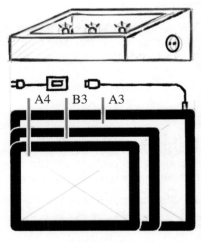

Tracing Pad

For more professional use, you can buy a **Super Slim Tracing Pad** with a LED light. They come in various sizes and are portable light weight with a body thickness of 8mm. The light is uniform without any flicker, no heat, no noise. The LED light source has a life span of 50 000 hours.
Standard models are powered by either a domestic plug with a transformer or with a USB connection to your computer. The HB (High Brightness) models are equipped with a power mod selector to adjust the brightness from 0% to 100%.

For more information contact *stephane-rudaz@bluewin.ch*

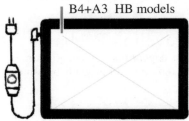

Drawing Disc, Light Box

The drawing disc is a circular piece of plastic, metal or wood containing an opal glass and pegbars.
The disc can be mounted on the light box, which has a circular hole for the disc to be turned.
A convenient box size is 700 mm in length and 560 mm in width. The front height will be 50 mm and the back height160 mm. The disc should have a diameter of 460 mm and the opal glass inside the disc a format of 320 x 240 mm

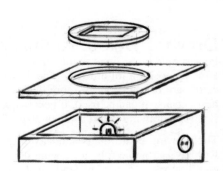

Drawing Board **without** Pegs

If no pegs are available, an L-shaped corner can be fixed to a drawing board. Fitting all the sheets into this frame for drawing and shooting procedures serves to control the registration of the drawings. The lack of precision caused by this method can be somewhat diminished by using broad lines and extremely simple forms.

Standard video Field guide

In standard video the screen proportions are **5:4** or 720 x 576 pixel.
Fieldsize **10** = 213 x 170 mm is a convenient format to work on size A4 paper with this format.

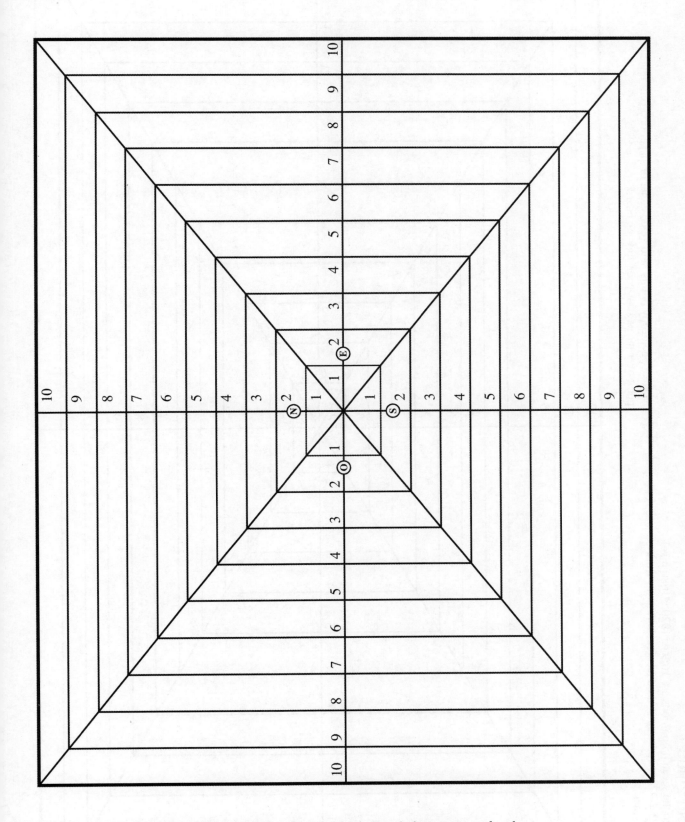

Make a photocopy of this field guide either on paper or a cel. Punch the paper or cel and put it over the pegs of your drawing board.

HD Field guide

In HD video the sceen proportions are **16:9** or 1920 x 1080 pixel.
Fieldsize **12** = 274 x 155 mm is a convenient format to work on size A4 paper with this format.

Make a photocopy of this field guide either on paper or a cel. Punch the paper or cel and put it over the pegs of your drawing board.

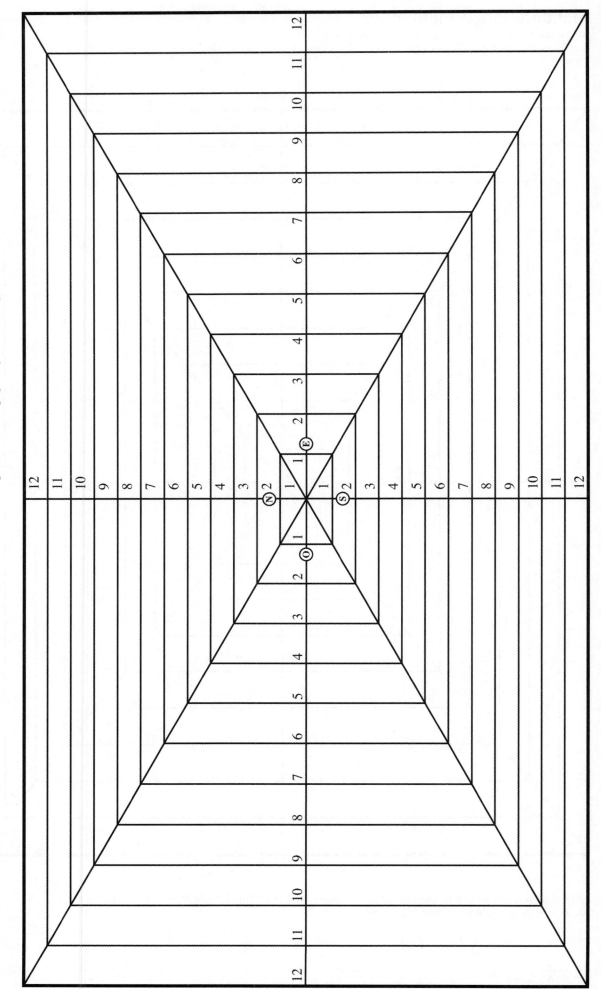

0108_Audio Recording

Like light, sound is produced by pressure waves in the air. To record an audio signal on a magnetic tape, the **vibrating waves** have to first be transformed into an **electric signal**. The tool that transforms the sound into an electrical signal is called a **Microphone** (mic). The electrical signal is converted by the **Tape Recorder** into magnetism and recorded in a magnetic form onto a sound tape.

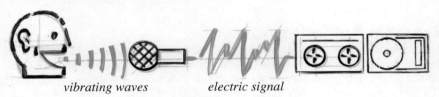

vibrating waves   *electric signal*

When the tape is played back, the magnetism is reconverted into an electrical signal and the speakers transform the electrical signal into vibrating waves. The sound coming out of the speakers to our ears is quite close to what has been recorded by the microphone.

electric signal   *vibrating waves*

Working with Film

Recording with film procedures means that all recorded sounds are transferred to 16mm or 35mm perforated magnetic tape. These tapes are edited to make a synchronized unity with the film visuals. The edited tapes are then mixed and transferred to magnetic or optical sound strip on the film.

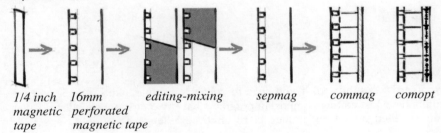

1/4 inch   *16mm*   *editing-mixing*   *sepmag*   *commag*   *comopt*
magnetic *perforated*
tape   *magnetic tape*

Working with a Computer

In computer assisted animation you have to distinguish between two different basic types of sound: digitized and synthesized. Digitized is analogue recorded and converted to digital which can be used in computer program. Synthesized sound is generated by the computer. According to these two types, there are two kinds of sound files: MIDI for synthesized sound and Waveform for digitized sound, MIDI (Musical Instrument Digital Interface) and AIFF (Audio Interchange File Format) or WAV (Windows Audio Video). MIDI is not an actual sound file, but a computer language that describes the various sound parameters. MIDI files are always in MIDI format.

Waveform files include AIFF and WAV files. AIFF and WAV are sound files formats in which a specific sound is digitally stored. Most of the current editing programs uses AIFF or WAV. To use a MIDI file in these kinds of program, the file has to be converted to AIFF or WAV.

Most of these formats can be converted into the others. Check which type of audio file fits into your production procedure.

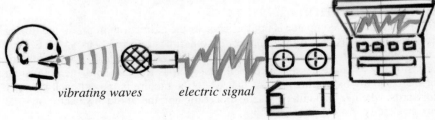

vibrating waves   *electric signal*

This is a basic list of equipment you might use when recording, storing, and distributing sound.

Microphone

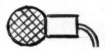

The quality of the microphone will directly affect the quality of sound recording. For each type of recording, there is a special microphone. Animation sound recording is mostly done in the studio. Therefore, a good choice is a general-purpose microphone.

Portable Audio Recorder

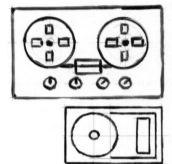

In animation, most sounds are recorded in a studio straight onto the hard disk of a computer. To record sounds outside of the studio, you may use a portable audio recorder. This can be done on analogue magnetic tape or for higher quality on DAT (Digital Audio Tape). In any case, you will need a microphone, headphones, cables, and a recorder. The sounds recorded on these devices have to be transferred either to perforated magnetic film for film editing or formatted as an audio file to be imported into a computer.

Attention must be paid to cables and jacks, as a defective cable or a loose jack can spoil the best recording equipment.

Keyboard

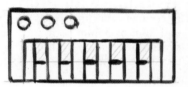

To create your own music, a MIDI keyboard is a useful tool. As the name suggests (MIDI = Musical Instrument Digital Interface), it is used to play and control a synthesizer program that can simulate and digitize musical instruments.

Mixer

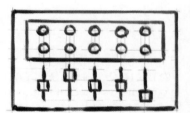

A mixer is a useful tool if you need to connect multiple audio sources to your computer. Most editing/composing programs have two or more soundtracks that can be edited, mixed, and influenced by effects or filters.

Speakers

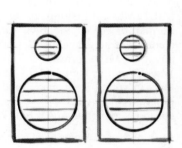

According to the way your animation is distributed, you would like to listen to the soundtrack under the same conditions. If the animation is distributed on television the TV-set built-in speaker or desktop speaker of the computer are good enough. For theatrical releases, the sound should be checked on a pair of professional quality speakers similar to the ones you would find in a movie theatre.

Synchronisation

If the sound in the computer is not the same as the animation program, the timing between the two is linked by a *time code*, sometimes referred to as SMPTE. This can be incorporated into a MIDI data stream, on a separate audio-style track, or occasionally by more complicated methods, such as RS422. This, the equivalent of the perforations in films, means that when the picture is moved backwards or forwards, whether on a video cassette or a computer, the sound always follows the image exactly.

0200_Animation Techniques

The word *animation* comes from the Latin word *anima*, which means *soul* or *vital breath*.

Animation therefore means to create life, to blow life into lifeless things.

There are most probably as many definitions of animation as there are animators. Frame-by-frame recording is known as a characteristic sign of an animated film. This definition applies only to single frame animated films. But what about animated films without single frame exposure, and what about camera-less animation and virtual reality films?

I like to look at animation as a total art, the perfect synthesis of many forms of art:

Fine Arts for visuals and animation techniques
Music for sound effects, voices, timing and rhythm
Dance for movement, time and space
Theatre for acting and performance, for emotions in images and sound
Literature and **Poetry** for the film's content, storytelling and narrative structures

A great Canadian animator and creator of magic films puts it this way:
*Animation is not the art of **drawings that move** but the art of **movements that are drawn**. What happens between each frame is much more important than what exists on each frame. Animation is, therefore, the art of manipulating the invisible interstices that lie between the frames.*
Norman McLaren

The definition of the British director, producer, and founder of ASIFA is:
Animation is design in motion. It is subject to the passage of time. Design, through animation, loses its identity as a static shape in time and space. Time and space are, therefore, the essential raw materials for animators.
John Halas

In my own opinion:
Animation is... I don't know... Anyway - it's a disease!
Robi Engler

Animation is a moving trade and by the time you read these pages, more and different animation techniques will have been created.

The synoptic chart is not meant to fence in the different techniques, but to clarify them and make you conscious of the fantastic and endless possibilities that lie within animation.

Your own dream technique is perhaps not mentioned on this chart but lies somewhere in between. Animation is like cooking. (Is this why so many animators are fine chefs?) Here are the ingredients, but you'll have to make your own menu. Creating is inventing, and the future of animation lies in the mixing of the techniques!

But don't forget that the techniques are not self-sufficient; they are the simple supporting structure for the film's most important thing: **the Content - your Story!**

0201_Synoptic Chart of Techniques

Animation

01/00 Animation without Film
01/01 Thaumatrope
01/02 Phenakistiscope
01/03 Zoetrope
01/04 Flip Book
01/05 Lanterna Magica

00/00 Kinetic Art
00/01 Animated Scale Models
00/02 Neon Signs
00/03 Traffic Lights
00/04 Spring Fountains
00/05 Christmas Decorations
etc..

Animation Cinema

Animation without Camera

Animation with Camera/Scan Single Frame Recording

Animation with Camera/Scan Continous Recording

02/00 Working direct to Film
02/01 Etching Film/Transparencies
02/02 Painting Film/Transparencies

02/03 Drawing Sound

08/00 2-D Computer assisted Anim.
08/01 Drawing to computer:
         Flash
08/02 Animation / Compositing:
         After Effect
08/03 Compositing / Editing:
         Première

09/00 3-D Computer Animation
09/01 Character Animation:
         Maya / 3-D Studio
09/02 Rendering / Special Effects:
         Fusion

03/00 Plane View / 2-Dimensional
03/01 Evolution Painting or Drawing
03/02 Animation Black/White Board
03/03 Cut-Out Animation
03/04 Silhouette Cut-Out Animation
03/05 Slice-Cuts Animation
03/06 Powder Animation
03/07 Paint-on-Glass Animation
03/08 Pastel Animation
03/09 Animated Painting
03/10 Etching Animation
03/11 Scratch-Off Animation
03/12 Filmographs
03/13 Visual Squeeze

04/00 StopMotion / 3-Dimensional
04/01 Animated Objects
04/02 Clay Animation
04/03 Pin-Art Animation
04/04 Pendulum Animation
04/05 Stop Motion / Armature Model
04/06 Pixillation

05/00 Relief Animation / 2.5-D
05/01 Animated Material
05/02 Bas Relief Animation
05/03 Collage Animation

06/00 Pegbar Animation / 2-D
06/01 Cel Animation
06/02 Drawing-on-Paper-Animation
06/03 Mixtures of Cel and Paper
06/04 Rotoscoping

07/00 Special Effects
07/01 Time-Lapse Cinematography
07/02 Chronophotography
07/03 Masks / Counter Mask
07/04 Split-Screen
07/05 Multi Exposure
07/06 Glass-Shot / Mirror-Shot

10/00 2-Dimensional Animation
10/01 Cybernetic Films
10/02 Stick Cut-Outs
10/03 Black Light (Black Theatre)

11/00 3-Dimensional Animation
11/01 Morphing
11/02 Puppets
11/03 Virtual Actors / Motion Capture

12/00 3-Dimensional / X-Effects
12/01 Chroma Key

0202_Glossary of Animation Techniques

00/00_Kinetic Art

These techniques include any human-made, reproductable movements like neo-signs, advertising display, indicator board, kinetic art, moiré patterns, fibre optics, mobiles, spring fountains, traffic lights, LED-Animations and blinking Christmas decorations.

01/00_Animation without Film

There are many different kinds of animations possible without any film, camera, projector or computer.

In this book there are a few examples: 01/01_**Thaumatrope**, 01/02_**Phenakisti-scope**, 01/03_**Zoetrope**, 01/04_**Flip-Books**, 01/05_**Lanterna Magica**,

All these early forms of cinematography create the illusion of movement and help to understand the basics of the cinema, like the function of the shutter and the persistence of vision.

These simple and easy-to-make devices are extremely interesting in a workshop, as the result is immediately visible.

02/00_Animation without Camera

These techniques use no camera to produce the film, but do use a projector to see the results.

02/01_Etching on 16 or 35 mm Filmstock or Transparencies

The emulsion of 16 or 35 mm filmstock, or ink applied to clear filmstock, is scratched off. The scratched-off parts can be coloured afterwards.
Example: Blinkety Blank - Norman McLaren 1954

02/02_Painting on 16 or 35 mm Filmstock or Transparencies

The animator inks and paints directly on clear film.
Example: Colour-Box - Len Lye 1935

02/03_Drawing Sound

This technique is close to etching and painting on film. The difference is that you cannot see the result but you can hear it. The drawings are made there where the sound head of the projector can *read* the pictures: the edge of the film: on the strip used for the soundtrack.
Example: Book Bargain - Norman McLaren 1937

Working with computer
When neither filmstock nor projector is available, the animator can paint and scratch on overhead projector transparencies and record the created images frame by frame into computer program. Obviously, the term *Animation Without Camera* doesn't apply any more to this procedure, but you will get all the original feeling of the scratch-and-paint technique straight onto filmstock

03/00_Animation with Camera or Scanner: Single Frame Recording

Plane View / 2-Dimensonal Animation

03/01_Evolution Painting / Drawing

Paintings and drawings are created and modified frame by frame under the camera.
Example: The Wave - Sabine Balasa 1968

03/02_Black or White Board

Chalk drawings on a blackboard are completed or modified frame by frame in front of your camera. For white boards, special felt-pencils and erasers are used.
Example: Minilogue/Hitchhikers - Krisfor Strom 2006

03/03_Cut-Out Animation

This easy-to-learn technique consists of moving cut-out objects, sometimes with jointed limbs, manually, frame by frame, under the camera.
Example: Mister Head - Jan Lenica 1959

03/04_Silhouette Cut-Outs

Same technique as above. To create the silhouette effect, black cardboard is used for the cut-outs. During recording procedure, the figures are placed on a sheet of glass and lighted from beneath.
Example: The Adventures of Prince Achmed - Lotte Reiniger 1926

03/05_Slice-Cuts Animation

Forms and shapes made out of coloured wax are mixed together to form a bloc. From this bloc, thin slices are cut to reveal the inner structure. At each cut a new film frame is exposed. In 1920 Oskar Fischinger invented the first machine to cut the waxbloc into thin slices. It took him two years to complete this film.

Instead of wax the creative animator can slice other matrials like vegetables, fruits, sausages and cakes. This is a truly original animation techniques. Who else then an animator could reveal the inner side of a cabbage or a banana ?!
Example: Wachsfilmexperimente - Oscar Fischinger 1922

03/06_Powder Animation

Fine sand or quartz powder is moved around with a brush and spatula on a plate of glass. For silhouette effect the glass surface can be lighted from beneath. The creative animator may also use ground coffee, salt, sugar or any kind of grain.
Example: Anima - Gisèle Ansorge 1977

03/07_Paint-On-Glass Animation

Water-based ink or oilpaints are used on a glass surface. The parts of the painting that are going to move, are removed and repainted, giving a soft, fluid aspect to the movement.
Example: The Street - Caroline Leaf 1978

03/08_Pastel Animation

Pastel colours are used on a rough, slightly sanded paper. A modification in movment is made by covering or erasing the part that is going to move. New lines and colours are applied on that part.
Example: La Poulette Grise - Norman McLaren 1947

03/09_Animated Painting

Coloured ink, watercolour or oil paints are the mediums used to paint shapes and forms which are recorded frame by frame.
Example: The Cow – Alexander Petrov 1989

03/10_Etching on Plaster

A thin layer of paint is applied on a bloc of plaster. This layer is scratched off to reveal the plaster underneath. To make the lines disapear, the lines are covered with the same opaque paint.
Example : Kafka – Piotre Dumala 1995

03/11_Scratch-Off Animation

Inked lines on a cel or glass plate are removed little by little. The camera is set to shoot in reverse frame by frame. In the projected film the lines appear to advance.
Example: Sarabande and Variation - Gilbert Vuillème 1964

03/12_Filmographs

Movements of camera and tabletop create the illusion of movement on still photographs and artwork.
Example: Cosmic Zoom - Wilson, Trickett, Dumas, Lanzello 1968

03/13_Visual Squeeze

Photos, artwork, paper cut-outs or real life film scenes are recorded on one or two frames. The projector will flash the images in rapid succession on the screen and create a sort of image avalanche.
Example: Frank Film - Frank Mouris 1973

04/00_Animation with Camera: Single Frame Recording
Stop Motion / 3-Dimensional Animation

04/01_Animated Objects
Manipulation of three-dimensional objects are recorded frame by frame.
Example: The Automatic Moving Company - Emile Cohl 1910

04/02_Clay Animation
Natural clay or modeling clay is manipulated and transformed right in front of the camera. Each change of the position is recorded in single frame exposure.
Example: The Sand Castle - Co Hoedeman 1977

04/03_Pin Art Animation / Pinhead Shadow Animation
Rows of pins are pressed in and out of a board, which is sidewards lighted. When the pins are raised and lowered they make a more or less long shadow on the board. Each change in the position of the pins is recorded in a single frame exposure.
Example: Here and the Great Elsewhere - Michèle Lemieux 2012

04/04_Pendulum Animation
Objects in movement, pendulums or mobiles, are shot with long exposure time (20 to 30 seconds). Each image shows the oscillation of the object. For the next frame, the position of the object or the camera is modified.
Example: Sap of the Earth - Alexander Alexeïeff 1955

04/05_StopMotion / Armature Models Animation
Three-dimensional models/puppets with an armature inside and jointed limbs are moved and recorded frame by frame.
Example: The Hand - Jiri Trnka 1964

04/06_Pixilation
Live actors move from point to point and pause to be recorded frame by frame in mostly artificial positions.
Example: The Neighbours - Norman McLaren 1952

05/00_Relief Animation

05/01_Animated Material
The manipulation of two-dimensional objects is recorded using single frame exposure.
Example: Vanish - Yoji Kuri 1980

05/02_Bas-Relief Animation
Two-and-a-half dimensional figures laying flat on a horizontal sheet of glass are animated and recorded frame by frame.
Example: The Passion - Jiri Trnka 1962

05/03_Collage-Photo Animation
Flat pieces of cut-out paper, leather, felt or photographs are animated and recorded directly in front of the camera. The movement is produced by replacing the whole picture or by changing an element within the picture. Camera and compound movements are used to focus on a particular part of the artwork.
Example: The School - Walérian Borowczyk 1958

06/00_Pegbar Animation

The name of this technique comes from a flat plate of steel with two or three pegs mounted to it, called a pegbar. This pegbar keeps the cels or paper in a steady and lasting relationship with each other. This is done by punching holes in all the cels or papers and putting them over the pegs on the pegbar. Pegbars are identical on both the drawing board and the animation stand.

06/01_**Cel Animation**

Cel is the short form for celluloid or acetate sheets. These transparent sheets are about 0.07 to 0.10 mm thick and used as a surface for inking and painting images. The cels are punched to fit over pegs. The high transparency allows combining up to four cels for a single image
Example: Au bout du Fil - Paul Driessen 1974

06/02_**Drawing-On-Paper Animation**

Thin bond paper (50 gsm) or tracing paper is punched to fit over the pegs. The fact that the paper is opaque means that the entire artwork has to be redrawn each time. A cel covering the artwork or cut-out elements can be used to create a foreground.
Example: Un Jour comme un Autre - Daniel Suter 1974

06/03_**Mixtures of Cel and Paper**

Drawings on thin bond paper are mixed with traditional Cel animation
Example: If I Were - If I Had - NRJ Production 1980

06/04_**Rotoscoping**

This technique consists of projecting a live-action film on a screen and tracing the moving parts you want in the animated film.
Example: Poursuite - Robi Engler 1980

The same technique is used to add animation to a live action film. The drawings are matched to live action and superimposed.
Example: Mary Poppins - Walt Disney 1964

07/00_Special effects

07/01_**Time-Lapse Cinematography**

Live actions are recorded frame-by-frame with a varying time-lapse between the frames. Normally slow processes are speeded up, leaving a long time interval between each exposure.
Example: Metamorphosis - Robi Engler, Ray Wong 1979

07/02_**Chronophotography**

Each movement is filmed in continuous exposure. On the optical printer a certain number of previous frames from each movement are reproduced by superimposition. The effect looks as if the film would keep the memory of the movement.
Example: Pas de Deux - Norman McLaren 1967

07/03_**Mask and Countermask**

The animated objects and the background are separately recorded. The superimposition is made with mask and countermask, either in the film laboratory or by compositing in computer program.
Example: Tango - Zbigniew Rybczynski 1980

07/04_**Split Screen**

By using several masks and the same number of scenes the screen can be divided into almost any number of parts.
Example: The New book - Zbigniew Rybczynski 1975

07/05_**Multiple Exposure**

This technique is used to combine in the camera two or more scenes, which cannot be recorded at the same time.

Superimposition

Like multiple exposure this technique is used to combine in the camera two or more pictures which cannot be recorded at the same time. The superimposed picture can dominate and burn-out everything which is behind on the film or both pictures can be of equal value with a translucent effect.

07/06_**Glass Shot**
Part of the scene is painted on a clear sheet of glass, which stands in front of the camera. The camera is recording at the same time both the painted picture and the scene behind.

Mirror Shot
There are two methods to combine two pictures in one shot:
Recording with a mirror placed at an angle of 45° in front of the camera which replaces the whole or part of the picture.
Recording with a half-transparent mirror placed at an angle of 45° in front of the camera in order to get a translucent effect of the whole or part of the picture.

08/00 2-D Computer assisted Animation

08/01_**Animated drawings to computer program**
Combination of the classical animated drawing technique assisted by computer program for scanning and colouring of characters and backgrounds.
Example: Les Volbecs - Robi Engler 1992

09/00 3-D Computer Animation

09/01_**Character Animation**
Virtual actors generated in a computer program and animated by key-frames. The animated characters are combined with 3-D backgrounds.
Example: Traces - Robi Engler 2010

10/00_Animation with Camera: Continuous Recording
2-Dimensional Animation

10/01_**Cybernetic Films**
Any film that uses a machine to create the picture. The artwork can be made of video signals, optical effects, mechanical or chemical patterns.
Example: Le Retour à la Raison - Man Ray 1923

10/02_**Stick Cut-Outs**
Cardboard figures, attached to a stick hidden by a foreground, can be moved either on the spot with a moving background or run along the foreground.
Example: Indonesian Shadow Theatre

10/03_**Black Light**
Black light reflects only on bright colours. Hands or the whole body of the animator are covered with black velvet and remain invisible.
Example: Prague Black Theatre

11/00_Animation with Camera: Continuous Recording
3-Dimensional Animation

11/01_**Morphing**
An early computer technique of recording the signals fed to a TV monitor by a programmed computer in single-frame exposure.
Example: Hunger - Peter Foldes 1973

11/02_**String or Hand Puppets**
The puppets are created as in classic puppetry and recorded with film or video cameras.

11/03_**Virtual Actor**
A character is created as a 3-D model in the computer. In key-frame procedure, the animator manipulates this actor with an electronic pen according to pre-recorded movements.
Example: Victor - Robi Engler 1998

Motion Capture
Another technique is to use a real live actor to animate the virtual actor through the technique of motion capturing.
Example: The Polar Express - Robert Zemeckis 2004

12/00_Electronic Video Animation

Electronics is a fast-moving trade. By the time you read this chapter, work in progress may have modified the following information.

12/01_Chroma Key

A technique of colour separation within a TV camera. A special blue colour is not recorded by one camera and is therefore invisible. All the non-blue elements of this camera can be incorporated into another camera's image.
Example: Tramway 12 - Robi Engler 2000

0203_Animation Techniques for Workshops

In theory, all the animation techniques are suitable for workshops. In reality, you will find yourself limited by equipment and time problems. Before you propose an animation technique to workshop participants it's good to remember a few facts.

There are more than twenty film animation techniques, which can be divided into four big groups:

01_Direct Animation, where artwork is animated under or in front of the camera. Direct animation needs a camera for each one, or two, participants. This applies also to animation created in the computer, it needs a computer and animation program for every participant.

02_Pegbar Animation, where the artwork is prepared away from the camera. In pegbar animation many animators can prepare the drawings and record them all with one single camera or computer.

03_Animation Without Camera, where the picture is made directly on filmstock and a projector is used to see the result.

04_Animation Without Film, where optical devices are constructed and the result is immediately visible.

There is an inversion of the time ratio between preparation work and recording in direct and pegbar animation:

Direct animation:	**preparation 10%**	**recording 90%**
Pegbar animation:	**preparation 90%**	**recording 10%**

Animation techniques also have to be chosen according to the experience of the participants and how much time you have. For beginners you could choose a technique without film, like Zoetrope or Flipbooks, so that the result can be checked immediately. Camera-less animation is also good for beginners to develop a sense of timing. The direct animation techniques need only little preparation; shooting can start right at the beginning and results are achieved faster than in pegbar animation. Pegbar animation is ideal when you have enough time and you want to make sure participants understand the basic principles of animation.

For participants with some experience don't forget that you can mix techniques. It shouldn't be either/or. Drawings and cut-outs, Animated objects and Clay animation, even Puppets and Cel animation are all possible combinations.

0300_Animation without Film

There are techniques for animation that don't require any film at all, such as using neon signs, traffic lights, flickering Christmas decorations, and so on. There are also projectors such as the *Lanterna Magica* and devices like *Thaumatropes, Phenakistiscopes, Zoetropes* that were invented long before cinematography was born, and certainly can be used in animation workshops.

Making these prehistoric toys is lots of fun and demands the same craftsmanship as any other filmmaking technique. There's no better way of seizing ideas like persistence of vision and the role of shutter movement in a film projector.

Another advantage of these techniques is that no expensive cameras or film stock is used, so there's no worry about film processing, no projector is needed and, best of all, the results of your work can be seen immediately.

A great number of participants can work at the same time, since there are no expensive technical equipment needed to work.

Approximate conversation table

5 mm	/ 0.5 cm	= ¼ inch
10 mm	/ 1 cm	= ½ inch
25 mm	/ 2.5 cm	= 1 inch
50 mm	/ 5 cm	= 2 inches
100 mm	/ 10 cm	= 4 inches
200 mm	/ 20 cm	= 8 inches

0301_Thaumatrope

By means of an optical illusion, this device gives you a good idea of the phenomenon called persistence of vision.

Take two cardboard discs and draw part of a scene on one and the rest on the other. Glue them together back-to-back, with a string through the centre, between the two discs. When the strings are turned between the fingers in a to-and-fro movement, the disc will spin around its axis and the two drawings will fuse into a single one.

Number of participants
Twelve approximately

Time required
Three hours minimum

Basic equipment
White cardboard
Fast drying paper glue
Staples
Cutter
Scissors
String
Coloured pencils or felt pens

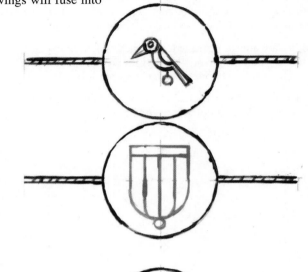

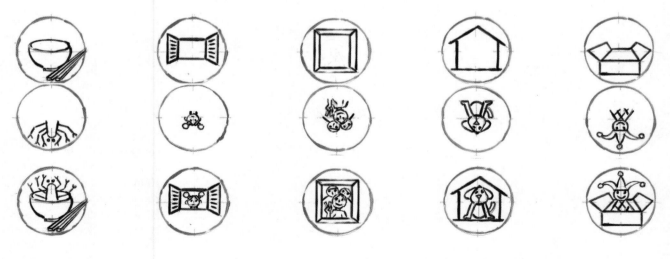

Hints
To stimulate the activity of the participants, you can draw a picture on one side of the disc and let the participants invent the reverse side.

Example:
Draw an empty rice bowl and chopsticks on one side
Let the participants decide and draw what is in the bowl: spaghetti or a cockroach?

Draw an open window on one side.
Let the participants decide and draw who is looking out of it: a child or a monster?

Draw a mirror on one side.
Let the participants decide and draw who is looking into it: one's self or friends?

Thaumatrope

Make photocopies of these drawings and mount them on a piece of cardboard. Make drawings on each disc. Cut along the traced lines. Glue the two backs together and glue a string through the centre in between the discs.

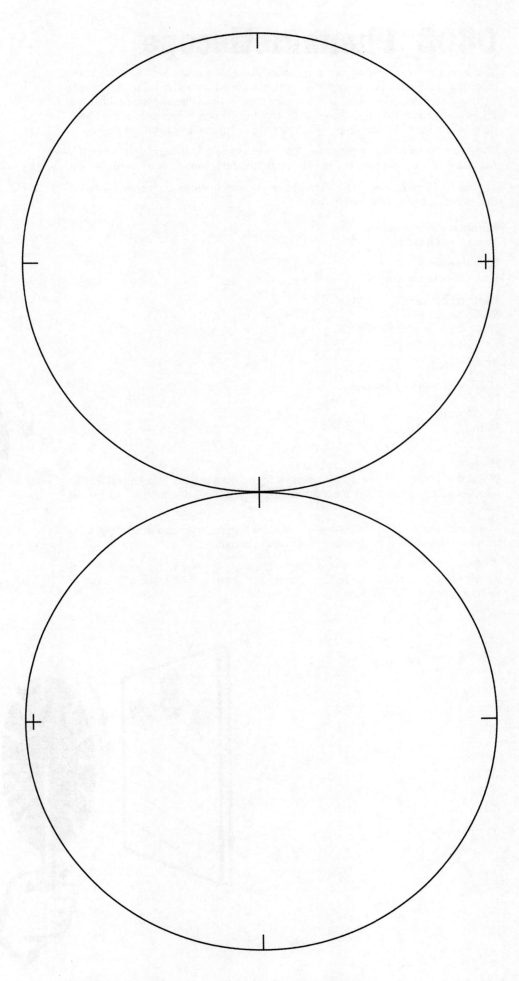

0302_Phenakistiscope

This circular device gives you a continuous vision of an action. It's a disc cut out of strong cardboard. There are 12 slots evenly spaced around the disc. In between each slot, a drawing is made. Start to make the first drawing, and then each drawing, slightly modified up to the seventh drawing. This is the climax of the movement. From here, the drawings will be developing again towards the first one.

The disc is attached with a pin through its centre to a stick of wood. Put yourself in front of a mirror, turn the disc, look through the slots, and see your picture move.

Try out cyclic movements like a mouth, or a flower, opening and closing, or a human walking cycle, or a bird flying.

Number of participants
Twelve approximately

Time required
Four hours minimum

Basic equipment
White cardboard
Black cardboard or black paint
Fast drying paper glue
Cutter
Scissors
Coloured pencils or felt pens
Pin
Wooden stick
Mirror

Hints
If you don't want to make a cyclic action, try out movements in perspective, like a rocket going to the moon, a car driving right up to you, or a football hitting the goal.

Make sure the back of the disc is either black cardboard or painted in black, to avoid eyestrain and a washed out effect on the drawings.

Whenever you want to show your Phenakistiscope art to a wider audience, you can record the drawings, taking two frames per drawing, and make a film out of your experience W*ithout film.*

Disc Front

Disc Back

Wooden Holder

Mirror

Phenakistiscope

Make photocopies of these drawings and mount them onto black cardboard. Make one set of drawings in the outer section in between the slots and another one in the inner section. Cut out along the traced line. Put a pin or a needle through the centre of the disc and attach it to a wooden stick.

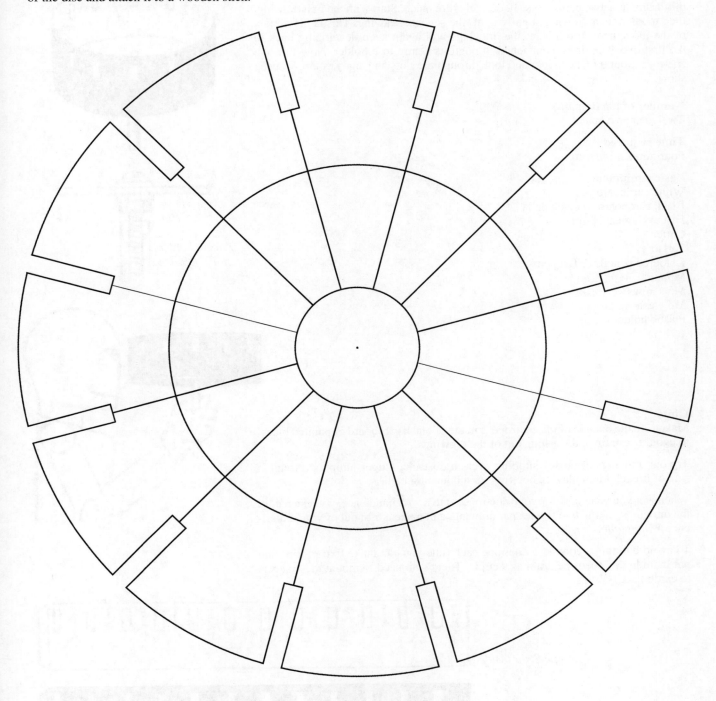

0303_Zoetrope

This cylindrical device gives you the continuous flow of a repeated movement. A strip of cardboard with vertical slots is attached to a bottom disc. On the inside of this drum, in between the slots, 12 drawings are made. Start with the first drawing, then modify each drawing slightly up to the seventh drawing. This is the climax of the movement. From here, the drawings will again keep developing back to the first one. The drum is attached through its centre to a holder. Now turn the zoetrope around in the holder and look through the slots and enjoy your own peep show!

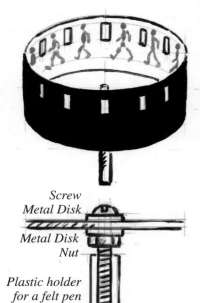

Number of participants
Twelve approximately

Time required
Four hours minimum

Basic equipment
White cardboard
Black cardboard or black paint
Fast drying paper glue
Cutter
Scissors
Coloured pencils or felt pens
M5 nuts
M5 screws
M5 washers
Plastic holder

Screw
Metal Disk
Metal Disk
Nut

Plastic holder
for a felt pen

Hints
Make sure the outside of the zoetrope is made of black cardboard or painted black, to avoid eyestrain and washing out of the drawings.

Try out drawings of horses jumping over an obstacle, a tiger jumping through a ring of fire, children playing hop frog, or a bouncing ball.

Whenever you want to show your Zoetrope art to a wider audience, you can record the drawings, taking two frames per drawing, and make a film out of your experience *Without film*.

To avoid building a complete Zoetrope each time you can make Extra Strips and put them in the Zoetrope drum as a circle. There's no need to mount these sheets to cardboard.

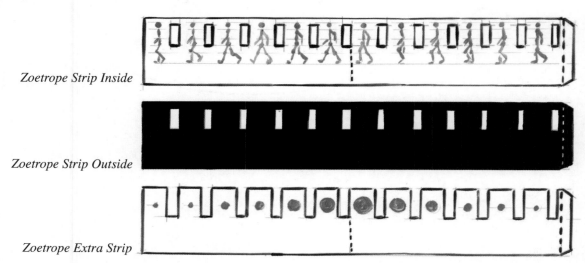

Zoetrope Strip Inside

Zoetrope Strip Outside

Zoetrope Extra Strip

Zoetrope Strip

Make photocopies of these drawings and mount them onto black cardboard. Make a drawing between each slot. Cut along the traced line, including the slots. Glue one strip to another to form a circle. Fold the bottom part along the dotted line and glue it to the cut out bottom disc.

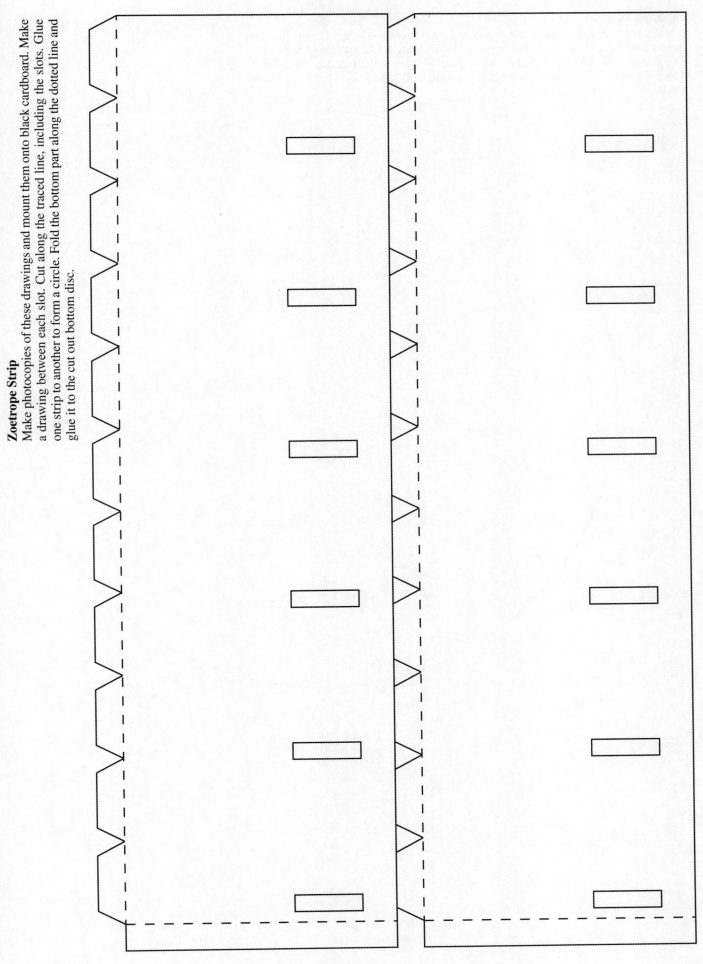

Bottom Disc

Make photocopies of these drawings and mount them onto black cardboard, then cut along the line. Make a hole in the centre and insert a screw (about 6 cm long) with a washer through it. A nut with another washer will attach the drum firmly to the screw. The screw is then put into a holder. Try the plastic holder of a used felt pen.

Zoetrope Extra Strip

To avoid building a complete Zoetrope each time, make photocopies of this Extra Strip and make a new series of drawings between the slots. Cut the strip out along the lines and glue one strip to another. Put it in the Zoetrope drum as a circle in a way that you can see through both, the slots in the drum and the slots in the Extra Strip. There's no need to mount these sheets to cardboard.

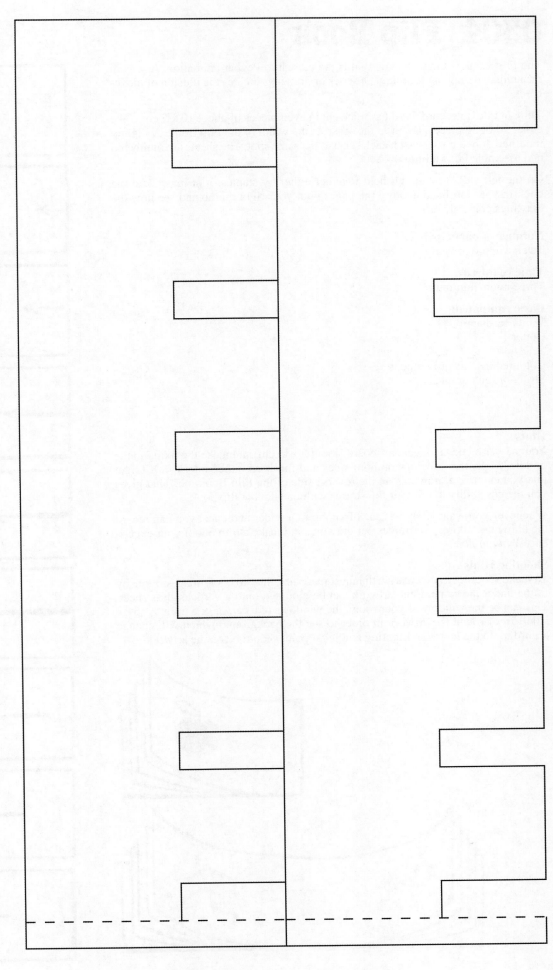

0304_Flip Book

The Flip Book is the technique that is the closest to Pegbar animation. Just as in the animated drawing technique, a series of drawings creates the illusion of movement.

Thin, but flexible, cardboard has to be cut in even pieces of about 10 x 5 cm. Take either 24 or 36 pieces. Use it in the sense of the width of the Flip Book. A slightly modified drawing is made on each sheet at the same spot. The sheets are numbered and assembled like a little book.

On the left side they are all held together either by staples or strings. Take the book in your left hand and flip the pages with your right thumb and see how the drawings come alive.

Number of participants
Twelve approximately

Time required
Three hours minimum

Basic equipment
White cardboard
Cutter
Scissors
Coloured pencils or Felt pens
String or long Staples

Hints
You may also take a longer cardboard, about 5 x 15 cm, and make the fixing in the middle. Make the drawings on both sides and flip it on either side. Don't forget that you can make drawings on the reverse side of the Flip Book too. That gives you the possibility to tell four flip stories with one double flip book.

Whenever you want to show your flip book to a wider audience, you can record the drawings, taking two frames per drawing, and make a film out of your experience *Without film*.

Shooting Hints
To make shooting more creative than just recording the flip book images frame by frame under the camera, the artwork can be mounted onto a vertical glass sheet. This can be the window of your room, the windows of a car, or of a train. A space is left free around the artwork in order to see the background which will change according to the location. Lighting and focal point should be on the artwork.

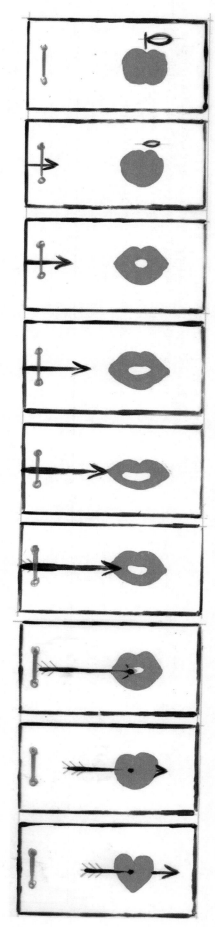

0400_Film Animation without Camera

A lot of people will tell you: *Filmmaking is wonderful; I'd love to do it, but there's all that expensive equipment -- I just can't afford it!*

This technique proves that you can afford it! Take outdated film stock and your pocket knife, start scratching, and you're a filmmaker!

In the digital age, however, its not as simple as that. Film stock is hard to find, film projectors are even harder to find, and finding someone who knows how to operate it properly is *Mission Impossible*.

Since you can't etch and paint on digital tape or onto a computer hard disk, you have to find a way to paint and scratch onto a clear sheet of plastic material and record it frame by frame with a DV camera or a scanner. Using this technique, of course, loses its camera-less characteristic and gets closer to the Etching and Painting Animation techniques.

0401_Etching and Painting on Film

This is not the technique you would choose to make a scientific film or a feature length movie, but when it comes to expressing visually the mood of a piece of music or the beat of a rhythm, there's really nothing like etching and painting directly onto film. That's why this technique is probably the best one for learning to work with one of the animator's most important raw materials: **Time**. Furthermore, the results can be screened immediately while the memory of what you have done is still fresh.

Number of participants
Twelve maximum

Time required
Four hours minimum

Basic equipment for working with film stock
Black leader film stock: Super 8mm or 16mm or 35mm
Clear leader film stock: Super 8mm or 16mm or 35mm
Scratching instruments: Needles, Penknife, Razor blades, Sandpaper
Permanent felt pens
Film holding block
Film projector: Super 8mm or 16mm or 35mm

Technique for working with film stock
Drawing on clear film with coloured ink, using a pen or a brush, or drawing with permanent felt marker.

Etching on black film by scratching into the emulsion with sharp instruments of your choice.

Mixed technique: either by scratching into the already painted film or by colouring the scratched-away parts of black film. Bits and pieces of real life films or slides can also be glued to the film stock.

Black and clear leader is available from any film laboratory. For black leader, you can also use unexposed and developed film; for clear leader, film stock exposed to bright light and developed.

Another method to make a clear film by yourself is to take any old film and wash it with warm water and a solution of bleaching powder (so-called) chloride of lime. The emulsion will wash out and you will get an entirely transparent film.

Considering the size of the image, it's easier to draw on 35mm film stock.

For etching on black leader, you'll have to work with underneath lighting. Anything from a light box to office lamp or pocket lamp will do. In order to know the field size to scratch on, a black mask with just the opening of one frame in the middle of the film holding block must be put over the whole length of the film guide.

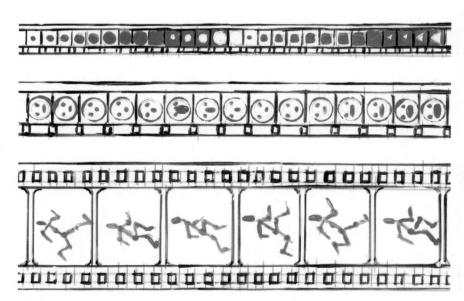

For etching and painting always work on the emulsion side of the film. To find the emulsion side you can take the film between your lips. The emulsion is on the dull, sticky side of the film. For one edge perforated film stock, the perforation of the film is always on the left side of the film guide.

Work from the top to the bottom of the film holding block. This means that you draw your first picture at frame no. 1 and then work down to frame no. 25. Then move the film upwards so that your 26th drawing will be at frame no. 1 of the film holding block.

Always make two or three drawings look identical before making a change. It's like shooting in *Twos* or *Threes*. This method makes your film slower and longer and the drawings maybe a little less jerky.

If you work on 16mm or even super-8 film stock a realistic looking drawing cannot be expected, since the frame to draw on is so small. Therefore, try abstract patterns and lines going length-wise over several frames.

Film holding block

Of course it's possible to put the film on your table and scratch away or paint, frame by frame.

However, if you want to control your work frame by frame, you need a film holding block. This is a simple-to-make object made of wood and a piece of plexiglass.

The plexiglass bottom lets the light through, which is especially important for etching on black leader. The two wooden ledges on each side are to guide the film, and the two wooden blocks at each end of the plexiglass are to reinforce the structure and to support the registration pin. This pin is made to hold the film in place during drawing. Take a nail, cut off the head and smooth it down with a file to a square form to fit into the film perforation. The whole construction is glued together with carpenter's glue.

The film guide in between the two wooden ledges must be exactly the same gauge of the film stock used. The field guide can be indicated directly on the plexiglass; or the field guide on the next page can be filmed with a camera using the same gauge of film stock as the one you want to make drawings on, and then put directly on top of the plexiglass.

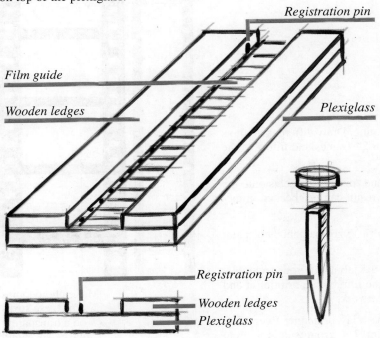

Registration pin

Film guide

Wooden ledges

Plexiglass

Registration pin

Registration pin

Wooden ledges

Plexiglass

Field size for film holding block
Film this document with film stock of the same gauge you are going to draw on.

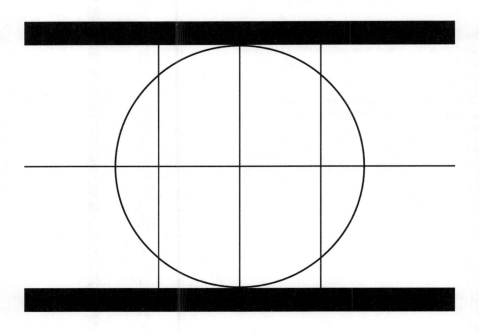

Hints

This is a good technique to develop your sense of timing. Draw different rhythms into the film by first making one picture every 12 or 24 frames and filling in the intermediate after.

Analyse a soundtrack (for example, drum strokes) and transfer the beats onto the film. On an editing table or a sepmag projector, the result can be checked immediately.

Use permanent felt pens, not the soluble ones. Don't use grease pencils or paint that will crack or wash out.

When ordering a print from the laboratory, inform the lab about your technique and the colours you used. Good labs usually clean the film before printing it and this way they might simply wash away your whole artwork.

A group project can be carried out according to the relay principle. Every 300 frames a drawing is scratched or drawn onto the film. The group sits in a circle and passes the film stock from one participant to another. Each one fills in the 299 in-between drawings according to the two given key drawings.

Make photocopies of these strips on a transparent plastic sheet and slip it in the film holding block.

0402_Etching and Painting on Transparencies

Recording pictures with a digital camera
At a time when film stock and film projectors are an outdated technology, there are still some animators who like to scratch and paint on film. The solution is to use sheets of transparent plastic and to etch and paint the images onto them. The working procedure is the same as working on film stock but the resulting pictures are recorded with a digital camera. The result is that it is no longer a technique without camera and therefore gets closer to the Etching and Painting Animation technique.

Number of participants
Twelve maximum

Time required
Four hours minimum

Basic equipment for working with digital recording
Clear plastic sheets (transparencies for overhead projectors)
Scratching instruments: Needles, Penknife, Razor blades, Sandpaper
Permanent felt pens
Any kind of opaque or transparent colours
Pen and Brushes
Masking tape

Equipment for digital recording
Animation stand
Light box or glass plate and two lights of 100 to 150W or 12V-50W
DV Camcorder
Cable from camera to computer
Computer program with stop-motion capture
Scanner
DV tape, CD-R, DVD

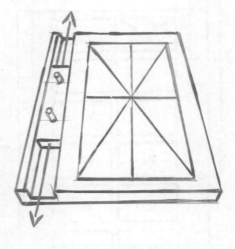

Technique for working with digital recording
Use a drawing board with the traveling pegbar moving south to north. Attach the field guide to the pegs and adjust the camera to frame field number 01. Put a clear and punched sheet of transparency over the field guide. Field number 01 is the first picture to draw and record. Next, move the traveling pegbar with the field and transparency up to field number 02 and make another slightly modified drawing at this place and record it. Proceed this way up to field number 06. Turn the field guide with the transparency 180° over and frame field number 07. Proceed by drawing and recording pictures up to field number 12. At this point, you may take another clear sheet and restart at field number 01, or you may work your way backwards from field number 12 to field number 01 by drawing over the existing pictures.

For drawing on transparencies you can use coloured ink with pen or brush, permanent felt marker or any other drawing material. Even sand, glue or cigarette burns and ashes are creative means to express a content.

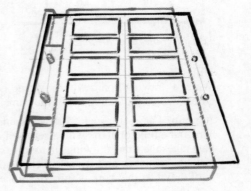

The working surface can be bottom- or top-lit. Bottom light makes transparent colours brighter, but throws opaque paint into shadows. Top light can bring out the three dimensional structure of the paint and other materials.
You may use water- or oil-based paint. Maybe you would like to try out colour ink or watercolour pencils, which can be dissolved with water and worked like an aquarelle.

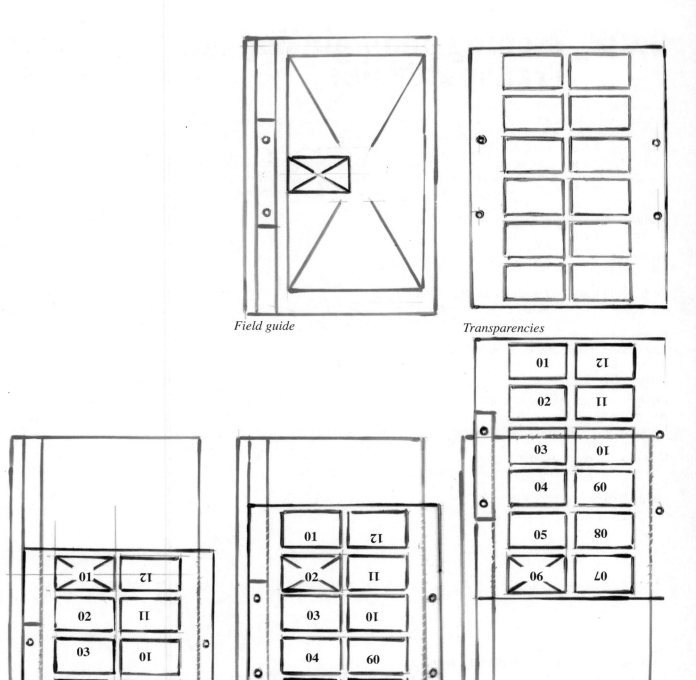

Field guide

Transparencies

Position of transparencies
for frame 06

Position of transparencies
for frame 01

Position of transparencies
for frame 02

Hints

When a drawing board with traveling pegbar is not available, you can manually adjust every single field under the camera.

A group of animators can work according to the relay principle in evolving cycles. The first animator starts with a series of drawings and records it. The next participant takes the same drawings in reverse order and makes new drawings over to the original sequence and records them again. All the animators add to the sequence until they feel the work is fully developed.

Make copies of this Fieldguide on transparent plastic sheets and use it as a support for your drawings.

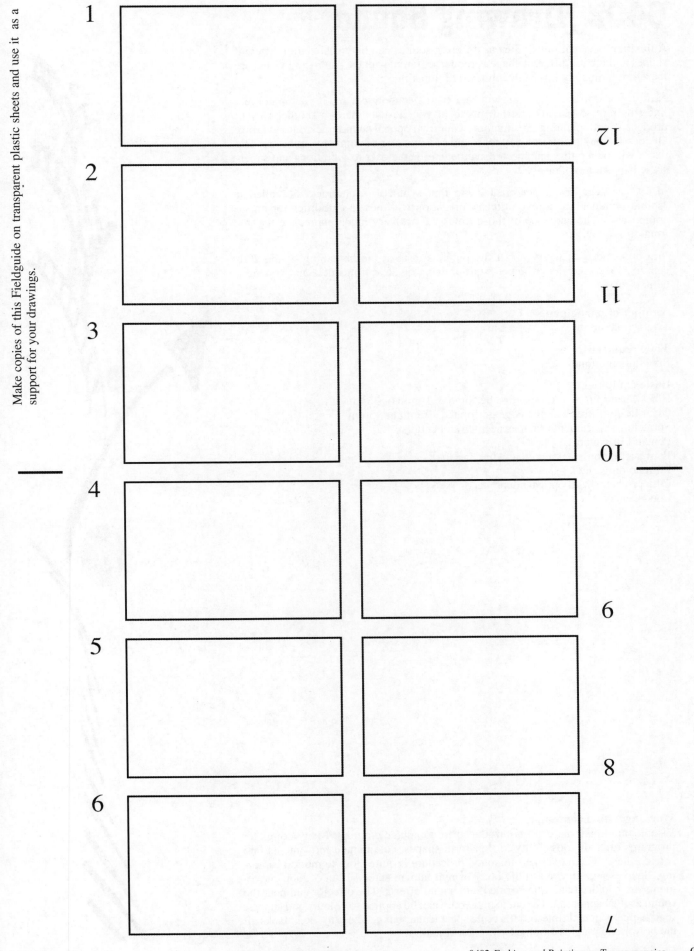

1   12

2   11

3   10

4   9

5   8

6   7

0403_Drawing Sound

Animation is visual music. Just as different sounds can be visualized in different shapes and forms, different shapes produce different sounds. Audio and visual are therefore intimately linked in animated filmmaking.

Now, if you don't want to start with an existing soundtrack, and if you do not feel like singing and playing instruments to fit your visuals, here is another way to produce sound: painting or scratching your own optical sound track onto the film. Of course, you do not get a perfect sound of a voice or a symphony orchestra. The result will be a rather unexpected synthetic effect, closer to vibrations and super-sonic bangs than to music.

In 1932, Oscar Fischinger created the first synthetic soundtrack, he called it "sound ornaments -- a revolutionary invention with new possibilities for music composers". The audience of those times did not very much appreciate the un-usual tunes though.

You don't need to worry about the public's taste at the beginning of the 20th century. Take your favourite pen, start drawing on clear film stock, and you are a composer!

Number of participants
Twelve maximum

Time required
Six hours minimum

Basic equipment
Black leader filmstock, one edge perforated, 16mm or 35mm
Clear leader filmstock, one edge perforated, 16mm or 35mm
Scratching instruments such as needles and cutters
Pen and Brush no.1
Permanent, non cracking, black drawing ink
Film holding block
Film projector with optical sound head
Loudspeaker

Working with a computer
Visual sound patterns can be introduced to computer program. Many computer programs offer the possibility to transform shapes, colours and movements into sound effects. The movement-to-sound procedure is quite close to motion captur-ing. Sensors are attached to the body of real human actors. Data of their move-ments are captured and transformed into sound effects. The director can hear the sound as it's happening. The same procedure can be applied to colours and shapes. It all happens in real time and it's quite spectacular, but needless to say, it lacks all the power and magic of frame by frame animation!

Technique: From mouth to ear

Sound is produced, just as light, by waves vibrating in the air. In the process of recording, the sound must be changed from vibrating waves into an electrical signal. The electrical signal is, in the case of optical sound, converted into an optical image of the vibrating waves.

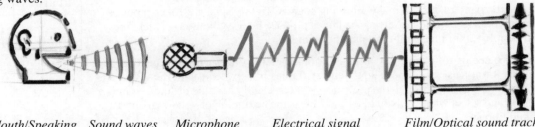

Mouth/Speaking   Sound waves   Microphone   Electrical signal   Film/Optical sound track

During playback, the sound patterns passing over the optical sound head of the projector are changed back into an electrical signal and transformed over a loudspeaker into vibrating airwaves

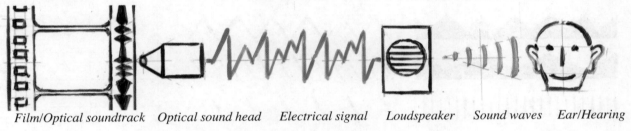

Film/Optical soundtrack   Optical sound head   Electrical signal   Loudspeaker   Sound waves   Ear/Hearing

The actual work involved in this technique is very similar to that of etching and painting on film. The real difference is, of course, that the result is not visual but audio. The drawings have therefore to be made where the sound head of the projector can "read" the drawings: on the edge of the film, opposite the film perforation.

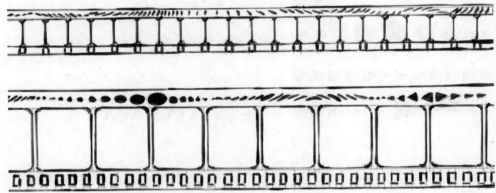

When drawing sound to film stock, there are two possible methods:

01_Drawing on the soundtrack on clear film stock with black, permanent ink, using a pen or a fine brush.

02_Scratching onto the soundtrack, either into the emulsion of black leader or you can first apply a small strip of black ink on clear leader and then scratch with sharp instruments of your choice.

Before you start your own film score, you must find out the kinds of sounds the different patterns are producing.

The sounds produced depend upon the size and shape of the forms. Shapes such as triangles, squares and circles with equal dimensions will produce bangs. Perpendicular strokes will make vibrating sounds. Tightly spaced strokes produce sharp vibrations, while loosely spaced ones produce heavy vibrations. Thick lines will amplify, thin lines will diminish the sound.

Take a piece of film and draw all the various patterns on that film. Repeat each pattern for at least 50 frames and 25 empty frames in between each effect. When you run the test film through the projector, you can clearly hear the different sound effects and select whatever you like best. This is the beginning of your own optical sound library.

Image Frames	Image Track	Sound Track
Image Frames		**Sound Frames**
		SF-1
		2
		3
		4
		5
		6
		7
		8
		9
		10
		11
		12
		13
		14
		15
		16
		17
		18
		19
		20
		21
		22
		23
		24
		25
		26
IF-1		
2		
3		
4		

Synchronisation of sound and image

For technical reasons, the sound head in a 16mm projector is 26 frames ahead of the image projection gate. If you are aiming for perfectly synchronised sound and image, this displacement must be taken into account.

In order to get picture and sound synced on your film holding block, the sound must be drawn 26 frames ahead of the image. The first frame on the sound side: **SF-1**, is synced with the first frame on the image side: **IF-1.**

0500_Animation recorded with Camera or Scanner

This is a collection of the great classical animation techniques. The common point of these techniques is that a camera or scanner is used to record the pictures. The use of either a film camera or computer program with frame-by-frame capture is the same in terms of the basic working procedures.

Except for the pegbar animation techniques all the other techniques are improvised, straight-forward animations. These direct animation techniques need very little preparation. The material to be animated is put directly in front of the camera and the shooting can start as soon as the camera is set up. The results can be checked much faster than if using planned pose-to-pose animation.

Direct animation techniques gives your animation a natural flow. It has the vitality of improvisation, and you may be surprised to see the animated material leading the way. On the other hand, you may lose control of the timing and your film may overcome a reasonable time length. This method also becomes really difficult if you have several characters interacting in the same scene.

Basically, there are three different groups of direct animation techniques:

01_Plane-view or 2-dimensional animation

02_Stop-motion or 3-dimensional animation

03_Relief animation or 2.5-dimensional animation

For most of the 2-dimensional animation techniques, a scanner can be used instead of a camera. It takes longer to scan an image than to capture it by camera, but the quality is better. The scanner is particularly useful for animated drawings on paper, or when using the cel technique, and for painting backgrounds. The scanned pictures can be worked over, registered, and adjusted using a computer program such as Photoshop, Illustrator, and Painter. The editing of the pictures files has to be made in a compositing program such as Final-Cut, Premiere, After Effects or Flash.

Don't forget that you can mix the techniques. Don't fence yourself in the schematic either/or dichotomy. You can easily combine drawings and cut-outs or animated objects and clay-animation, or even puppets and cel animation. Anything is possible; **the only limit is your imagination...**

This page is for your own sketches and scraps.

0501_Animated Painting or Drawing

This is a plane-view animation technique. The camera looks horizontally or vertically at the artwork.
The main characteristic of this technique is that you can only add to the drawings but not erase. If you work with opaque paint, parts of the drawing can be painted over and therefore covered.

Number of participants per camera
One or two

Time required
One hour minimum

Basic equipment
Two lights of 100 to 150W or 12V-50W or LED 12W
Animation stand or Tripod
Paper
Colour or Grease pencils
Coloured ink or paint
Brushes
Masking tape

Equipment for digital recording
DV-Camcorder
Cable for camera and computer
Computer
Computer program with stop-motion capture
Scanner, Printer
DV-tape, CD-R, DVD-V

Equipment for film recording
Film-camera
Film stock
Exposure meter

Technique
A painting or drawing is created, completed or modified directly in front of the camera. Shooting in two's is good for all but the slowest or fastest movements.

Hints
For beginners: Don't move the camera; no zooms or pans.

Give rhythm to the film by changing the number of frames exposed in each additional step.

Work according to a soundtrack.

Mix this technique with cut-outs.

Indicate the field size with masking tape on the working surface.

Zoom out to discover the whole picture as different from the close-up.

Use Picture turn-around to discover a new and unexpected element.

Reverse shooting or editing
Use a surprise element by adding the most important factor at the end when the picture is almost completed.

Picture turn-around

Drawing on a starch-paste surface

A interesting version of the *Animated Painting or Drawing* technique is to use starch powder and mix it with water in order to get a thick pulp or paste. This pulp is poured into a flat, square glass recipient and placed under the camera. According to the thickness of the pulp, you can use front or back light. The drawings are made with a brush and watercolours. The effect produced by the contact of the watercolours with the starch surface is surprising and improvised.

This technique also permits you to move the watercolour strokes and thus to animate the drawings.

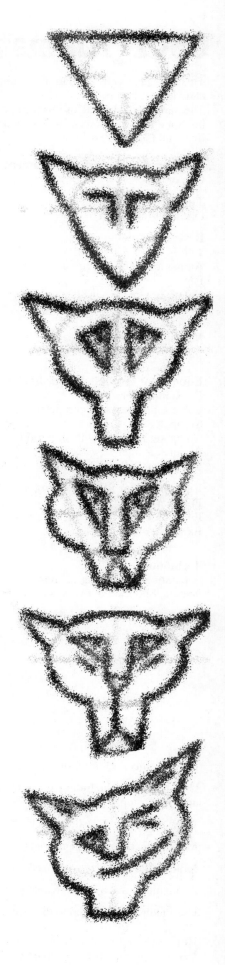

0502_Animation on Black- or White Board

This is a very fast, expressive and low-cost technique, and things really move here! This is of course not the technique to demonstrate the functioning of a diesel motor or a precision watch movement, but it's great to animate fluttering butterflies, a fearless goldfish or growing buttercups.

Number of participants per camera
Two to three

Time required
One hour minimum

Basic equipment
Two lights of 100 to 150W or 12V-50W or LED 12W
Animation stand or Tripod
Blackboard (chalkboard) or Whiteboard
White and colour chalk
Eraser for blackboard
Felt pens and eraser for whiteboard
Masking tape

Equipment for Digital recording
DV-Camcorder
Cable from camera to computer
Computer
Computer program with stop-motion capture
Scanner, Printer
DV-tape, CD-R, DVD-V

Equipment for film recording
Film camera
Film stock
Exposure meter

Technique
This is a plane-view animation technique where the artwork is upright or horizontal, and the camera is facing it at a right angle.
A drawing is created, completed or modified directly in front of the camera.
There are three possibilities to do so:
01_creating the drawing from the beginning to fully developed
02_completing or modifying an existing drawing
03_partly erasing and modifying a drawing to create movement

Standard exposure is two frames for each movement, except for the fastest or the slowest movements.

This technique can be applied on black or whiteboard, but it's either/or.

Using whiteboard offers brilliant colours but the white surface also causes eyestrain.

Some felt pens look like watercolours.

On the blackboard, erased parts always leave marks behind. This is not necessarily a disadvantage if you make use of it –– as speed lines, for instance!

Hints
With this technique a group of participants can produce a harmonious result if each participant continues the work of the previous one.

Indicate the field size on the board.

Use indirect light to prevent reflections.

Avoid camera movements (zooms or pans).

Use tracing paper or cels with guidelines indicated, and with the outline of the image sketched. This way you are assured that the subject is in the correct position and size.

If you use the board in a horizontal position, this technique can be mixed with cut-outs.

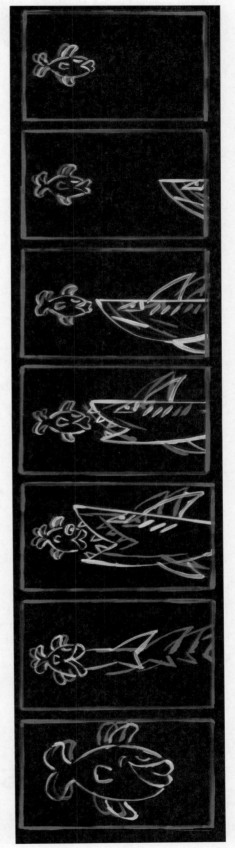

0503_Cut-Out Animation

Cut-out animation is a simple but wonderful animation technique. No special drawing abilities are necessary. If you don't want to draw, cut characters out of magazines. It's great to match Queen Elizabeth's head with a Yeti's body. Cut them out and move them around in front of your camera.

Collage animation

Number of participants per camera
One or two

Time required
Four hours minimum

Basic equipment
Two lights of 100 to 150W or 12V-50W or LED 12W
Animation stand
Assorted coloured cardboard
Clear and coloured cels or plastic sheets
Scissors
Cutter
Fast drying glue
Eyelet puncher and eyelets
Fine string
Masking tape

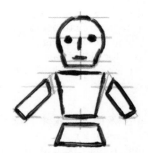

Jointless cut-outs

Equipment for digital recording
DV-camcorder
Cable from camera to computer
Computer
Computer program with stop-motion capture
Scanner, Printer
DV-tape, CD-R, DVD-V

Equipment for film recording
Film camera
Film stock
Exposure meter

Cut-outs with jointed limbs

Technique
This is a plane-view animation technique where the camera points down at the artwork at a right angle. Take two frames for each movement except for the fast and slow ones. You should be aware of the possibilities and limits of cut-out animation.

Don't expect the smooth movements of pegbar animation, but take advantage of jerkiness.

The details of the painted figures and the background make up for the lack of natural movement. Turn the disadvantages into advantages and make cut-outs look and behave like cut-outs.

Silhouette cut-outs

There are five basic types of cut-outs for animation:

01_Collage animation

02_Jointless cut-outs

03_Cut-outs with jointed limbs

04_Silhouette cut-outs

05_Cut-outs of each movement

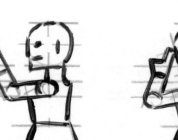

Cut-outs of each movement

01_Collage Animation

This technique is somewhere in between cut-outs and animated material. Flat pieces of newspaper, photographs, napkins, or even your stamp collection can be animated directly in front of the camera. The movement comes by replacing the whole picture or by changing a part of the picture. Also, make use of camera zooms and pans.

Most collage animation is done in visual squeeze. This involves an *avalanche* of pictures, often structured to a sound track.

Collage animation is a good technique to tell a story. Cut out pictures from newspapers and magazines and tell a story about the horror of war or the beauty of tropical flowers. Take your family photo album and tell the story of your dynasty in twenty seconds.

02_Jointless Cut-outs

This is very simple technique, easy to cut out, but more delicate to animate. Pieces can be cut out of almost any kind of material: cardboard, paper, felt or other cloth, plastic, or the skin of a water buffalo.

A frequently used material for cut-outs is drawing paper with a thin layer of metal in-between the sheets. This paper is quite stiff so it can be painted on and cut out easily. The cut elements are animated on a background which is on top of a magnetic board. These loose parts can be moved with precision, as they stick firmly to the metal background, lie really flat, and don't fall down even when animated vertically.

Another good technique is to make cut-outs of transparent coloured plastic with lighting from beneath. Wherever a cut-out of one colour overlays another, mixtures of colours appear in those areas

03_Cut-outs with Jointed Limbs

The body and limbs can be cut out of any durable material. Each part is painted and coloured separately, then cut out.

The parts can be assembled either with **Eyelets** or **Metal Fasteners.** The joints will be visible unless you fix them to the body by gluing them behind the limb, which has to be able to move.

Another method to make joints invisible is to punch a hole in the body and glue the punched-out disc to the limb. This **Punched-Out-Joint** is then fitted into the hole of the body part.

The easiest way to make invisible joints is to attach both parts with a thin **String-Joint**. Make a small hole in the body part and introduce a piece of string, which is then taped to the body and limbs.

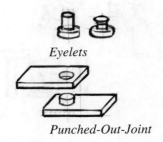

Eyelets

Punched-Out-Joint

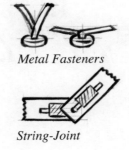

Metal Fasteners

String-Joint

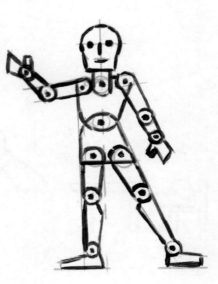

04_Silhouette Cut-outs

This technique uses the same construction methods as jointless or jointed cut-outs. However, you don't need to worry about colouration, or visible or invisible joints. The figures are made out of black cardboard, and even the metal joints (if any) are painted black to avoid reflections. For shooting, the figures are placed on a sheet of glass and lit from beneath.

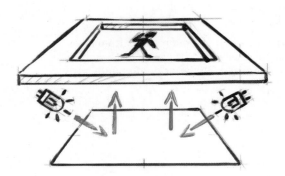

05_Cut-outs of Each Movement

This technique is somehow in-between pegbar and cut-out animation. The preparation time is longer than for the usual cut-outs, but you catch up during the shooting.

The principle is to mix animated cut-outs and still cut-outs. When the whole object moves, each phase is cut out entirely, e.g. a walking cycle. When only parts of the body are moved, e.g. sitting figure turning the head, only the moving parts are cut out and jointed to the still part. The animated parts are used over and over again, especially in cyclic movements.

The cut-outs can also be mounted to cels and used just as in pegbar animation.

Still part   *Moving parts*   *Composite image*

Hints

You must find some way to prevent cut-outs from moving out of place, as there's no previous drawing to tell you where to put them back. You can try a thin layer of rubber cement or double-sided tape. There are, of course, sprays available for this purpose. Personally, I use a piece of masking tape made into a tiny loop.

To avoid shadows around the edge of your cut-outs you can use a glass pressure-plate to hold them down and keep them flat.

Another method to avoid shadows is to use a simple multiplane animation stand. A few centimetres of space between the background and the figures is enough to diffuse the shadows

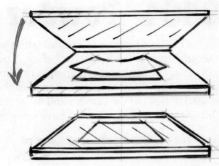

Glass pressure-plate

To keep cut-out's flat during the colouring procedure and on your animation table black self-adhesive plastic wallpaper is mounted to the reverse side of the drawing paper before cutting them out. This also avoids reflections when used on a multi-level stand.

Transparent cels or plastic sheets can be coloured and scratched to create a texture. The semi-transparent cut-out pieces create a sense of depth when they are animated on top of each other. Moreover, you can flip these pieces and use them with the back side up.

Front   *Back*

Still another method is to paint both sides of the figures, so you can just turn them over if you want to animate them the other way around or change the expression.

Turn around to change expression

Don't forget to indicate the field size on the table top. Fix the camera so that it faces the artwork right side up, and the lamps at an angle of 45 degrees in order to avoid reflections from the glass plate.

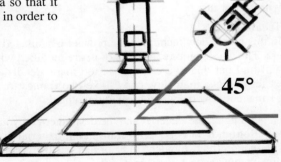

Indicate the Fieldsize
Lamps at an angle of 45°

Working with a Computer

Computer programs has entered the world of cut-out animation. The Inverse Kinetic Principle allows you to connect individual parts of a character and animate it just like a puppet with invisible strings. The same program offers the possibility to work on multiple levels with foreground, middle, and background. Special effects, lights, camera, and compound movements, as well as editing can all be handled together at once.
Besides, all computer program with Stop-Motion recording comes with a feature called **Onion Skinning**. This is a handy invention for cut-out animation because it allows the previewing of the new position before you capture the frame.

0504_Powder Animation

One of the best powder animation artists pretended not to be able to draw a straight line on paper. Even if I never believed her, there is something true about it. I've seen many workshop participants, cameramen, producers and editors who never made a drawing in their lives, and yet they were perfectly able to move powder around in front of the camera and to create beautiful animation. After all, why not? Did anybody ever ask you to have drawing abilities to play in a sand box?

Number of participants per camera
One or two

Time required
Three hours minimum

Basic equipment
Animation stand
Light box or glass plate and two lights of 100 to 150W or 12V-50W or LED 12W
Masking tape
Granulated material such as fine quartz sand
Brushes of different sizes
Spatula
Comb

Equipment for digital recording
DV-camcorder
Cable from camera to computer
Computer
Computer program with stop-motion capture
Scanner, Printer
DV-tape, CD-R, DVD-V

Equipment for film recording
Film camera
Film stock
Exposure meter

Different kinds of fine, granulated material such as coffee, sugar, salt, rice or flour can be used. For a transparent effect, you can animate fine coloured glass or plastic grains. Other particular effects can be obtained by using metallic powder or coloured glitter. The best powder is probably very fine grained quartz sand. The sand can be picked up at construction enterprises or at the beach. Copacabana has a good name for quality sand, next time you spend your holidays there, don't forget to take a bag back home! The sand is sifted until it reaches the fine grain quality you're looking for. This sand has a natural sand colour that looks beautiful on a dark background. If you want to work with coloured sand, you can dye it with colour ink.

Technique
In this plane view technique the powder is animated directly in front of the camera. The whole picture, or parts of it, are modified with brushes and spatulas. You will find out that you can't make too many details and that fast movements are easier to make than slow ones. Take two frames for each movement to ensure a permanent flow from one form to the other.

Depending on the material and the desired effect, you will have to adapt the lighting. Bottom light is good for transparent material like grained glassware or for a silhouette effect. Incident light brings out the colours of the sand and the three dimensional aspect of the material.

Hints
Work on a glass plate so the material will move around freely.

Use material of only one colour; different colours should be placed on different levels (multiplane) if you don't want to mix them up.

The camera should be mounted to the carriage so that the artwork is right side up when sitting in front of the animation stand.

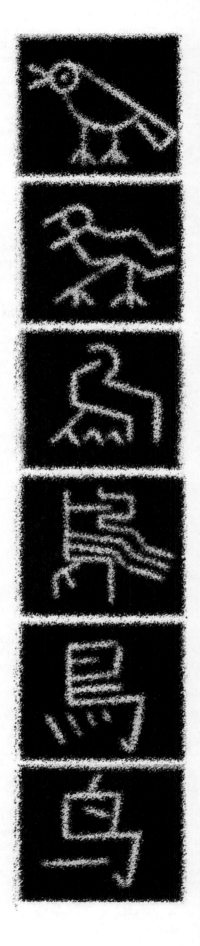

0505_Paint-on-Glass Animation

This is a child of the happy union of animated painting and powder animation techniques. As a matter of fact, it uses paint, but the paint is animated very much like the movements in powder animation.

Number of participants per camera
One or two

Time required
Three hours minimum

Basic equipment
Animation stand
Light box or glass plate and two lights of 100 to 150W or 12V-50W or LED 12W
Masking tape
Acryl or Oil Paint
Brushes of different sizes
Spatula
Comb

Equipment for digital recording
DV-camcorder
Cable from camera to computer
Computer
Computer program with stop-motion capture
Scanner, Printer
DV-tape, CD-R, DVD-V

Equipment for film recording
Film camera
Film stock
Exposure meter

Technique
The working surface is a clear sheet of glass. This surface can be bottom- or top-lit. Bottom light makes transparent colours brighter, but throws opaque paint into shadows. Top light can bring out the three dimensional structure of the paint.

You may use water or oil based paint. Perhaps you would like to try out coloured ink or watercolour pencils, which can be dissolved with water and worked like an aquarelle. In order to make the watercolour adhere to the glass surface you may add a few drops of oxgall to it.

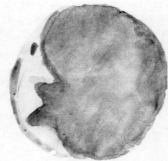

Hints
You will soon find out that you can't make too many details and that fast movements are easier to make than slow ones. The movement in this technique is sort of a permanent dissolve. Parts of the painting or the whole painting are metamorphosed one into the next one. This gives a soft, fluid aspect to the film, which resembles powder animation and can hardly be achieved with any other technique.

If you work with oil paint and the recording will take several days the paint will dry out and become hard. Add a little bit of Vaseline to the paint in order to prevent the oil paint drying too fast. According to the animator who uses this technique, the oil paint will stay soft for at least 10 years ! Time enough to finish your work comfortably.

0506_Pastel Animation

This is one of the youngest children in the family of animation techniques. It's very close to the paint-on-glass technique, but done with pastel crayons or chalk on rough paper.

In this plane-view technique, the camera is looking at right angles to the artwork either horizontally or vertically. The vertical position of the artwork has the advantage that all the dust falls straight to the floor or into a bag prepared for it. In any case, it is a dust-producing technique. Some way to collect the dust must be found; try your vacuum cleaner.

The working surface is a rough, slightly sanded paper and the pastel colours are applied heavily to this surface. A modification in movement is made by erasing or rubbing off the part, which is going to move, and then new lines and colours are applied to that part. Just like in the paint-on-glass technique, the whole picture or part of it can be metamorphosed one into the other.

Black and rough photo-cardboard is the best material to bring out the bright pastel colours and to avoid reflection which may appear with glossy surfaces.

0507_Etching Animation

This technique consists of applying a thin layer of black paint or china ink onto a sheet of glass or a piece of flat plaster cast. In fine art shops you will find scratch-boards (scraper-boards) already covered with a fine layer of chalk, which is just perfect for this technique.

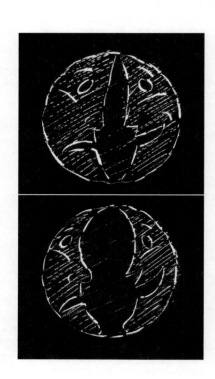

The sheet of glass or the cardboard is top-lit under the camera. The black layer is scratched or etched with a knife, or any other sharp tool, to show the white plaster or chalk underneath. The scratched lines will disappear, if you cover them with the background colour. Make sure the covering colour has dried before you continue the shooting; the difference between dry and wet colour might show on the screen.

The scratched-out lines and shapes can also be coloured by gouache or watercolour. Several layers of colours applied to the sheet of glass allow the discovery of different colours according to the depth of the etching.

In the silhouette version of this technique the sheet of glass is covered by black opaque paint and the plate is bottom-lit. The layer of black paint is scratched with a knife, or any other sharp tool. The scratched parts will appear white. The scratched lines will disappear if you cover them with the black opaque paint. No excuse here *to wait for the ink to dry;* with back light, there is no difference between dry and wet paint! To bring some colours into this technique, the lines can be coloured by transparent ink, or sheets of transparent and coloured plastic can be placed underneath the glass plate.

0508_Pin-Art Animation

Thanks to the popular pin-boards the traditional technique of pinhead-shadow animation has had a happy revival. *Alexandre Alexeieff* and his wife *Claire Parker* invented the technique of pinhead-shadow animation in 1933 and made their first-film, *Night on the Bald Mountain*, inspired by the music of *Moussorgsky*. Alexeieff was first of all an engraver and the visual effect he achieved with his invention was that of an animated black and white engraving.

Jacques Drouin and *Michèle Lemieux* from the National Film Board in Canada are some of the few artist to continue to work in this technique.

Number of participants per camera
One or two

Time required
Three hours minimum

Basic equipment
Tripod
Two lights of 100 to 150W or 12V-50W or LED 12W
Spotlight
Pin board
Spatulas of different sizes

Equipment for digital recording
DV-camcorder
Cable from camera to computer
Computer
Computer program with stop-motion capture
DV-tape, CD-R, DVD-V

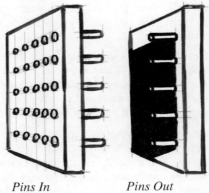

Pins In   *Pins Out*

Equipment for film recording
Film camera
Film stock
Exposure meter

Technique
The basic principle of this technique is that pins are pushed in and out of a white surface.
This surface is lit from one side. When all the pins are inside the board, the surface looks white with small black dots like an engraving. By pushing the pins from behind out of the board, the pins create a dark shadow on the white board. When all pins are pushed entirely out, the surface of the board looks black. By pushing the pins in and out, an image with various intensities between black and white can be created on the board. The visual effect is indeed that of a black and white engraving.

The pin-board is mounted upright in front of the camera. With various instruments like spoons, the pins are pushed in and out of the board.

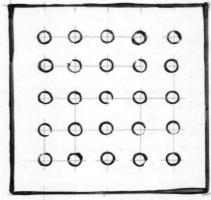

Pins In

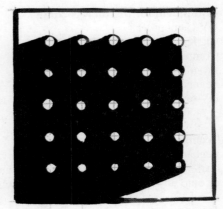

Pins Out

Hints
You will soon find out that you can't make too many details and that fast movements are easier to make than slow ones.

The movement in this technique is a sort of permanent dissolve. Parts of the image or the whole images are metamorphosed one into the next. This gives a soft, fluid aspect to the film, which resembles powder animation and can hardly be achieved with other techniques.

0509_Pegbar Animation

In pegbar animation, there are two ways to proceed:

Straight ahead animation is improvised animation. The animator creates drawing after drawing, very much like in powder- or paint-on-glass animation.

Planned animation is when the animator breaks down the movements into strong poses, key-drawings, and in-betweens. The planned animation requires an exposure sheet for recording.

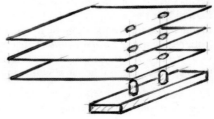

Punched cels /paper Pegbar

This is the traditional technique of all cartoon films, from Max Fleischer to Tex Avery and Walt Disney. All the big production lines have been built upon this system. It's the pegbar technique that permit's one to set up these production lines. Pegbar is the only technique where the actual animation work is done not under but away from the camera. This technique permits dividing animation work into different jobs such as key animation, in-betweening, tracing, colouring and recording.

Animation board

The name of this technique comes from a flat plate of steel with two or three pegs mounted to it, called the pegbar. This pegbar keeps the punched cels or paper in a steady and lasting relationship to each other. This is done by punching holes in all the cels or papers and putting them over the pegs on the pegbar. Pegbars are identical on both the drawing board and the animation stand.

If no pegs are available, a corner registration system can be used instead. An L-shaped piece of cardboard controls the registration of the paper or cel sheets. During the drawing and recording process, the lower left corner of the sheets are put into the cardboard corner. The lack of precision caused by this method can be somewhat diminished by using broad lines and extremely simple forms.

L-shaped cardboard

Number of participants per camera
Twelve approximately

Time required
Six hours minimum

Basic equipment
Two lights of 100 to 150W or 12V-50W or LED 12W
Animation stand
Masking tape
Office hole puncher
Coloured grease pencils or felt pens

for each participant:
200 sheets of white bond paper, format A4 about 50 to 60 gsm
a few clear acetate cels
Drawing board with pegbar or L-shaped corner

Equipment for digital recording
DV-Camcorder
Cable from camera to computer
Computer
Program with stop-motion capture
Scanner, Printer
DV-tape, CD-R, DVD-V

Equipment for film recording
Film camera
Film stock
Exposure meter

Technique
Pegbar animation means animating drawings. Drawing with pencils, brush, charcoal, felt pens or any kind of instrument onto paper, cels, cardboard, banana leafs, or onto any kind of support. Each drawing is made on a separate sheet of paper or cel.
To create continuity of movement, each new drawing has to refer to the previous one. The closer you make one drawing to the other the smoother and slower the animation will appear on the screen. The transparency of the cels and paper allows the previous drawing to be seen and a slight modification can be made for the new one. Each drawing is numbered in order and registered on the exposure sheet.

Drawing Means Omitting

While planning the characters for the film, don't forget that you'll be drawing them several hundred times. So if you want to finish your film within a reasonable period, you must simplify the structure of your characters. A complicated figure can be very expensive in terms of time and energy invested. Every extra piece of clothing may take you hours of work.

From reality to abstraction: Simplified drawing

Repeat movements

This is a standard in pegbar animation, because you can use the same drawings as a cycle without making new drawings. Take advantage of cyclical movements, like humans or animals walking, dancing elephants, an eye or a mouth that opens and closes...

In **Straight-ahead animation**, the animator would start with the first drawing and then make each drawing slightly modified up to the climax of the movement or to the end of the cycle.

In **Planned animation,** the animator would draw first the beginning and the end of the movement, then the Key-drawings, and finally make the In-betweens.

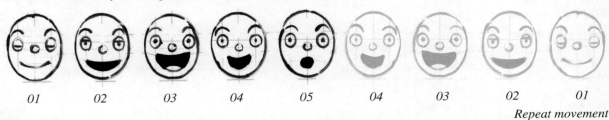

Repeat movement

Metamorphosis

Growing and morphing procedures are classic in animation. Planned animation is used to melt one drawing into the other. In a metamorphose that takes 5 drawings to transform A into B, the animator would draw number 1 and 5 first and then the in-betweens by splitting. The first in-between would be the number 3 drawing, which is the perfect in-between of 1 and 5. Then you would continue the splitting by making the number 2 in-between 1 and 3 and the number 4 in-between 3 and 5

Metamorphoses

Hints

To create a large number of drawings in a limited time, the drawings must be simplified to the maximum (outline drawings or stick figures).

Each participant uses one colour for the animated drawings and adds more colours only when all the drawings are finished.

Everybody uses the same field size.

To save time during shooting, a whole pile of drawings can be put under the camera. The drawing on top of the pile is recorded, then lifted, and so on.

Shooting holds: Take advantage of holds, but be sure that holds in a wobbling animation keep wobbling, and don't look like a freeze frame. You should make two or three copies of the hold and then shoot them alternatively. This gives the same wobble to the hold as to moving parts.

Shooting Hints

To make shooting more creative than just recording the images frame by frame under the camera, the artwork can be mounted onto a vertical glass sheet. This can be the window of your room, the windows of a car, or of a train. A space is left free around the artwork in order to see the background which will change according to the location. It is a good idea to use small size artwork like A5 or even as small as a flip book. Light and focal point should be on the artwork.

0510_Cel Animation

One of the possible applications of the pegbar technique is cel animation. *Cel* is the short form of celluloid, or acetate, sheets which are used as a surface for inking and painting images. The cels are punched to fit over pegs. The high transparency permits combining up to four cels for a single image.

Cel animation was the classic animation technique used by all studios until the late 1970s when computer technology became reliable. The hand drawn cel animation had no chance to compete, since cel animation is labour intensive and therefore expensive. In artistic, hand-crafted animation, cels are however still used either in the classical hand-drawn way or in a mixture with other techniques, particularly with drawing-on-paper animation.

In cel animation, the rough layout drawings are cleaned, and these *cleans* are then traced onto a clear sheet of cel with pen and ink.
Felt pens with ink that adheres to the smooth cel surface can also be used. Tracing is done on the front side of the cel. Painting or opaquing is done on the reverse side of the cel so the ink line will not be disturbed. The painted part will look opaque and flat on the front side.

A photocopy procedure is also used to transfer the drawings from paper to cels with the advantage of preserving the artistic quality of the original line drawings.

Layout Drawings

Number of participants per camera
Twelve approximately

Time required
Six hours minimum

Basic equipment
Two lights of 100 to 150W or 12V-50W or LED 12W
Animation stand
Masking tape
Office hole puncher
Pen and ink
Brush and acryl colour paint
Coloured grease pencils or felt pens

for each participant:
100 sheets of clear acetate cels
Drawing board with pegbar or L-shaped corner

Traced Cleans

Equipment for digital recording	Equipment for film recording
DV-camcorder	Film camera
Cable from camera to computer	Film stock
Computer	Exposure meter
Program with stop-motion capture	
Scanner, Printer	
DV-tape, CD-R, DVD-V	

Painting on the back of the cel

Planned Animation
Cel animation is always associated with planned animation. None of the classical animation feature films could have been made without a script, storyboard, layout, posing, key animation, in-betweens and exposure sheets. Planned animation requires a vision of the finished animation which means precise control over the production procedure from idea to screen.

In opposition to improvised animation, the important thing here is the result and not so much the making of it. Yet both approaches have in common starting with an idea. In planned animation, the idea is researched and visualized according to general film design, character, and background concepts. The storyboard and animatics are the next steps. The storyboard leads to layout and posing. In planned animation, the animator works according to an exposure sheet. This helps the animator to make precise key drawings and in-betweens The exposure sheet can be based on a pre-recorded soundtrack which is crucial for lip-sync animation.

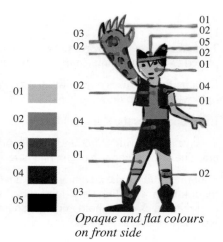

Opaque and flat colours on front side

0511_Drawing-on-Paper Animation

Drawing-on-paper animation is similar to the line test in cel animation. But with this technique, it's not just a test but the lines on paper are the actual drawings for the film. Nowadays the drawing-on paper technique has become the new standard. In the digital production procedure, the drawings are no longer traced to a cel and hand-coloured, but scanned and coloured in a computer. The scan and the compositing computer program has replaced the animation stand and film camera, but the drawings-on-paper remain.

Technique
In order to animate one drawing, close the previous one; you have to refer to the last drawing you made. To see the previous drawing while making the next one on a new sheet of paper, you would prefer the paper to be transparent.
This can be done either by using very thin paper (50g/gsm) or transparent tracing paper. The other method is to use a light box. The light under the drawings shines through the papers and you can see the previous drawings in transparency. A slight modification can then be made for the new one. Each drawing is numbered in order and registered in the exposure sheet.

Hints
The drawing-on-paper animation technique is an interesting one for workshops because it's fast and economical. Moreover, all the participants go through the whole job, from line drawings to coloration.
Characters and backgrounds must be very simple, as everything has to be redrawn for each frame. Even when the drawings are made very precisely they are never identical, so the projected picture seems to wobble. This is inevitable with this technique and must be accepted as such.

Number of participants per camera
Twelve approximately

Time required
Six hours minimum

Basic equipment
Two lights of 100 to 150W or 12V-50W or LED 12W
Animation stand
Masking tape
Office hole puncher
Coloured grease pencils or felt pens

for each participant:
200 sheets of white bond paper, format A4 about 50 -60 gsm
Drawing board with pegbar or L-shaped corner

Equipment for digital recording
DV-camcorder
Cable from camera to computer
Computer
Program with stop-motion capture
Scanner, Printer
DV-tape, CD-R, DVD-V

Equipment for film recording
Film camera
Film stock
Exposure meter

Improvised Animation
Drawing-on-paper animation is good for both direct and improvised animation. To improvise is to create without preparation. You can start with a subject: an image, a sound, a movement... When you are writing a letter to a friend, you know the general content, you know the beginning and maybe the end, but you don't know all the details in-between. It's through interaction that you move forward. Drawing-on-paper animation can be interactive, where one drawing leads to the next. Each drawing develops out of the previous one. The important thing with this approach is the process of discovery and not so much the final result.

When working with this technique, you can forget everything you've heard about cels, multi-levels, backgrounds, inking and painting. Take a ream or two of bond paper, your favourite pencil, and start drawing. And keep drawing, drawing, drawing...

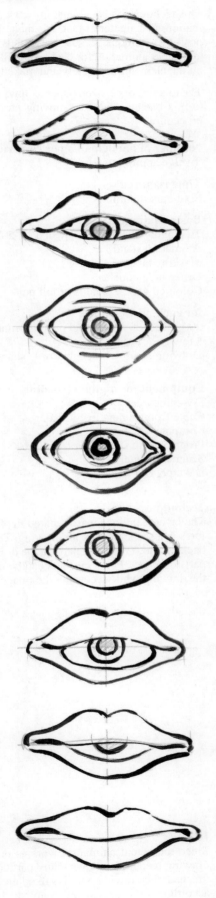

0512_Mixtures of Cels and Paper

This technique is somewhat in-between cel animation and drawing-on-paper animation. As a matter of fact, this manual technique is quite close to the digital compositing technique because it uses cels and paper cut-outs as layers for foregrounds and paper animation for background layers. By using computers, you may capture all the elements separately and make the mix in the compositing program.

The mixture of cels and paper technique is, however, still used whenever you want to mix backgrounds and moving parts straight in one shot during the recording procedure.

Number of participants per camera
Twelve approximately

Time required
Six hours minimum

Basic equipment
Two lights of 100 to 150W or 12V-50W or LED 12W
Animation stand
Masking tape
Office hole puncher
Coloured grease pencils or felt pens

for each participant:
200 sheets of white bond paper, format A4 about 50 - 60 gsm
a few clear acetate cels
Drawing board with pegbar or L-shaped corner

Equipment for digital recording	**Equipment for film recording**
DV-camcorder	Film camera
Cable from camera to computer	Film stock
Computer	Exposure meter
Program with stop-motion capture	
Scanner, Printer	
DV-tape, CD-R, DVD-V	

Technique
The layer technique was invented in order to avoid redrawing the parts of the pictures in a scene that are not moving. This applies especially to the foreground and background. These still parts of the drawings can be made on a cel and the moving parts on paper. Paper cut-outs can be mounted to a cel. This cel must be put over the drawing while recording the image.

White Bond Paper

Foreground Cell

Composite Image

Hints
Since the actual animation work is done away from the camera, the animated drawing technique allows many participants to be occupied at once. When all is finished, the drawing board is fixed under the camera and the drawings are filmed according to the previously established exposure sheet.

0513_Rotoscoping

Originally rotoscoping was used to combine animation with live-action film. Walt Disney used the rotoscope technique to give a realistic look to *Snow White* and her *Prince Charming*.

The interesting and creative part of rotoscoping is to manipulate the live-action film as a base for drawings and paintings. It is by drawing over the live action that you make important decisions about the speed and rhythm of the animation, the framing, the background, the graphic style, the texture and colour.

The live-action used for rotoscoping can be old film stock or you may want to shoot and edit live-action so the basic material will fit the exact needs of the project. In both cases, rotoscoping means redrawing the pictures of a live-action film frame by frame.

Nowadays most rotoscoping is done in a computer. The live action is imported into computer program, where the animator can trace straight over the live action footage.

Number of participants per projector/camera
One

Time required
One day minimum

Basic equipment
Two lights of 100 to 150W or 12V-50W or LED 12W
Animation stand
Tracing paper or bond paper 50 - 60 gsm
Drawing board with pegs
Office puncher
Coloured pencils, ink, or paint

Equipment for digital procedure
DV-camcorder
Cable from camera to computer
Computer
Program with stop-motion capture
Scanner, Printer
DV-tape, CD-R, DVD-V

Equipment for film procedure
Projector with single frame projection
or camera with rotoscope unit
or editing table or film viewer
Table with frosted glass and mirror
Film camera
Flm stock
Exposure meter

Technique
Rotoscoping can be done by using film stock either in rear projection or viewing on a editing table with a luminous screen. However, today's video and digital tools have replaced film procedures in most cases.

Choose the digital or film procedure according to your equipment.

Hints
If the only purpose is to redraw the live-action in the same realistic manner, it's not really worth doing rotoscope animation. Motion capture can do it better better and faster !

The more you manipulate the original live-action film, the more interesting the animated film becomes.

Try to change the pace and framing of the original live action film.

Look for cyclic movements, without overdoing it.

Digital Procedures

With the digital method, the live-action sequence is imported into a computer drawing program, where the animator can draw with an electronic pen on a separate layer, straight over the live-action footage. When the drawings are finished, the live-action layer is deleted and the rotoscope drawings can be played on the screen.

Another procedure, somehow in-between the all-computer and the hand-drawn animation is the following: just as before, the live-action is imported into a computer drawing program. A sheet of glass with a pegbar is placed over the computer screen. The live action is played frame by frame and the movements are drawn on a transparent tracing paper straight from the screen. This technique needs recording of the drawings before viewing the animation.

Film Procedure

The live-action film is projected frame by frame to punched paper or cels. The part of live-action that interests you for the animated film is traced or painted on those supports, which are numbered and then can be filmed or scanned to be used in the traditional pegbar technique.

There are a few different possibilities for projecting the live-action film onto a drawing board:

If your camera is equipped with a rotoscope unit, you may load the camera with the live-action film and project it onto the animation table.

An editing table or a simple film viewer can do the same job, although the tracing will be harder, because the image is not so bright and sharp, and putting the tracing paper over the screen may lack precision.

The best way is to find a projector that can project frame by frame without burning the film. An old projector can be modified by taking the lamp house out of the projector and projecting over a mirrored prism. The image can then be projected either to a wall or over a mirror to a frosted glass inlaid in a table.

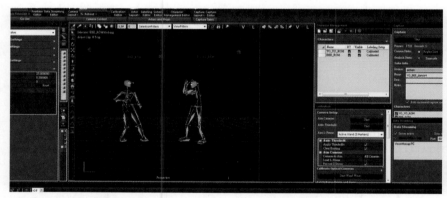

Motion Capture / Mocap

This technique is somehow in-between rotoscoping and stop-motion animation and consists of translating human movements to otherwise lifeless characters. Motion capture sensors are attached to the body of a human actor. Data of his movements are then captured by a virtual actor and processed in real time. The director can monitor the action as it's happening. This system can be applied to live broadcasting with characters on a virtual set.

Early attempts to capture real life movements have been made by *Eadweard Muybridge* and *Etienne-Jules Marey* in the 19th century. Their work is still widely used as visual references by classical animators.

The films made to this day show smooth and realistic movements, so realistic that all the power and magic of frame by frame animation is lost and gone for ever ! But animation is a moving trade and future animators will use Mocap in a creative and not too realistic way. No doubt, the real actors will learn how to behave like cartoon characters and then the frontier between Mocap and Frame-by-frame animation will be invisible.

0514_Animated Objects

Animating objects in stop-motion is another easy and really low-cost technique. No need to make thousands of drawings or to create complicated brushwork. Put your favourite objects, such as tins, bottles, pipe cleaners, or your own drawing material (since you don't use it for this technique!), in front of the camera and move it around.

There are two basic types of animated objects:

01_Still objects, such as bottles, stones, plastic letters for your titles, etc.
02_Movable objects, such as packages, paper foldings, wires, puppets, etc.

Number of participants per camera
Three or four

Time required
Six hours minimum

Basic equipment
Two lights of 100 to 150W or 12V-50W or LED 12W
Tripod
Projector light source or slide projector
Masking tape
Large roll of paper for diorama background
Coloured cardboard
Scissors and Cutter
Wire
Variety of objects of your own choice

Equipment for digital recording
DV-camcorder
Cable from camera to computer
Computer
Program with stop-motion capture
DV-tape, CD-R, DVD-V

Equipment for film recording
Film camera
Film stock
Exposure meter

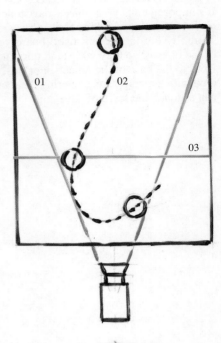
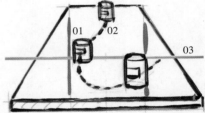

Field guide_01
Guideline_Spacing Guide_02
Focus Line_03

Technique
Stop-motion animation is ideal for illustrating principles of animation such as movement in time and space. For precise animation indicate the **Field Guide** on the table top and draw the **Guideline** and **Spacing Guide** as well as the **Focus Line.** Study the size of the objects and the distance to move them. Figure out the number of frames and the distance in millimetres between each move. With practice you will get the feeling for moving your objects around, and you won't use the guideline *crutch* any longer.

Moving objects must be done carefully to ensure smooth animation. Slow movements are harder to animate than fast ones. To assure smooth motion, objects are usually animated in *Ones*.

Shooting in reverse is necessary whenever objects out of order rearrange themselves into precise order. Setting the camera on reverse shooting and starting with the objects in their desired order produces this effect. Then you break down the movement by taking one frame for each position until they are in complete disorder. In projection, the orderly situation, which was first in shooting, will be last on film.

Low dramatic camera angle

01_Animation of Still Objects

It's important that your objects have a **Solid Base** to stand on. Fixing tall objects to a hard, smooth ground is possible by using a tiny piece of **Double sided Adhesive Tape**. If your tabletop is a soft board you can attach a **Drawing Pin** to the base of the objects, so they will stand upright. Still another method is to use a **Magnet** fixed to the base of the objects. For this, the whole animation table has to be covered with a metal plate. Covering the metal plate with one or more sheets of paper can regulate the force of adhesion.

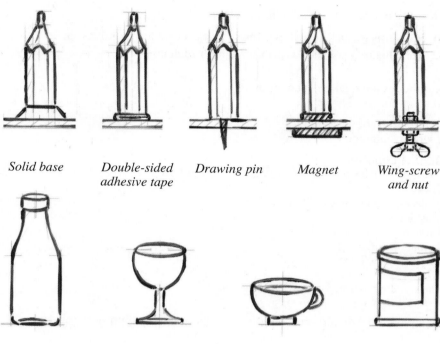

Solid base   *Double-sided adhesive tape*   *Drawing pin*   *Magnet*   *Wing-screw and nut*

02_Animation of Movable Objects

A movable object is a volume that can be moved in itself. Usually it is associated with toys and puppets, but not necessarily. It could be a flexible card box or a sack of flour. As a general rule, self-made objects are more fun to animate than toys you buy in a shop.

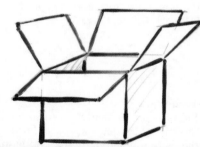

The inner structure of puppets *(see: 0516_Stop Motion_Model Animation)* may be constructed from a variety of materials such as metal wire. Electric or flower wire is good enough and comes in a variety of thicknesses. Make the skeleton flexible enough to move in all directions. The skin over the skeleton can be made out of any scrap material you find: cloth, foam, clay, paper. There is no limit to your imagination.

In specialized shops for exhibition material and toy shops you will find all sorts of articulated materials with plastic joints. This material is perfect for the articulated interior structure of a puppet. These puppet structures, dressed up differently, can be used over and over again.

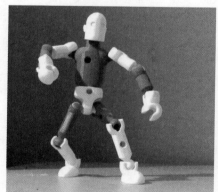

A 3-D printer can be used to make body parts for armatures with moveable joints

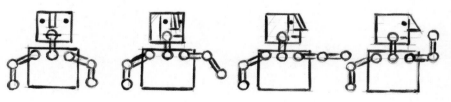

Light and Shadows

Light plays a creative part in object animation. Often the atmosphere of a film comes more from the lighting than from an elaborate background and objects. In object animation, the light is very much used as in a stage setting. For a flat light with no shadows, use one or two strong halogen lights pointed to a reflecting white surface, e.g. the ceiling. For dramatic light effects with shadows, use a spotlight projector or a slide projector focused on the objects being animated.

The shadows of objects can be projected to the ground where the objects are animated or to the background.

A **Backlight** throws the object into silhouette and gives a strange look to the scene. In the shape of the shadow, the object loses it's three-dimensional identity. It becomes a flat shape and bizarre deformations may appear.

Backlight

Camera Angles

Camera angles show the position of the camera (the filmmakers and viewer's point of view) in relation to the picture. For the animated objects, the technique of camera angles is an easy job. Just move the camera and you will get an entirely different atmosphere.

In a **Horizontal shot**, without shadows, the scene looks neutral.

The **Down-looking shot** can clarify a scene and explain the relationship between the subject and the background. The shadow projected to the ground underlines the weakness of the subject.

The **Up-looking shot** gives the impression of power and strength. The shadow projected to the background adds to the menacing look of the subject.

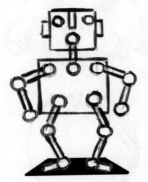
Horizontal shot

Down-looking shot

Up-looking shot

Hints

Take advantage of the three dimensions by creating foreground, middle-ground and background. Move the objects not only sideways in front of the camera but also towards and away from it, creating in and out of focus effects.

Indicate the field size and the focal line on the tabletop.

For more dramatic effect, mount the camera horizontally at the same level as the animation table or even in a up-looking position

In order to avoid shooting your own hand, use the same hand to move the objects and to release the frames.

A good basic background is a large roll of paper, taped to the wall and used as a horizonless smooth cove. Another method is to mount the paper roll upright as a *Cyclorama* background. This set-up is good to make horizontal camera pans.

To make objects *fly*, nylon string is not recommended, for the movements can not be controlled sufficiently. Use a clear **Sheet of glass** across the field size and animate the object on this invisible surface.

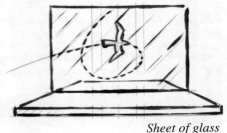

Sheet of glass

0515_Clay Animation

The modeling-clay technique is one of the most spontaneous and expressive kinds of animation. Take advantage of this material's properties, make your characters look like clay-figures, and make them move with all the expression inherent in this material. Clay is always in movement: the object is ready to be metamorphosed from a dog to a man, to a snake and back again.

Number of participants per camera
Three or four

Time required
Six hours minimum

Basic equipment
Two lights of 100 to 150W or 12V-50W or LED 12W
Tripod
Table
Spotlight or Slide projector
Masking tape
Large roll of paper for diorama background
Coloured cardboard
Scissors and Cutter
Modeling clay
Soft, non-hardening plasticine
Potter's clay

Equipment for digital recording	**Equipment for film recording**
DV-camcorder	Film camera
Cable from camera to computer	Film stock
Computer	Exposure meter
Program with stop-motion capture	
DV-tape, CD-R, DVD-V	

Potter's clay can be purchased at fine art- and stationery shops. It usually comes in monochrome brown or grey colour. Objects of Potter's clay must be covered overnight with a wet cloth or a plastic bag to keep them from drying out.

Modeling clay can be purchased at stationery shops and toy shops. It comes in a wide range of colours. White plasticine can be dyed to your taste.

Different sorts of soft plastic or jelly purchased in toy and gadget shops can be animated using plane view animation. If the material is transparent, bottom light can be very effective.

Technique
In this three-dimensional technique the clay object is modified directly in front of the camera. Take two frames for each movement and make use of the three dimensional form of the objects by using a spotlight for shadow effects. Move the objects not only parallel to the camera but also towards and away from it.

Metamorphosis

Background
Three types of backgrounds can be considered:

A ***still background,*** such as in puppet or object animation. It's a good idea to create a circular background to avoid shadows from the corners and to allow the camera to pan without going out of field from one side to the other.

Part of the ***background can be made of clay*** and integrated into the action (e.g. a mountain transforms into a house).

The ***whole background is made of clay*** and acts according to the film's plot (e.g. out of the ground a tree, a house or a mountain grows or disappears).

There are three basic types of clay animation.

01_ Start like a sculptor from a fresh piece of clay and create whatever you want. Take two frames for each phase of the development. The projected result appears to be a sculpture that is sculpted all by itself.

Sculpture

02_ Similar to puppet or object animation, the clay is shaped around a metallic structure with movable limbs. An advantage over puppets, is that parts of the figure, for instance the face, can be animated to change the expression.

Metallic structure

03_ The object is entirely out of clay metamorphosing from one figure to another These figures should be simple with a solid base to stand on in order not to fall apart.

Metamorphosis

Light
Light plays a creative part in clay animation; it can either give relief to the material or flatten it. Use the light as in stage lighting to create atmosphere: Low lights and dim shadows for morning mood, flat light from above with no shadows for high noon, long black shadows for evening. Blue filters create a night atmosphere and yellow filters create bright sunshine.

Using basic lighting from above to avoid double shadows from the camera and the animator plus a spotlight from one side for relief is most effective.

Position of light sources

Hints
To benefit from the material's character, don't use them as still figures, but let the clay be in movement to allow transformations and metamorphoses.

For beginners: use only one or two clay colours, one dark and one clear.

Indicate the field size on the background.

For beginners: no zooms, pans, or tilts.

Fix the camera horizontally on the same level as the animation table or in an up-looking position for a dramatic effet.

To achieve a continuous animation with a group, each participant can pursue the work of the previous animator or each participant starts his animation with a round ball of clay and finishes the same way.

0516_Stop Motion_Model Animation

Stop-motion films with armature models are enjoying a powerful comeback. Traditionally Czech masters, like *Jiri Trinka* and *Bretislav Pojar,* occupied this field for a long time. Recently, animators from all over the world are rediscovering this technique. Sophisticated and expensive armatures with mechanics to move eyeballs and mouth positions help to create animations, in which it is hard to see the difference between an armature model or a 3-D computer character.

This chapter is more concerned with low cost self-made armatures used for training purposes. The animation of these models with an aluminum wire armature and a modeling clay body is very much the same as with professional armatures which can easily be purchased on the internet.

Number of participants per camera
Two or three

Time required
Four hours minimum (shooting time)

Basic equipment
Two lights of 100 to 150W *or* 12V-50W *or* LED 12W
Spotlight *or* Slide projector
Stage with perforated table top
Tripod *or* Traveling camera device
Masking tape
Scissors and cutter
Electrical drill with slow speeds
Pliers
Screw drivers
Hacksaw
Sculpting tools
2 mm aluminium wire
(thicker or thinner according to the model)
M4 nuts
M4 wing screws
Two-part epoxy glue
Hardening modelling clay

Equipment for digital recording
DV-camcorder
Cable from camera to computer
Computer
Computer program with stop-motion capture
DV-tape, CD-R, DVD-V

Equipment for film recording
Film camera
Film stock
Exposure meter

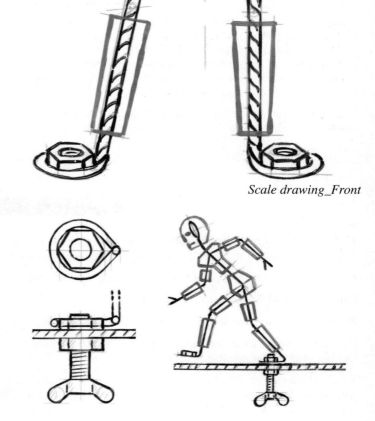

Scale drawing_Front

Wing-Screw and Nuts
to tie-down one foot of the model

Construction / Armature

Plan your armature by making a scale drawing and indicate the proportions and measures of head, body, arm and legs.

Use 2 mm aluminum wire and cut twice the length from hand to toe of the model The loose ends of the wire are put into a drill and the other are held by the end with pliers.

Slowly twisting the two wires together will reinforce the armature and make it easy to bend, to hold it steady and not spring back. This twisted part will be for the leg, body and arm of one side of the body. Repeat this procedure for the other side of the body. For the head, neck, and body, another wire is twisted according to the scale drawing.

These three parts are assembled and held together by the hips and chest. Two-part hardening clay is used to form these parts of the body as well as parts of the arms and legs. Hands and fingers can be shaped with thinner wire and the core can be modeled with hardening clay or two-part epoxy glue.

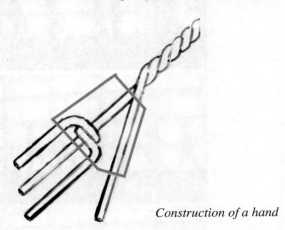

Construction of a hand

Animation

The animation of models is a difficult job, both physically and mentally. Physically, it is hard because you will have to work for hours in front and under the stage. For each step, the tie-down screw under the table top has to be changed from one foot to the other.

Mentally, it is hard because every step has to be planned and coordinated with the camera and compound moves. The interaction of several characters on the stage makes the job certainly more interesting, but certainly not easier.

In order to have the model stand upright, tie-down screws are used to hold each foot in a steady position on the tabletop. An M4 nut is fixed into each loop of the feet and glued to the wire with two-part epoxy glue. On the stage, the feet are tied-down with wing-screws through the perforated table top. A low camera angle or a thick carpet will hide the holes in the table top.

Hints

Take two frames for each movement.

Make use of the three-dimensional form of the objects by using a spotlight for shadow effects.

To create a depth of field feeling, move the objects towards and away from the camera.

Indicate the field size on the background.

For beginners: no zooms, pans, or tilts.

Fix the camera horizontally on the same level as the animation table or in an up-looking position for a dramatic effect.

To achieve a continuous animation with a group, each participant can pursue the work of the previous animator by taking over the model and animating a squence of his or her own.

Scale drawing Profile

To make use of the new technologies you may use a 3-D printer to make body parts and armatures
Draw the pieces in a 3-D program and feed it to the printer.
The machine will print any number of parts and joints.

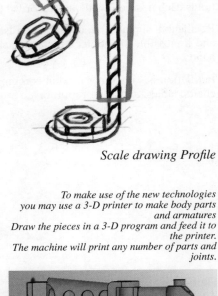

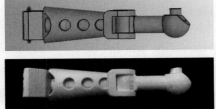

0517_Pixillation

Pixillation - nobody really knows where this funny word comes from. Most probably it was created by *Norman McLaren*, an artist of the *National Film Board* in Canada. Most of Pixillation is done with live actors. The actor gets into a strong pose and holds the position while the camera is recording one frame. Good actors are able to jump into the air and look as flying humans in the finished film.

Don't confuse Pixillation with Time-Lapse Cinematography, where natural live movements are filmed frame by frame in order to speed up the action, for instance, a flower opening.

Number of participants per camera
Any number of participants.
The more participants the more difficult it will be to direct them. You can try it with one hundred, but you need the voice of an army officer, or a megaphone to direct them.

Time required
Two hours minimum

Basic equipment
Tripod
Megaphone *(to communicate when you are shooting outdoors)*
Enough light for indoor shooting
Suitable background for indoor or outdoor shooting

Equipment for digital recording	Equipment for film recording
DV-camcorder	Film camera
Cable from camera to computer	Film stock
Computer	Exposure meter
Program with stop-motion capture	
DV-tape, CD-R, DVD-V	

Technique
This technique can be used outdoors with natural light and indoors with artificial light. In pixillation, each movement is created artificially by live actors as if they were puppets. The actor breaks down the movement into a series of poses and holds each position while it is recorded frame by frame.

Real actors slip around, appear, and disappear across a wall or a fence. Fantastic and impossible situations are created, such as people flying or walking on their hands.

Pixillation is sometimes used in combination with animated objects. In this case, chairs, tables, and other furniture are moved around in a mixture with live actors.

Hints
Avoid camera moves like zooms, pans, and tilts.

Indicate the field size on the set or the outdoor scene.

Indicate the guide line for actors.

With many actors you have to be very directive, or else the shooting will become completely disorganized.

0518_Time-Lapse Cinematography

Time-lapse cinematography is one of the privileged techniques for documentary animation filmmaking. Time-lapse cinema is observation and documentation of a slice of time in the life of self-moving objects. From an academic point of view, this technique belongs to the group of Special effects.

It is scientifically used to speed up natural movements such as the growth of plants, the opening of flowers, the movements of clouds, sunrises and sunsets.

Time-lapse cinematography squeezes time and can show in a short time the activity of workers in a plant, the movement of traffic in a street, people entering and leaving a cafeteria or a super-market.

Audiences are surprised to see within seconds the construction of a fifty storey building or the coming and going of people and cars in a parking lot.

Number of participants per camera
Two or three

Time required
Three hours minimum

Basic equipment
Enough light and set for indoor shooting
Suitable background for outdoor shooting

Equipment for digital recording
DV-camcorder
Cable from camera to computer
Computer
Program with stop-motion capture
DV-tape, CD-R, DVD-V

Equipment for film recording
Film camera
Film stock
Exposure meter

Technique
Before filming any action, it is necessary to determine the total number of frames to be made. This number of frames determines the length of the entire scene and the length of the time interval between exposures. This calculation is easy to make.

First you have to decide over what time period the action should be filmed. Let's say you would like to show the activity in a cafeteria during lunch time. The time to be covered would be from 11:00h to 14:00h, which is 3 hours or 180 minutes.

Next is to decide how long you would like to see this action on the screen. In this case, the projection time film should be about one minute or 60 seconds. Assuming that the film will be projected at 24 fps we need 60x24 frames or 1440 frames These 1440 frames must be made within the 180 minutes, so you divide 1440 by 180 and obtain 8 frames per minute, or an interval of 7.5 seconds between each exposure.

Hints
If you film outside with natural light, the light will considerably change during the shooting. An automatic shutter can be helpful, but it might influence too much the exposition of each frame. Best is to use the automatic shutter to measure the average light and set the shutter to manual during recording.

Shoot or composite the sequence in reverse. To make a building disappear is more surprising to an audience than to see the construction of it.

Avoid camera moves like zooms, pans and tilts.

If you use a film camera, the shooting time can be quite long and tiresome. The participants have to take turns with each other on the camera.

This is not a problem, however, if you work with a computer. Frame by frame capture programs always comes with a time-lapse feature. You may set this timer to capture a frame according to any number of seconds, minutes or hours.

0519_Animated Scrap-Material

Scrapbooking has become fashionable and is seriously competing with the traditional photo album or diary. So, why not animate and put life into your memories An airplane or metro ticket, coins from countries you traveled through, the bill of a unforgettable and overpaid intimate dinner for two, newspaper clips, a sketch from your hotel window, the photo of your beloved ones at sunset, etc. Nothing can resist your desire to communicate a slice of your life.

Animated scraps are, in a way, documentary animated films. They tell stories of happy holidays, of broken hearts or simply show the evidence and become the testimony of what you carried in your pocket or bag on a particular day, in a particular year.

Since just about anything can be animated, why not open your drawers and take out all the rubbish you've been keeping for ages? Look at all the needles, pins, nails, buttons, matches, chewing gum, pens, screws, confetti, strings, and what have you, and then make a decision: animate it - or throw it away!

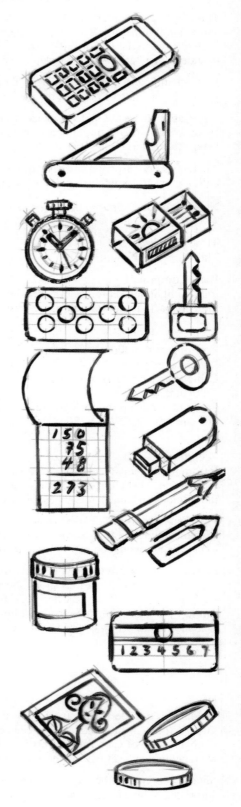

Number of participants per camera
One or two

Time required
Four hours minimum

Basic equipment
Two lights of 100 to 150W or 12V-50W or LED 12W
Animation stand
Masking tape
Scrap material of your own choice

Equipment for digital recording
DV-camcorder
Cable from camera to computer
Computer
Program with stop-motion capture
DV-tape, CD-R, DVD-V

Equipment for film recording
Film camera
Film stock
Exposure meter

Technique
This is a plane-view animation technique. The camera points down to the artwork at a right angle. The material is animated directly under the camera. Take two frames for each movement.

The stage can be lighted either by bottom light or incident light. Bottom light is good for transparent material or for a silhouette effect. Incident light brings out the three-dimensional aspects of the material

Hints
Scraps should not only be thrown on the table in front of the camera. They have to be animated, coming in an going out of the frame. The pages of a diary or an agenda can be turned over, a watch can indicate the time of shooting, a mobile telephone or a digital camera can display photos. A drawing can be animated in a sketch book, and so on. The limit is your own fantasy and imagination!

The term documentary film lacks a precise definition. In most so-called documentary films, it is impossible to know what is documentary or what is fiction. Documentary animation belongs most probably to the range of doc-fiction film.

However, if you consider your scrap film as a truly documentary animation, there is no room for fiction. Be honest, do not cheat by selecting objects which do not belong to the pretended content.

To achieve a continuous animation with a group of participants, each animator can pursue the work of the previous animator by using the Relay Principle.

0520_Bas-Relief Animation

To my knowledge, the world's first animated film made with the Bas-Relief technique was a Czech film called *Roman's Basou*. More widely known to the public is the film *The Passion* by *Jiri Trnka* (1962). *Trnka's* film is actually a mix of stop-motion and Bas-Relief Animation.
Kihachiro Kawamoto was certainly inspired by his master, *Jiri Trinka*, when in 1976 he made *Dojoii Temple*, which is a masterpiece mix of stop-motion and cell animation.

Number of participants per camera
One or two

Time required
Four hours minimum

Basic Equipment
Two lights of 100 to 150W or 12V-50W or LED 12W
Spotlight or slide projector
Animation stand
Masking tape
Bas-relief material of your own choice

Equipment for digital recording
DV-camcorder
Cable from camera to computer
Computer
Program with stop-motion capture
DV-tape, CD-R, DVD-V

Equipment for film recording
Film camera
Film stock
Exposure meter

Technique
Basically, this is a plane-view animation technique, but the materials are half 3-dimensional models and objects. The part pointing to the camera is in 3-D relief, while the the part behind, and therefore invisible for the camera, is flat.

The camera points down to the artwork at a right angle. The material is animated-directly under the camera. Take two frames for each movement.

The tabletop can be lit either by bottom light or incident light. Bottom light is good for transparent material.

A spotlight, or the beam of a slide projector, brings out the three-dimensional aspects of the material.

To animate characters and objects with long floating appendages like long hair, scarfs and skirts, the Bas-Relief Animation is the right technique. It is in fact much easier to animate these things horizontally on a flat surface than upright. To avoid shadows around the character you can animate on a sheet of glass like on a multiplane animation stand.

A 3-D printer can be used to make the objects. Create and draw the pieces in a 3-D program and feed it to the printer. The machine will print any number of parts and joints.

Hints
For beginners: avoid zooms, pans and tilts.

The camera should be mounted to the carriage in a way that the artwork is the right way up when sitting in front of the animation stand.

To achieve a continuous animation with a group of participants, each animator can pursue the work of the previous animator by using the Relay Principle.

Page for your own drawings.

0600_Grammar of Animation

What really makes animation different from painting, design, or sculpture is that it is subject to the passage of time. It depends perpetually on the principles of motion. What happens in between the frames is more important than the static state of one frame. The static shape loses its identity in time and space. In fact, time and space are the essential raw materials the animator works with every day.

Time and space are not easy to grasp. You cannot see or touch them, but there they are, in between the frames. Animation is not so much *art in movement* but *the art of movement.* Animation is design in time and space. It is the movement that gives life and meaning to your film.

Most students coming out of art school do not know how to handle time and space because they learned all about colours and shapes but have never heard about time and space. Moreover, in big studios animation has always been divided into specialties: designers for the characters and background; specialists for the movement breakdown; and so on. An animator must be concerned with both. Real satisfaction in this trade comes from the union of design and motion.

This chapter is intended to make time and space something real and show you how to put your hands on the invisible. There are people with a built-in sense of timing. They are usually good dancers or play a musical instrument; but even if you do not think that you belong to that species, your sense of timing can be developed by simply using the trial and error method!

Sense of Time

The passing of time, to be the master of time, to control it, to stop it, to manipulate it and to travel in time have always occupied and fascinated humankind. Artists, scientists, and philosophers have worked all around the subject. Whatever the results of these thoughts, one thing is certain: we all stand in a time-space framework and have to accept it whether we like it or not.

Time is omnipresent and everybody has theoretically the same amount of it, even if some people give the impression that they have more of it! However, there are people who work professionally with it: musicians, composers, dancers, actors, choreographers, filmmakers and of course, animators.

In animation, time is not only an essential raw material, it is first of all a material over which the animator has complete control. By making a film, the animator becomes a true master of time; he or she can expand or squeeze time, twist and turn it, or cut it into pieces – 24 pieces for every second – in order to fit it with his or her exact needs.

Developing a kin-esthetic sense, or a sense for timing, is for the animator as important as developing a sense for colour, framing and camera moves.

In live-action filmmaking, as in music and dance, the artist works with a sense of time, one which is related to real time. One minute in the recording of a live movie is one minute of real time. The animator works with fractions of real time. This time is split up into 24 units per second. One frame is the smallest unit in the composition and it takes 24 pictures to fill one second. To check the timing, animators need to record the pictures and play them back. Just as a composer can only check his or her music when musicians perform it.

Trying to explain timing and the sense of time with words is just as absurd as trying to explain music with words. To understand music, one has to listen to it; to understand timing in animation, one has to see it.

There is no standard of good timing in animation. All timing depends on the situation. What is good for one situation might be bad for another. The only valuable criterium is how it looks upon projection. Does it fit the intention of the character? Does it show what you want to say?

Nature produces natural movements, but what is the meaning of all these movements? What do they express? How can these movements be simplified or even exaggerated to express your ideas, feelings and emotions?

Correct timing gives meaning and expression to the movement. Of course an object can just be moved from A to B and the result will be movement, but not necessarily animation. In reality, things do not just move like robots; they move in meaningful ways.

The movement itself is not so important as the question, *Why this movement?* What is the motor of the movement? Which thought, which feeling, which emotion, which action or reaction is the motivation behind this movement?

Improvised or Straight-forward Animation
This is the method used in all direct animation techniques, such as cut-out animation and stop-motion. Using the animated drawing technique the animation will have a natural flow. It will have the vitality of improvisation; and you may be surprised to see your character taking over the animator's job.
On the other hand, you may lose control over the timing and your character may go out of the model-sheet. This method becomes really difficult if you have several characters interacting in the same scene.

Planned or Pose-to-Pose Animation
This is the technique used in all industrial studio productions. The animator, as well as the director, has full control over all actions. It is clearly structured and proceeds according to an exposure sheet calculated animation. The animator will work from strong pose to strong pose. The work can be split up in key drawings made by experienced animators and in-betweens made by newcomers.
There is a danger that the animation will look mechanical; you may miss the natural flow of the straight-forward animation. There will be a good or bad surprise when you make the line-test.

Combination of Improvised and Planned Animation
In all animation there are bits of improvised and parts of planned animation. The improvised method can be used to first sketch out the action and then decide which will be the strong poses. The strong poses or key drawings can be timed down and put in an exposure sheet. To fill the gap between the keys, the in-betweens can be inspired by the improvised sketches.

Most important for dramatic pose animation is to anticipate the actions. A move in a particular direction is reinforced by an initial move in the opposite direction. The action itself is reinforced by the use of stretch in the direction of the aim. Squash is the reaction to what happened before; it's the end of the action.

0601_Time and Space = Timing

Whatever action you draw or animate will always take place on a trajectory within a given space or distance and within a given time.

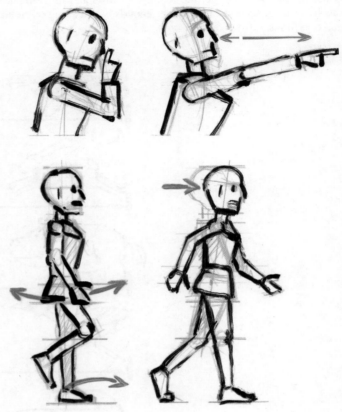

Something is going to move from A to B along a given guideline at a given speed. The animator draws the guideline and figures out the speed.

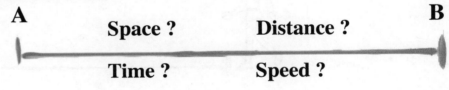

A   **B**

Space ?   **Distance ?**

Time ?   **Speed ?**

To imagine the movement and the speed, the animator must become an actor; not only a *Romeo* or *Juliet*, but also a Fish, a Turtle, a Bird or a Car. You must slip into the skin of the object and imagine what you'd do if you were in it's place. It's only when you feel the wings, when you pick at worms, and when you are chirping that you can animate a bird.

Timing depends very much on what kind of object you animate. Different types of action call for different speeds. Imagine the action, distance, and speed; feel it, act it out, and try to figure out the timing. Tap the beat of the action several times with a pencil on your table and measure the time with a chronometer.

Sooner or later you will get the feeling for time and movement. Think of all actions in terms of seconds. Count the seconds by speaking out loud: one-thousand-one, one-thousand-two, and so on.

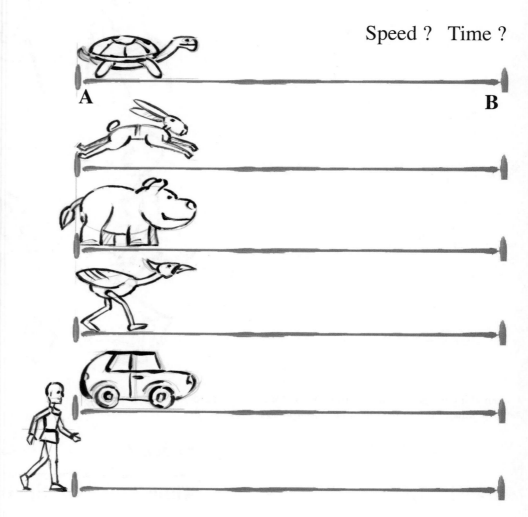

Speed ?   Time ?

A   B

Don't think only about the object, but also consider the condition in which it moves and its state of mind. What makes the object move? What's its motivation, its purpose? A turtle rushing to the beach might go faster than a car in a downtown traffic jam.

State of mind ?

Conditions ?

A   B

A good sense of timing is very important to get the right speed of action for every movement. Intuition for timing can be developed with practice.

Studying music is very helpful for the animator because in every natural movement there is music. The rhythm of the human walk, of waves, of a flying bird, or a bouncing ball - it's all music and can be timed-out for a movement break-down. Use your hands to trace out the movement of the object in the air to animate it, or consider the camera and compound moves. Go over the movements and measure them with a chronometer several times to get an average timing.

Movement in time is easier to express in an acoustic way than in a visual structure. Structured visuals in space and time can therefore be better understood if they are backed by acoustics. The tic-tock of a watch and the movement of a clock hand are good tools to measure time.

To animate a car going from A to B, you need to know into how many phases you have to break down the movement. First, figure out the time it will take the car to go this distance, considering the size of the car in proportion to the distance and its *state of mind* (for example, is it an ambulance or a leisurely cruising car?).

Distance : 100 mm
Time : 4 seconds

A   **B**

Suppose it takes 4 seconds for the car to move from **A** to **B** you will find the number of phases by using this simple formula:

$$\frac{\textbf{Time of action in seconds} \quad \text{x} \quad \textbf{Projection speed in frames per seconds (FPS)}}{\textbf{Number of frames recorded of each phase (exposure-shooting rate)}} = \textbf{Number of phases}$$

The speed of a sound projector is 24 or 25 frames per second (FPS). 24 FPS is used for film projection. 25 FPS is used for TV and video playback.

The normal recording ratio in animation is two frames for each phase. Shooting in "twos" is good for all but the slowest and the fastest of actions.

The 4 seconds of the action multiplied by the projection speed of 25 FPS is divided by the 2 frames exposed on each phase, yielding a product of 50, which is the number of phases required.

4 x 25 / 2 = 50

To know the length of each step, the distance from A to B has to be measured and divided by the number of phases. For a distance of 100 mm divided by 50 phases, the length of each step will be 2 mm. When this scale is drawn on the guideline, you are sure that the car is running from A to B in exactly 4 seconds.

00   **10**   **20**   **30**   **40**   **50**

This page is for your own drawings.

0602_Guide Line_Spacing Guide

In order to indicate the way the car moves from **A** to **B** you have to draw its own guide line. This Line is only here to guide the drawings and will be invisible in the film.

If you want the car to go from **A** to **B** in 4 seconds' time the guide line has to be divided into 50 parts. This is the spacing guide.

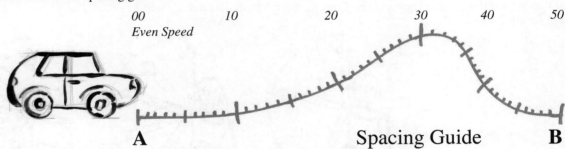

The car may not move continuously at the same speed along the guide line. This difference of speed will influence the spacing guide. Very likely the car will slow down going uphill and speed up going downhill. The purpose of the spacing guide is to indicate the different speeds.

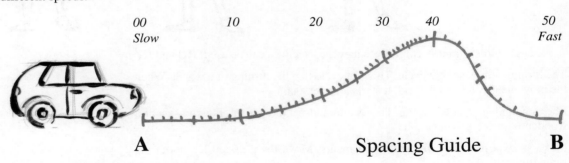

The closer the phases are to one another on the spacing guide, the slower the action will be. The more you space them apart, the faster the action. Sooner or later you'll get the feeling for movement and time and you'll be able to animate simple motions without a guide line or spacing guide.

It's only when you have settled the questions of the rhythm and flow of the action that you can actually start animating and/or drawing.

0603_Extremes_In-Betweens

To get the feeling for the movement of an animated character you have to do some acting yourself. Put yourself in front of a large mirror and go into a few acting exercises. Observe your movements and time them out.

The extreme positions or key drawings are the main poses in the action. Each key drawing shows the most expressive characteristics of the action.

In the animated drawing procedure, the key drawings are made first. To show the path of action, the extreme positions are linked by the **Guide Line**. The movement breakdown is indicated on the **Spacing Guide** and shows the position of the in-betweens.

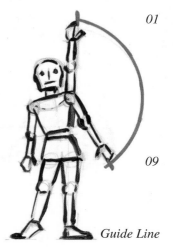

Guide Line

Movement Breakdown

Finish all the extremes of an action before breaking down the movement. The number and position of in-betweens is determined by the speed of the action and indicated on the Spacing Guide. You may have to make only three in-between drawings for a fast movement while nine or more will be necessary for a slow one.

The best method is to use the splitting principle. Make the middle drawing first and continue to split the action until all the in-betweens are finished. For example, in making a series of drawings between 1 and 9, make 5 first, then make 3 and 7 and finally 2-4-6-8.

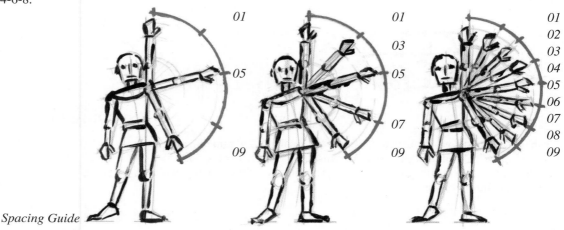

Spacing Guide

In the case of this gymnast, two different cycle principles can be used: **RO** and **RZ**

The turning arm is an **RO cycle.** This is a cycle like the turning of a wheel. When the movement comes to the end, it starts all over again.

The moving leg is an **RZ cycle.** This is a to-and-fro movement, like the saw of a woodcutter when sawing a tree.

Make an exposure sheet for both movements. Move the arm and leg not at the same time, but alternately.

Remember this is an important rule in animation: Move one thing at a time !

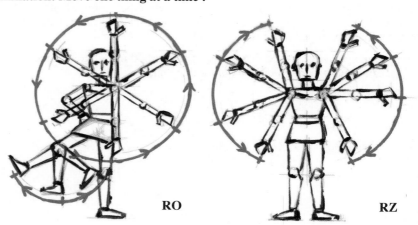

RO   **RZ**

Instructions for In-Betweens: Spacing Chart

While you're drawing the extremes, the instructions for in-betweening should be indicated directly on the drawing. This Spacing Chart is used to indicate the number and position of the in-betweens you have figured out. The numbers at the beginning and the end of the scale are the key drawings; the strokes in-between are the number of drawings to make. A stroke closer to one extreme is to be slowed down at one end of the action.

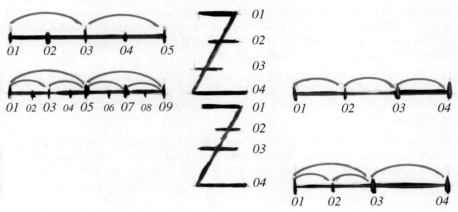

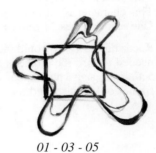

The same principle of in-between drawings applies to the transformations and metamorphoses of one form to another. The key drawings **01** and **05** are superposed and the in-between drawings are made according to the splitting principle, by first drawing **03,** then **02** and finally **04**.

01 - 03 - 05

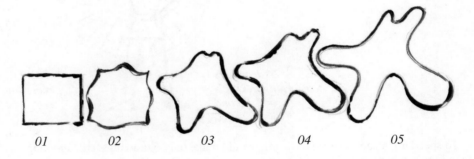

01   02   03   04   05

Check the Results

When you have finished a series of extremes and in-betweens, then you would like to see what this action is going to look like before cleaning, inking, colouring and finally recording the drawings.

Flipping the Drawings

Take a bunch of drawings in one hand and with the other hand flip it like a large flip-book. Try to let the drawings fall at an even speed. This is the moment to check for minor adjustments of the action. If a movement appears to be too fast, you'll need more drawings; if too slow, you must eliminate some of them.

Pencil Test

Today, most animators make a digital pencil test. The rough pencil drawings are captured by a camera or a scanner into a computer. The drawings are recorded precisely as indicated on the exposure sheet and played back in real time. The pencil test is the moment of truth. If the pencil test shows that the action is not what you expected or the characters are out of the model sheet, then you are *back to the drawing board !*

0604_Exposure Rate_Action Speed_Arcs

Most animation is exposed at the rate of two frames per drawing, which means twelve drawings per second. Basically, the fewer frames recorded on each drawing, the faster the object will move; and conversely, the more frames, the slower.

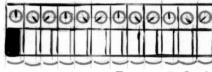

*Exposure in **One's***

In other words the slower the action, the more drawings will be needed; the faster the action, the fewer will be needed. Exposing in ***Two's*** is good for all standard actions. Animation exposed in ***One's*** is used for smooth movements and actions moving at high speed. Exposing in ***Three's*** is good for slow motion but needs the in-between drawings to be close to each other.

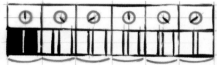

*Exposure in **Two's***

Movements filmed for longer than 3 frames tend to have a staccato flicker. This jitter or strobe effect occurs at the point where the persistence of vision can no longer bridge the gaps between two still pictures and the illusion of continuity is interrupted.

To avoid a strobe effect and to animate an object smoothly, it is best not to leave a wide gap in between one position and the next. The more overlap, the smoother, and of course slower, the animation will be.

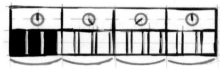

*Exposure in **Three's***

Action Speed

This character is turning his arm around at the rate of one second per each turn. One second takes 24 frames. Recording in *Ones* would mean 24 drawings.

Recording in *Twos* would yield an economy of 50%. Only 12 drawings would be needed to turn the athlete's arm around in one second. In order to speed up the action the same number of drawings could be recorded in *Ones*, producing 12 frames or half a second for each full turn.

24 drawings
*recording in **One's***
= 1 second

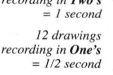

12 drawings
*recording in **Two's***
= 1 second

12 drawings
*recording in **One's***
= 1/2 second

To speed up the action even more you would make only 6 drawings, still shooting in ***One's***, which would make 6 frames or 1/4 second.

For speeding up even faster, you could make fewer drawings to the limit of three. Shooting in ***One's*** makes 3 frames, or 1/8 second, for each turn.

Three is the minimum number of drawings that still gives the impression of a continuous flow. Using only two drawings will bring the effect of a jumping to-and-fro movement.

6 drawings
*recorded in **One's***
= 1/4 second

3 drawings
*recorded in **One's***
= 1/8 second

Speed Lines

When the animated object is moving fast and there are only a few drawings, there is a big variation from one drawing to the next. A shorter exposure rate will help to bridge the gap between the drawings.

For faster speeds, in addition to recording in **One's**, the object has to be deformed towards the main direction of the action. At high speeds, at the limit of the number of drawings and deformation, the drawings blend into a continuous flow of motion.

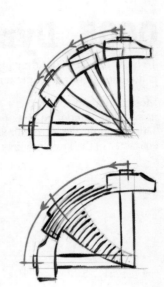

When it comes to even higher speeds, speed lines or blurs are drawn to carry the flow of action. These flow lines immediately follow the animated object. They are the action lines left on the drawing. The same effect is used in comic strips when the action is simulated to be fast. The speed lines can be rendered with dry brush, fine ink lines or grease pencil. The colour of speed lines has to match the moving object. The best is to use a mixture of the colour of the object and the background.

Arcs

All human movements, and many mechanical moves as well, happen in arc form. The principles of force and drag apply to the hand position. Movement along an arc line gives a dynamic flow to the action and helps to bridge the gap between the individual drawings.

0605_Dynamic Movement

To blow life into your drawings, to make them jump out of your drawing board, it is not enough to repeat them mechanically only by changing the position.

Most important for efficient and dramatic animation is to create dynamic movements. This cannot be done by straight-forwardly adding one drawing to another. This dynamic has to be already kept in mind when planning the posing of the character in the key drawings.

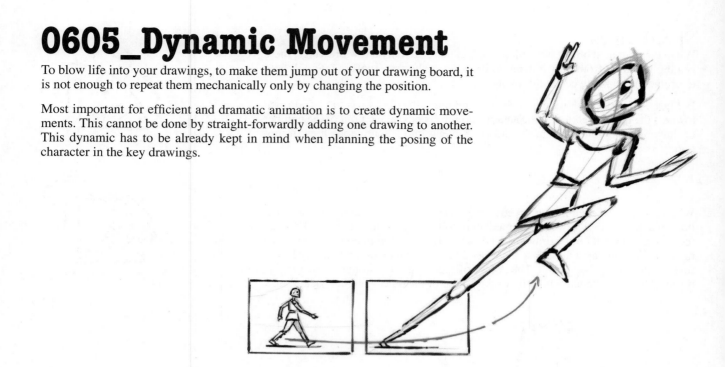

Stretch and Squash

Dynamic movement requires **Anticipation** of the coming action. A move in a particular direction is reinforced by an initial move in the opposite direction. The action itself is reinforced by the use of **Stretch** in the direction of the aim. **Squash** happens at the end of the action. It is the reaction to what has just happened.

Take a football and let it bounce up and down on a table. Draw what you see. If you only draw what your eyes can see your drawings will look stiff and unnatural on the screen. To create the illusion of natural movement you must make unnatural looking drawings. But still, the deformation of your drawings is based on the natural behaviour of the bodies in movement.

The animator can exaggerate actions and reactions controlled by physical forces. To create the illusion of natural movement, a Softball will look like a pancake when it touches the ground, like a banana when it bounces up, and during the relative resting state it will take its original round form.

Important: No matter how much you squash or stretch the **bouncing Ball,** it will change his shape but **never its volume !**

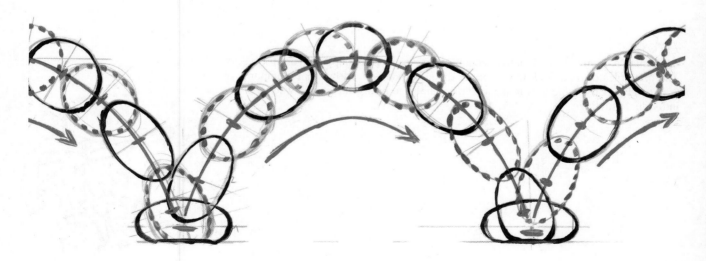

The same principles apply to a **bouncing Cardbox** or a **bouncing Sack of flour**. Just as the bouncing ball these objects will squash or stretch but never never lose their original size or volume. If the volume increases or decreases they would look like the object is growing or shrinking.

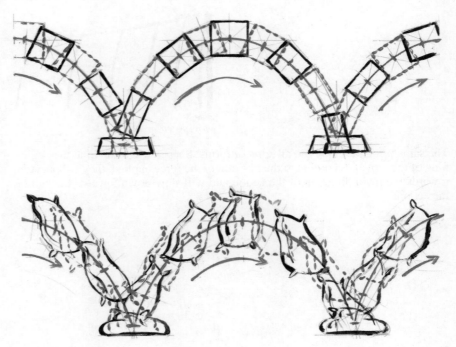

Force and Drag

Actions and reactions controlled by physical forces apply also to straight lines. Take a plastic ruler and wave it through the air. Draw what you can see. How does it look on the screen? To make the movement look natural the straight line will bend. In animation this is called **Drag.** Imagine the ruler being dragged through water; it will bend in the opposite direction of the movement.

The drag of an action is not the same when the force that drives the ruler is applied in the middle or at either end. The ends of the ruler always drag behind the point where the force is applied.

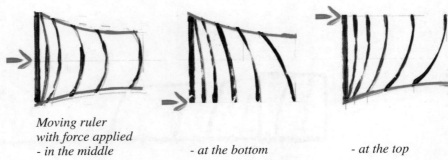

Moving ruler
with force applied
- in the middle   *- at the bottom*   *- at the top*

Natural movements never just suddenly start or end. There is acceleration at the beginning and deceleration at the end of the movement. In animation these are known as *Slow-ins* and *Slow-outs*.

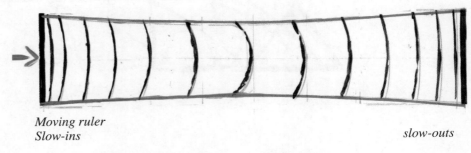

Moving ruler
Slow-ins   *slow-outs*

Follow-through

Imagine that the same force that drives the ruler will make it suddenly come to a stop. The parts of the ruler opposite the base where the force is applied will continue to move before they come to a rest. This principle is called **Follow-through.**

Moving ruler

Sudden stop
Follow through

The same principles apply to all sorts of forms. Shapes will **slow-in** at the beginning of the move. According to the position of the force applied, they will **stretch** towards the main direction of the action and will slow down towards the end of the action.

Shapes will bend over, when they come to a sudden stop. This gives the action a natural flow and will also help the viewer's eye to bridge the gap between the drawings.

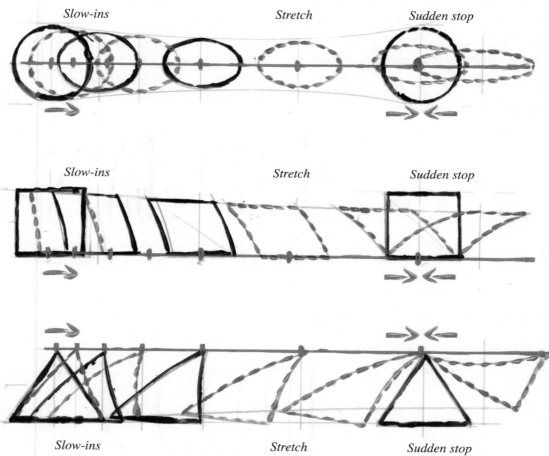

Slow-ins   *Stretch*   *Sudden stop*

Slow-ins   *Stretch*   *Sudden stop*

Slow-ins   *Stretch*   *Sudden stop*

In very much the same way a character will behave when he is on the move, how much it will stretch and squash depends on the character itself.

This cartoon character will move, walk, run and jump before he makes a sudden stop caused by an obstacle: the famous cliff !

Walk *Stop* *Anticipate* *Jump*

Stretch *Squash* *Run* *Sudden stop*

A realistic character will not behave like a cartoon character. Yet even a hyper-realistic character will bend his knees and curve the spine for squash and straighten the legs and spine to get a stretch.

Squash and stretch are part of every moving creature. They are based on physical laws discovered and described by *Isaac Newton* in 1678.

Walk *Stop* *Anticipate* *Jump*

Stretch *Squash* *Run* *Sudden stop*

Weight and Material

Exaggeration and deformation is stereotypical in animation. The degree of deformation of an object depends not only on the forces applied to it but also on its weight, material and elasticity. These three spheres are different in weight and material. They will fall onto three different surfaces. The movement of the spheres and their impacts on the surfaces will be different for each case. They will behave according to their inner structures. Until they move and act, you will not know what material they are made of.

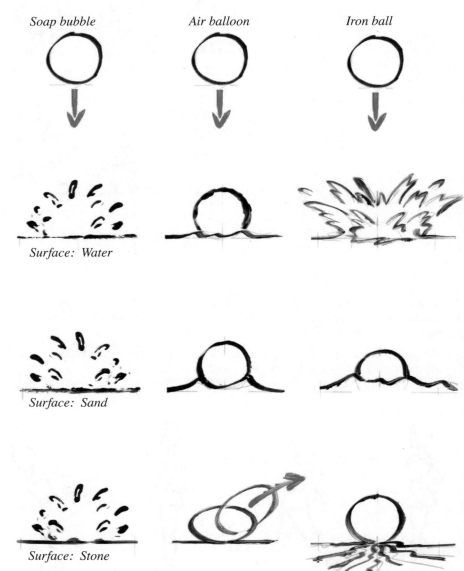

Soap bubble   *Air balloon*   *Iron ball*

Surface: Water

Surface: Sand

Surface: Stone

However, as strongly as you express the deformation, the object itself should never lose its principal characteristics. Even though exaggeration is one of the keys to smooth animation, it can be overdone, which results in an artificial appearance. Adapt these principles to what your film project requires and to the style of your drawings. And, don't overuse stereotypes.

0606_Action Line_Strong Poses _Silhouettes Test

Before you start drawing, think about what really makes things move. Why do they move? What force is behind the movement? In most human action, the driving force is the state of mind, the personality, and the attitude of the character.

When making the movement, think of the overall action. First draw the general line - **the Action Line** - and add the details later.

Action Line

The action line is the backbone of the movement: an invisible connecting line found in any action, which illustrates forces and movement and how they relate to each other.

In hitting and pulling - at the extreme points of the movement - the action line goes right through the body, from the toes to the fingertips

hitting a punching-ball

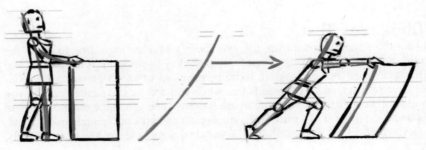

pushing a box

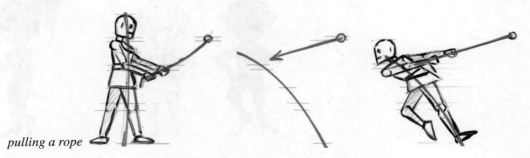

pulling a rope

Strong Poses

The action line applies also to poses. Strong poses are the key positions and turning points in any animation. A strong pose is the key to the quick understanding of the action. In the strong pose, the position of every part of the body is important to express the character's feelings and emotions.

At your service !   *Blue Monday !*   *I'm the winner !*

What's that ?   *Look up there !*   *Here I come !*

Silhouettes Test

During the screening of a film, the eye doesn't have enough time to study the action of any single drawing. Therefore, every key position must be as clear and unmistakable as you can make it. Extreme positions of an action should be readable even in silhouette. That means that when you opaque the whole drawing you should still be able to see what the figure is doing. The silhouette test is the key to this understanding. It is a must for commercials and educational television - and, in fact, wherever the message has to be punched across clearly and unmistakably.

0607_Follow-Through_Arc Line_Overlap

Like the other rules of animation, the follow-through principle is based on the observation of natural behaviour. It applies especially to objects and characters with loose appendages, such as neckties, dresses, tails, long hair and so on.

These parts, being merely attached to the character or object, must follow the path of motion established for them. Follow-through is generated by the main action of the object. The round or curved line on which the objects follow the action is called the **Arc line.**

Guide Line

Arc Line

The follow-through principle is also applied to make animations smooth and fluid. Just as with speed lines and deformation, it helps the viewer's eye to bridge the gap between drawings. In running and stopping the tail will follow the motion of the body.

If the object or character turns around or stops suddenly, the trailing appendages will continue to follow their established paths of action until they come to a natural rest.

Overlap_Animate **one** thing at the time

Just as not every part of the body stops at the same time, not every part of the body is moving at the same time. In animation this principle is called **Overlap.** The very moment the character starts to walk, his foot and leg will move first, then he moves his body and his arms will follow, and the weight of his body will pass from one leg to the other.

The same applies when the character comes to a stop. The feet will stop first, then the body, and finally the arms will come to a rest. This comes to one of the most important principles in animation: **Animate only one thing at the time**

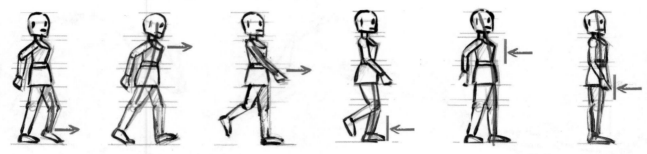

Character start to walk and stops

Overlap and Follow-through

A character with a skirt and long hair or any other appendages will act in a combination of the overlap and follow-through principles. When the character starts to move, the skirt will move forward with his leg. As the body moves forward, the skirt and the hair will drag behind. The faster the character moves, the more the skirt and the hair will float behind him.

When the character comes to a stop the skirt and hair will follow the main action and continue into that direction before they come to a stop at the end of the action.

Character with long skirt starts, runs and stops

0608_Anticipation_Stretch_Squash _Takes

When you are planning the drawings along the action line, you should always remember that every action has an expectation, a movement, and a result. In animation this is usually expressed as **Anticipation**, **Stretch**, and **Squash.**

Actions are better understood if there is first an anticipation. The more and the longer you anticipate, the more you draw attention to the movement. A football will duck down, as if by an invisible force, before it takes off to hit and smash into the goal post. When a character points his finger at something there should be an opposite movement first before the pointing action. A sitting character will move his body first backwards before getting up. As a general rule, the more anticipation you use, the more stretch and squash you produce.

Anticipation Stretch Squash

Anticipation *Action*

Anticipation *Action*

Takes

In a more psychological situation, anticipation is used before a character is going into a **Take**. A take is used when a character is being surprised. It is an over reaction to an event that the character is looking at. Before being surprised he takes a closer look. Then comes the anticipation before going into the surprise-take. This gives more impact to the stretch that will follow.

No matter whether the change in action is a change of body movements or a change of facial expressions, the efficient anticipation always first moves in the clearly opposite direction to that of the Take.

Looking *Closer look* *Anticipate* *Take* *Back to normal*

Looking *Closer look* *Anticipate* *Take* *Back to normal*

Anticipation

Anticipation means moving back before you move forward – or moving down before you move up.

Anticipation is therefore the preparation for the actual movement. Before the frog jumps, it crouches. Before smashing an uppercut to a punching ball, the boxer draws back his fist. Before a kick-off, the football player draws his leg back and even the ball ducks into the ground before being hit.

Stretch

Stretch is the release of anticipation. It's the action itself. During this movement, the frog's body, the boxer's fist, the football player's body and the football stretch in the direction of their aim.

Squash

Squash is the result of anticipation and stretch. At the end of the action, there is reaction! Squash occurs when an external force is stopping the movement. The body of the frog is squashed when it touches the ground. The boxer's fist, face and the punching ball take the form of a sausage. The football hitting the goal post, instead of scoring, will be flat as a pancake.

0609_Newton's Law of Motion

Although animation is based on the laws of nature, the animator can distort or ignore them. Animation is one art where the impossible becomes possible. It's magic to make houses grow like mushrooms, airplanes behave like flies and walk over the famous cliff without falling into the abyss...

But ... before you make a distortion of natural laws, you'd better know the laws.

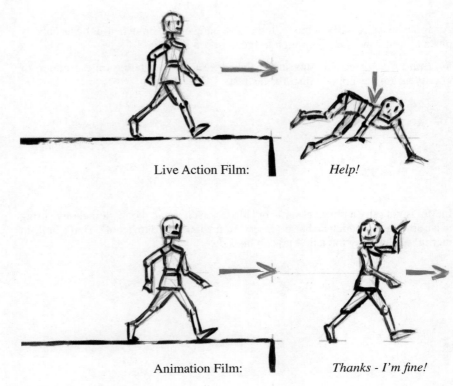

Live Action Film:

Help!

Animation Film:

Thanks - I'm fine!

Sir Isaac Newton said it all in 1687. We just have to apply his statements to animation:

Lex prima
Every body remains in a state of rest (inertia) or uniform motion unless acted upon by a force.

Lex secunda
The rate of change of the movement of a body in a given direction is in proportion to the resulting force that is applied to it in that direction.

Lex tertia
For every action there is an equal and opposite reaction.

These statements may sound very complicated, but since you will come across these laws in everyday animation, it's worthwhile having a closer look at them.

First of all, let's clarify **Inertia** and **Motion**.

Inertia
Every body continues in a state of rest...

A body in a state of rest has to look like its still! Caricaturing, exaggeration and deformation are some of the basic ways of *animating* a state of rest. The degree of deformation depends very much on the weight and elasticity of the object.

An apple on a tree will not move. It will just hang on the branch, as long as nobody picks it, or it is not heavy enough to break off on its own.

Sir Isaac Newton would stay under the apple tree, meditating on the notion of gravity as long as nobody disturbs his rest.

Inertia is not only a physical state, but also a psychological one. Somebody sitting in a train seat for which he has no reservation will be hard to get off. That's built-in inertia! He has Newton's first law on his side.

A car with flat tyres is not just heavy; it's fantasically heavy and looks like it is nailed to the ground.

A cat will rest and sleep as long as it can't get its teeth into something juicy and meaty.

Motion
Every body continues in a state of uniform motion...

To show a body in motion, it's not enough to merely move it along the guideline. Every detail has to indicate the continuity of motion, and the direction and speed of the object. Movement calls for deformation. By drawing the deformation, the illusion of life will be reinforced. The degree of deformation very much depends on the weight, elasticity, and speed of the object.

One day in the year 1726, the apple became too heavy to hang on the tree any longer. It broke away from the branch and, attracted by the force of gravity, was on its way, in a state of uniform motion, descending to the ground.

Sir Isaac Newton, still under the apple tree, would continue to think about gravity, as long as the apple doesn't attract his attention.

A passenger who arrives late to the platform will run for his or her life to catch the train and - although not recommended – may jump onto the moving train.

A car starting off has to first overcome some initial inertia. It's heavy and hard to move, yet the interior force of the engine pushes it forward. Once it has overcome the inertia, it's on the move. A fast-moving car will be **off** the ground and stretch in the direction in which it is propelled.

A goldfish never stops moving, even when it sleeps.

Newton's Law Number 1

Every body continues in a state of rest or uniform motion unless acted upon by a force.

Eureka ! I've got it !

State of Rest

Sir Isaac Newton will continue to be in a state of rest until he sees the apple, attracted by the force of gravity, on its way down to earth. Then, like *Archimedes* years before, *Isaac* exclaims: ***Eureka! I've got it!***

The apple, in a state of motion, will continue to descend perpendicularly to the ground.

The deaf gentleman sitting in your reserved seat will probably not get up unless you make him clearly understand what you mean.

Uniform Motion

A car on the move will stretch in the direction of its destination and nothing will stop it moving straight forward. To stop the car there must be an obstacle or somebody has to action the brakes.

The goldfish will sleep as long as no evident danger appears to him.

Newton's Law Number 2

The rate of change in the movement of a body in a given direction is in proportion to the resultant force applied to it in that direction.

Overcoming Inertia

It is too late for further comments; the apple's state of motion will be stopped by *Sir Isaac Newton's* head, because it is obstructing the path of the apple descending perpendicularly to the ground. Thus, *Newton* will overcome his state of inertia and discover the theory of gravity.

The clearer you explain the situation to the deaf gentleman who is occupying your seat on the train, the greater the chance of getting him out of it.

Stopping the Motion

To stop the car, another force must be applied: either friction or obstruction. Friction acts only on the wheels; they will stop, but the chassis will still go on. Recall that your body is projected forward when your car comes to a sudden stop (and how the airbag hits your nose).

With obstruction, the car will stop suddenly and tend to *wrap* itself around the obstacle. The faster the car goes, the greater the distortion (squash) will be.

The hungrier the cat is, the harder she tries to catch the fish and the more evident it will be for the fish that danger is approaching.

Sir Isaac Newton's Law Number 3

For every action, there is an equal and opposite reaction.

Hungry, not only for revenge, *Sir Isaac Newton* will strike back. He sinks his teeth deep into the juicy apple, and then the apple will have a lesson at its own expense: for every action, there is an equal and opposite reaction.

The deaf gentleman may not fully understand what you mean and could act according to *Sir Isaac's* Third Law!

The car will also be rejected after it hits an obstacle.

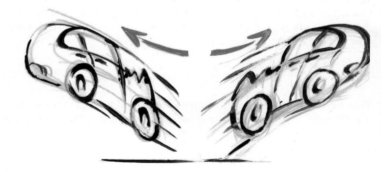

The goldfish could remember that it is hungry too.

0610_Frames-per-Second Charts

Film and Digital projections don't have the same speed.

A film projector needs 24 frames per second to project a continuous movement. This is the minimum number of frames required for a sound projector to reproduce the original and audible sound.

In the era of silent films, the projector speed could be anything between 12 and 18 frames per second. Nowadays, these films are projected at 24 FPS and this is why they look like they are speeded up with funny actor's movements.

Digital projection needs 25 frames per second. This is based on the 50 Hertz electrical system. Every frame is composed of 50 half frames which comes to 25 full frames every second.

Animators usually work with 24 FPS, because it's easier to divide in 12, 8, 6, 4, 3 and 2 frames. In television projection, these animations will be slightly faster, but not significantly visible to the eye of the audience.

Cinema-Chart
24 Frames per second

Seconds	Frames	Minutes	Frames
1	24	1	1440
2	48	2	2880
3	72	3	4320
4	96	4	5760
5	120	5	7200
6	144	6	8640
7	168	7	10080
8	192	8	11520
9	216	9	12960
10	240	10	14400
11	264	11	15840
12	288	12	17280
13	312	13	18720
14	336	14	20160
15	360	15	21600
16	384	16	23040
17	408	17	24480
18	432	18	25920
19	456	19	27360
20	480	20	28800
21	504	21	30240
22	528	22	31680
23	552	23	33120
24	576	24	34560
25	600	25	36000
26	624	26	37440
27	648	27	38880
28	672	28	40320
29	696	29	41760
30	720	30	43200
31	744	31	44640
32	768	32	46080
33	792	33	47520
34	816	34	48960
35	840	35	50400
36	864	36	51840
37	888	37	53280
38	912	38	54720
39	936	39	56160
40	960	40	57600
41	984	41	59040
42	1008	42	60480
43	1032	43	61920
44	1056	44	63360
45	1080	45	64800
46	1104	46	66240
47	1128	47	67680
48	1152	48	69120
49	1176	49	70560
50	1200	50	72000
51	1224	51	73440
52	1248	52	74880
53	1272	53	76320
54	1296	54	77760
55	1320	55	79200
56	1344	56	89640
57	1368	57	82080
58	1392	58	83520
59	1416	59	84960
60	1440	60	86400

Televison-Chart
25 Frames per second

Seconds	Frames	Minutes	Frames
1	25	1	1500
2	50	2	3000
3	75	3	4500
4	100	4	6000
5	125	5	7500
6	150	6	9000
7	175	7	10500
8	200	8	12000
9	225	9	13500
10	250	10	15000
11	275	11	16500
12	300	12	18000
13	325	13	19500
14	350	14	21000
15	375	15	22500
16	400	16	24000
17	425	17	25500
18	450	18	27000
19	475	19	28500
20	500	20	30000
21	525	21	31500
22	550	22	33000
23	575	23	34500
24	600	24	36500
25	625	25	37500
26	650	26	39000
27	675	27	40500
28	700	28	42000
29	725	29	43500
30	750	30	45000
31	775	31	46500
32	800	32	48000
33	825	33	49500
34	850	34	51000
35	875	35	52500
36	900	36	54000
37	925	37	55500
38	950	38	57000
39	975	39	58500
40	1000	40	60000
41	1025	41	61500
42	1050	42	63000
43	1075	43	64500
44	1100	44	66000
45	1125	45	67500
46	1150	46	69000
47	1175	47	70500
48	1200	48	72000
49	1225	49	73500
50	1250	50	75000
51	1275	51	76500
52	1300	52	78000
53	1325	53	79500
54	1350	54	81000
55	1375	55	82500
56	1400	56	84000
57	1425	57	85500
58	1450	58	87000
59	1475	59	88500
60	1500	60	90000

0700_Vocabulary of Animation

Animation is a unique visual language that needs no speech bubbles like a comic strip or lip sync dialogue like a live-action film. Take the opportunity to get the content across in a non-verbal way, with the use of **Shapes, Framing** and **Compsition, Light** and **Shadows, Colours** and **Values of black+white, Movement** and **Sound.**

These elements are the Vocabulary of Animation.

To develop animation like a non-verbal language, you must think in terms of visual and sound structures. Visual thinking is a shortcut to generating ideas straight from forms, colours, and movements instead of passing through letters and words. Forget how ideas were verbally expressed in literature classes and look at them from a purely visual point of view.

Non-verbal language can be developed. Watch a TV programme with the sound turned off and look at picture books with no text or in a language you don't understand, then see how much or how little of the message comes through.

Try to express the sentiments and emotions of Shakespeare's *Romeo and Juliet* by creating forms and colours that go with this unhappy love story.

Visual thinking and expression means thinking in direct relationship with seeing and feeling, with eyes and hands. Visual expression is related to drawing, but not only that. It also could mean modeling with clay, cutting and tearing paper, bending wire, or moving sand.

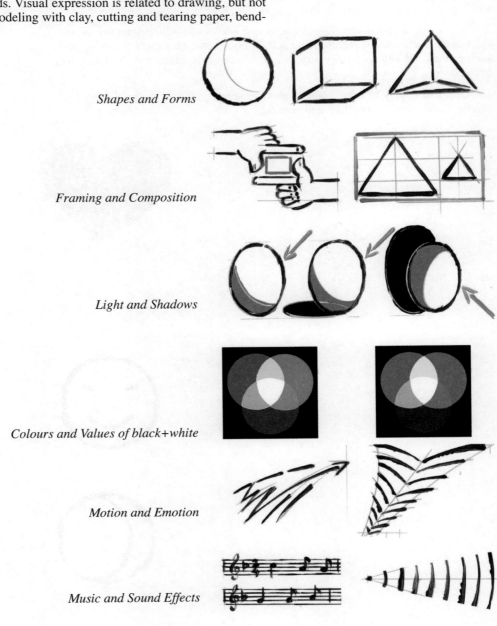

Shapes and Forms

Framing and Composition

Light and Shadows

Colours and Values of black+white

Motion and Emotion

Music and Sound Effects

0701_Visual Language

One of the current ideas circulated about animation is that to make animation one has to have good drawing abilities. As an animated filmmaker, your professional background might be as an illustrator or a cartoonist, but you might just as well be a painter, a sculptor, musician, dancer or a ... pastry chef. Most people get blocked very early in school from being creative. They learn that they can't draw, can't sing, and so on.

If knowledge of the visual arts were applied to verbal expression, we would be a world of illiterates. There are visually talented people just as there are verbally talented poets and speakers. The impulse to imagine and to draw is universal in young children; if education would encourage the drawing impulse, then everyone would know how to draw.

No one lacks imagination either. It is sometimes difficult, however, to contact your imagination and to direct it. Like seeing and drawing, directing imagination can be developed.

The worst is, when you are afraid of drawing and imagining, then you exclude yourself from a creative procedure: **Visual Thinking.**

Classical education concentrates on printed words and verbal expressions. The training of the eye and the resulting visual thinking is still the exclusivity of a small group studying in art schools.

Yet, we live in a visual age. Television, comic books and advertisements unload their daily avalanche of pictures to a totally non-prepared society. Looking and seeing is an activity to be developed, not a passive experience to be taken for granted.

Looking and seeing, to think visually and to express yourself in visual language, can be learned just like writing and reading.

Bye, bye words
Hello pictures !

0702_Visual Writing = Drawing

To work efficiently with pictures, you must know their structure and the elements they are made of. The basic elements you have to deal with in visual arts are very simple. Put your pen to paper and the first thing it will do is to make a **Point**. It all begins with a point. The point is the origin of all visual creation, the germ of all shapes and forms. The point is the symbol for the **Zero-Dimension**, a tiny, inert surface. The point symbolises immobility, inertia, it's the opposite of movement. But it expects to be moved, it's energy is loaded. Move your pencil on the paper and the point will lose its lifeless identity - it becomes a line.

Point 0-D

The point is the transitory state of growth, the egg, the germ. It's the atom of movement, departure - the sun, rays, explosions, fireworks. It's the stone thrown into the water to make circles.

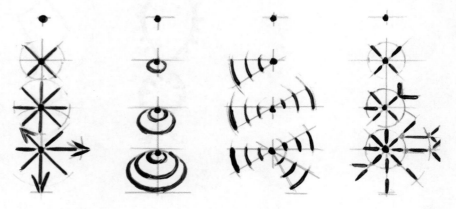

Lines 1-D

Movement is the origin of all creation and development. Move the point on the paper and it becomes a **Line** - the symbol for **One Dimension** (1-D). The line is the prolongation of the point, the link between two points. The crosspoint of two lines is the origin of a new point. Growth of the line is created by moving, by multiplication of a point. The line is the skeleton, the backbone of forms. It's a measure of distance and time. It is liberated energy, rays, explosions, arrows. What sort of line? Thick, thin, precise, wiggling, straight, curved, hesitating, elegant, energetic, strolling, hurried, alone, or accompanied?

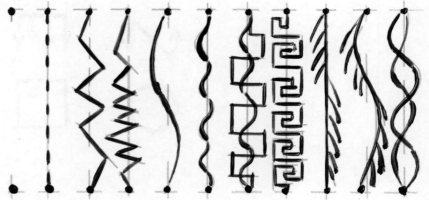

Borderlines

What happens *between the lines* ? Is there still a line or is it already a surface? If it is neither line nor surface, is there a concept in between? Is it the illusion of a surface? A line is a border, a limit for movement and forces. Multiplied lines tend to lose their identity and make place for a surface.

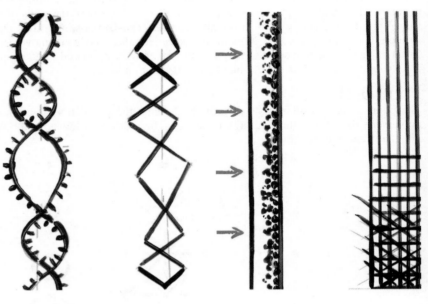

Surface 2-D

In between the lines, surfaces are created. The line generates surfaces by developing, by expanding. The line pushed sidewards becomes a **Surface**. This space is the symbol for **Two-Dimensions** (2-D). What kind of surface? Square, round, or triangular? Geometrical or organic? Curved inside or outside? Negative or positive? Black or white?

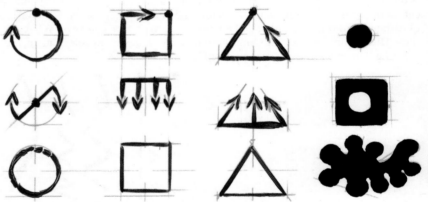

Volume 3-D

The surface that goes into the third dimension becomes a **Volume**. What kind of volume? Round or pointed? Soft or hard? Light or heavy? The volume is the symbol for **Three-Dimensions** (3-D). Perspective is a new element, adding space to distance.

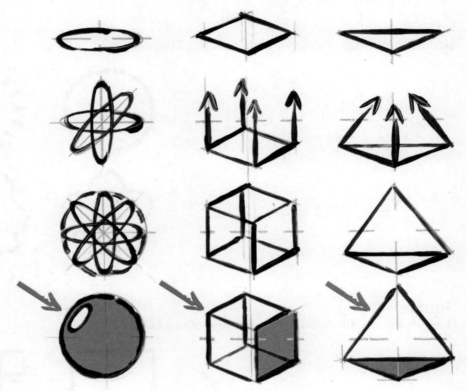

Observe the path from the Point to the Volume, the energy it takes to move a **Point** to a **Line**, the line into a **Surface**, and the surface into a **Volume**. These elements are the vocabulary for Shapes and Forms. It's with these elements that pictures are formed

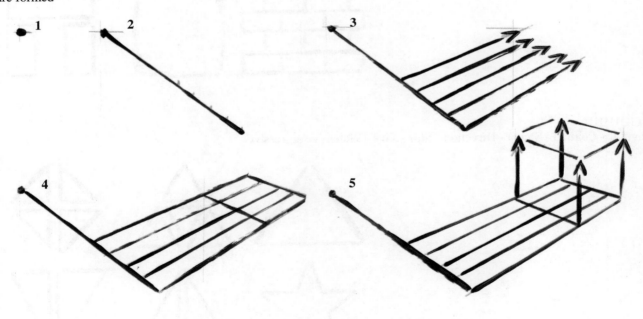

0703_Forms and Shapes

Look at the different forms and shapes and try to associate ideas with them. What does a Circle symbolize ? A Square ? A Triangle ? What can you make out of them? Express you feelings by using these elements.

Circle
Soft - Smooth - Moist - Tender - Full - Fat - Sun - Water - Air

Square
Hard - Solid - Earth - Rigid - Stone - Strong - Quiet - Consolidated

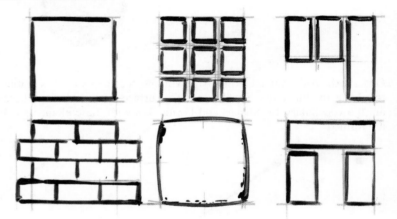

Triangle
Angular - Pointed - Sharp - Direction - Star - Fire - Violent – Aggressive

0704_Composition

The composition is the arrangement of the different elements that form the pictures of the film. These elements can be shapes and forms, but also colours, lights and shadows. The way you arrange them gives the picture a meaning and sense and will guide the viewer's eye to what you want him to look at.

Even more than in painting, composition is paramount in animation. Composition draws the viewer's attention to the key elements in order to make sure the message is clearly transmitted to the audience.

What is the meaning of the position of a form within the frame? In which way will the composition affect the meaning of the message?

Composition is also used for aesthetic reasons. Maestros of painting such as *Rembrandt Harmenszoon van Rijn* and *Leonardo Da Vinci* used these rules in a most efficient way.

Here are a few principles you may use, unless you intentionally want to get away from rules. But as always, to break rules efficiently, you better know them beforehand!

The **Centre of interest** is the thing that you want your audience to see first. It is the most important thing to communicate within the frame — and you have to decide what is the priority and what is secondary.

The **Centre Framing** is the classical, but the also the dullest, composition.

The **Off-Centre Framing** brings visual tension and life into the frame.

 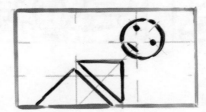 

Dividing the screen into thirds can be used is to get away from the centre position and approaching something like the Golden Rule.

Nose-room is the term used for framing actors in profile or three-quarter frontal position with space in front of them. Unless you want to give the impression that the actor is turning his back to audience, you should allow enough space in front of the nose in order to indicate that the actor is communicating with the audience.

 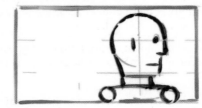 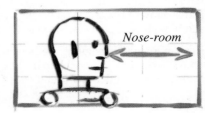

Diagonal composition can be used to establish priority and secondary values. Take the example of the jar and fruit plate: even when both are of the same importance, diagonal composition can be used.

  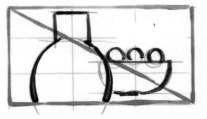

Triangular composition gives a solid base to the picture and the centre of interest is clearly indicated.
Triangular composition can be used with centre as well as off-centre framing.

0705_Framing
_Camera Fields_Field Sizes

Framing is of the greatest importance in animation, even more than in painting where the viewer can look from one part of the picture to the other, and for as long as he likes to do so. In cinema, the audience has no other choice but to look at the framing that is on the screen, and for only as long as the filmmaker decides to show the picture.

Within the frame, the animated parts attract the spectator's eye, but framing imposes a limit to this information.

Camera fields and angles are not only important for drawing attention to certain parts of the artwork, but they have an influence on the dramatic expression of each scene. Just as the camera operator looks through the viewfinder to establish the camera's field and angle, the animator plans the viewer's angle and field size on the drawing board or on the three-dimensional set.

To choose the field size means to limit the information of a given piece of artwork to that particular field. The TV cut-off for any field size must also be taken into account.

To express the camera fields, every manual uses different terminology. The following terms are standard expressions using the human body as a reference:

EXC	Extreme Close-Up	Eyes, Mouth, Hands, very close
CU	Close-Up	Face, close up of an object
MCU	Medium Close-Up	Shoulder or Breast
MS	Medium Shot	Waist field
MLS	Medium Long Shot	Famous American field
LS	Long Shot	Knee field
EXLS	Extreme Long Shot	Feet field

Use two **L-shaped pieces of black cardboard** or **your own hands** to study the various possible framings for a given picture.

Field Sizes

In animation, field sizes are expressed according to measures, which were originally referenced in inches. A one field is one inch wide; a two field is two inches wide, and so on up to the standard 12 field, or the maximum of a 15 field.

In HD video, the screen proportions are **16:9** or 1920 x 1080 pixels.
A **field size 12** - 274 x 155 mm - is a convenient format to work on a size A4 paper.

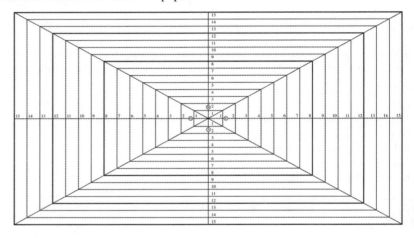

In standard video the screen proportions are **5:4** or 720 x 576 pixels.
Field size 10 - 213 x 170 mm – is a convenient format to work on a size A4 paper

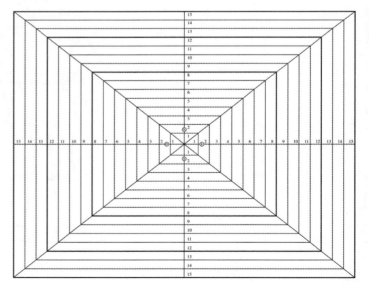

+0705_04

Make a photocopy enlargement of this **Field Chart** so that the **1-Field** will become **1 inch** (25 mm) wide.

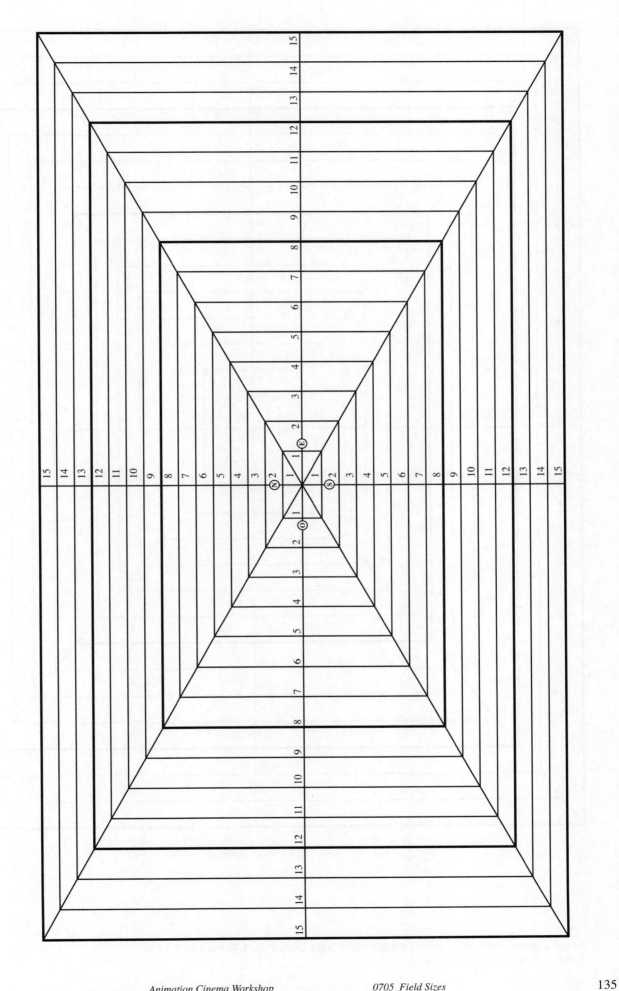

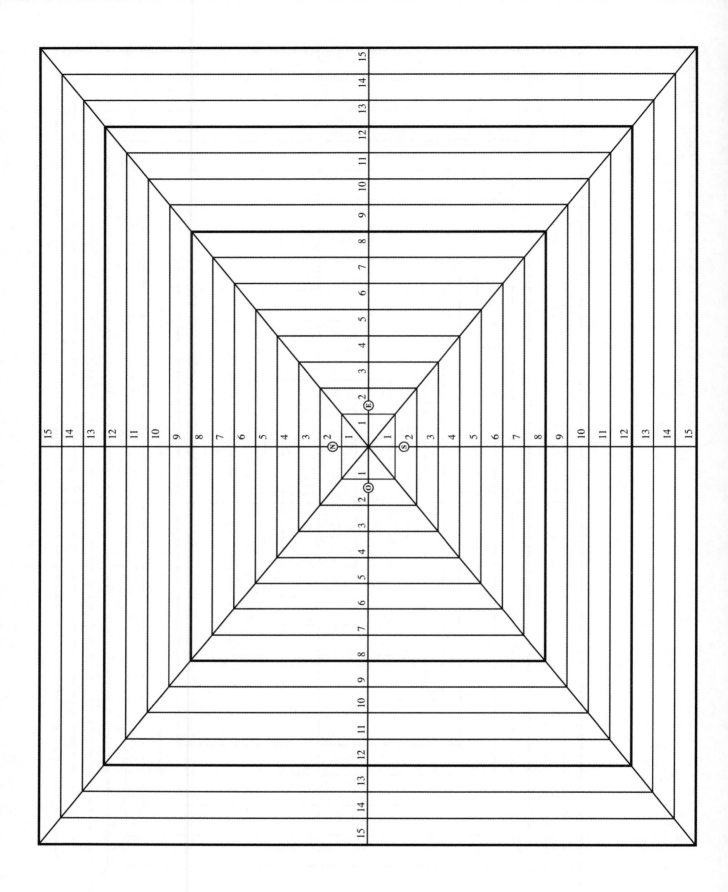

Make a photocopy enlargement of this **Field Chart** so that the **1-Field** will become **1 inch** (25 mm) wide.

0706_Camera Angles_Points of View

The camera angles show the position of the camera (the filmmaker's and viewer's point of view) in relation to the picture. The choice of the angle is always of dramatic value. Like all rules, these values can be denied and changed by filmmakers. There are three standard camera angles to be distinguished:

Human eye level - Horizontal shot
This natural, horizontal vision allows the camera to approach, to draw back or to turn around the subject.

For a horizontal shot, the horizon line is approximately in the middle of the field. The scene looks neutral; anything can happen and everything depends entirely on the action of the subject

Birds-eye view - Down-looking shot
The viewer looks at the scene from a higher point than the subject he is observing. Mostly the angle is oblique (30°- 45°), but the point of view can be up to vertical, like a geographic map.

The down-looking shot is a scene viewed from a high perspective. It presents an image of weakness and passivity. The character looks *crushed*, suggesting inferiority. The greater the distance between the subject and the viewer, and the smaller the subject is in relation to its environment, the more lost and weaker the subject will appear. The function of a down-looking shot may also be to clarify a scene, by showing a geographical map of the action.

Worms-eye view - Up-looking shot
The audience looks at the scene from a lower point of view than the subject he is observing. This point of view gives value to the character, the set, and to the whole scene.

The up-looking shot expresses a feeling of danger and terror. The scene looks dominant and even fearsome, giving the impression of power and strength. The lower you set the horizon line and the closer you approach the subject the more menacing it looks.

0707_Light and Shadow

Just like in painting and theatre staging, the play of light and shadow creates the ambiance and atmosphere. Think of the fascinating shadows of leaves created by moonlight or a street-lamp on a wall. Think of the magic of light and shadow created by candlelight or the flames in a fireplace.

Every object has a life in light and a life in shadow. Use these double lives by showing the objects with or without shadows, or show only the casted shadows.

The position of the light source is a creative factor itself. A light hitting an object from above or from beneath changes the dramatic impact of the scene entirely.

Make your own observations, perform experiments, and test your conjectures against what you see.

Light

Light is everywhere in our world. We need it to see: it carries information from the world to our eyes and brains. Seeing colours and shapes is second nature to us, yet light is a perplexing phenomenon when we study it more closely.

Light acts like a **stream of small particles** which flow from a source. If not interrupted the light streams in straight lines until it hits an object or loses its force and fades away.

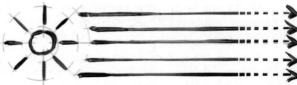

Light also acts like **waves**, instead of particles. This explains how rainbows work, when the light waves hits the waterdrops and break into different lengths corresponding with colours.

In fact, light is both a **stream of particles** and **waves.** This **wave-particle duality** of light is one of the most confusing, and wonderful, principles of physics.

Light behaves according to specific rules. If the straight lines hit a mirror or any other reflecting surface it bounces back at the same angle it hits them.

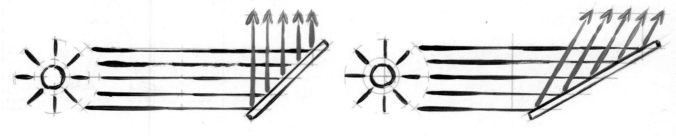

Shadows

Not all shadows are equal. There are in fact two very different kinds of shadows that occur in any object: **Form shadow** and **Cast shadow.**

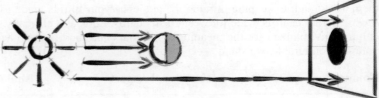

Form Shadow   *Cast Shadow*

A **Form shadow** is the shadow on an object on the side that is not directly facing the light source. A form shadow has a softer or less defined edge to it than a cast shadow. It is lighter than a cast shadow because it's not created directly by a blocked light source. Form shadows are subtle shadows; however, they are essential for making a subject appear three-dimensional rather than flat.
The play of light and shadows on an object reveals the structure and the texture of it's material, which can be according to the amount of light valued or flattened.

A vertical light source, flat and without shadows, stands for a midday ambiance and long shadows evoke sunsets and evenings. A low position of the light and soft shadows creates an early morning ambiance.

A **Cast shadow** is what we generally think of as a shadow. It's a shadow created by an object blocking the light source. For example, the shadow of a head, created by a light source that falls on the ground or a wall.
A cast shadow is darker than a form shadow and it has quite a sharp, definite edge. However it's important to remember that a cast shadow isn't a solid thing. The further a cast shadow is from the object that's creating it, the lighter and more transparent it gets, and the softer or less-defined its edges become.

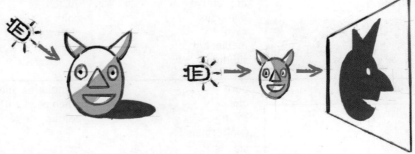

A back light throws the object into silhouette and gives a strange look to the scene. In the shape of the silhouette, the object becomes a flat shape and loses its three-dimensional identity.

The shadows projected behind an object make it seem powerful and menacing. The cast shadow may appear in bizarre deformations

0708_Colours

Colours create mood. Remember the standard meanings of colours and apply them to animation, keeping in mind the audience your film is made for. The following colour chart is made for western standards. Look at it critically. Check the cultural environment for the meanings of colours and modify them according to your own cultural background.

Colour	Emotional Aspect	Visual Aspect	How to use
Red	restless aggressive stimulating, exciting activating dramatic	very attractive warm living	*Best used* as accent colour *Overuse* overpowers and irritates
Orange	stimulating comforting in small doses cheerful	brilliant warm glowing	*Best used* as accent colour *Overuse* tires easily
Yellow	stimulating bright sunny	highly luminous warm cool and fresh	*Best used* for children summer / spring
Green	tranquillising restful passive soothing	natural colour down to earth growth cool	*Overuse* monotonous
Blue	depressing melancholy introspective tranquil soothing	atmospheric soft transparent	*Overuse* makes things cold and empty
Purple	impressive pompous royal melancholy subduing	austere cold atmospheric	*Best used* in small amounts as accent colour
White	pure clean fresh death-related*	stimulating and positive when used with other colours	*Best used* for accent *Overuse* causes eye strain
Grey	neither calming, nor stimulating	neutral	*Best used* with other colours *Overuse* dull
Black	isolating dignified nocturnal depressing death-related*	beautiful as background for colours	*Best used* with other colours *Overuse* negative

* Death related colour is **White** in traditional Asian culture and **Black** in Western culture.

0709_Focal Point

In cinematic language, Focal Points are used to direct the viewer's attention to the point of interest on the screen.

This can be achieved with the composition of the scene and by using colours and light effects to guide the viewer's eye.

Less important parts can be also be out of focus, while the focal point is in sharp focus.

A soft focal point can be a light area on the set, while less important parts are in the shadows.

The strongest focal point is a spotlight pointing at and limiting what you want the audience to look at.

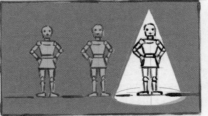 

0710_Reflections_Animation as a Mirror

Just as with light and shadows, reflections are part of the animation vocabulary. Reflections are used to create emotions, like reflecting moonshine on a lake or reflecting trees in a river.

In reality, there is only one body. To show another one, we use reflections. For the viewer, two events happen at the same time, and in the same image. Reflection creates this illusion and provides a new experience in perception.

Reflections represent another life of what is being reflected. If the shadow is the darker part of the character, then the reflection could be qualified as the lighter part. Make use of this double life by showing one or another face of the object and express feelings and emotions through it.

To discover the phenomenon of reflections the animator can use a mirror. Observe your environment in a convex mirror, in a Christmas tree decoration, or in a soap bubble or a water drop. What you see in a water drop is nothing less than the whole world.

Look into a deep pond or a quiet lake and observe your face. Drop a tiny stone into it and see what happens to your face. Observe the reflection of a water lily, a water bird or boats on a lake.

In **Stop-motion animation,** a sheet of glass or any other glossy surface can be used to show the effect. In the **Drawing techniques**, the reflection must be drawn just like the subject itself. In **Computer assisted animation,** many programs offer the possibility of creating shadows and reflections.

Animation as a Mirror

Much has been written and lectured about *Cinema as a Mirror*. Many artists use the cinema to mirror themselves or the souls of others. Animation is a privileged tool to look at yourself. Just as the artist uses the self-portrait to introspect himself and tell the outside world about his deep feelings, animation can be used to look at ourselves, mirror the feelings and communicate to the audience a content which otherwise would be invisible. Animation can mirror personal states of mind and tell stories without words.

A mirrored image of your face is an imaginary landscape of your inside. Imaginary landscapes are necessarily mind-scapes, ways of thinking, states of mind, spiritual attitudes, mind-benders, and revelations. They are certainly mind-readers and divinations, mind-setters and keys to the doors of imaginary worlds.

To look into a mirror and draw not what you see, but what you feel, is to experience your own mind-scapes. You may experience dreams that come true, adventurous phantasms, hallucinations, fantasy, extreme euphoric happiness or depressing sadness.

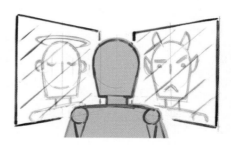

0711_Depth of Field_In and Out of Focus

Depth of field creates a feeling of space. This illusion can be achieved by several visual means.

A **Foreground** can be put on a separate level and hide part of the background. The animation happens in between the two levels and suggests that the action takes place in space.

The **Colours value** of the different levels of the set can fade progressively into the background colour and suggest distance.

Shadows of objects and characters may suggest perspective and depth of field.

In and Out of Focus

The **Foreground** and the distant **Background** can be out of focus and create the illusion of space.

0712_Background_Set_Foreground_Multiplane

The purpose of a background or a set is to establish the context of the film. You want to tell the audience where the action is going to take place. The film design and the graphic style of the characters will have an influence on the type of backdrop you will make. The style and colours of the background will create the mood of the scene. Use just enough background to create that atmosphere and let the imagination of the audience do the rest.

The viewer's eye looks more for content and relationships than for details. A flat colour background can be more efficient then detailed, naturalistic scenery. Too many details distract from the most important thing: the Action.

The soundtrack can replace a great part of the background and save you time and money. The sound of twittering birds or the blowing horns of cars will indicate that the action is situated in the countryside or in a town.

A **Background** is a two-dimensional image on which the animation takes place. Drawings and cut-outs move around in front of the background.

The **Foreground** on a two-dimensional background is often used as an overlay.

A **Set** is a three-dimensional area for stop-motion animation. Puppets and animated objects move around in a set.

A **Foreground-Set** is used very much like a wing on a stage. An out-of focus foreground creates the impression of space and depth in a scene.

The **Multiplane** combines the advantages of two and three-dimensional animation. It offers many possibilities for creating the effect of space and depth. It's most effective use is in long truck-ins or truck-outs.

For more about the technique of Backgrounds, Foregrounds, and Multiplanes, see Chapter *1000_Production*

0713_Perspective

Humans, through the eyes and brain, are searching for comprehension of what they see. Perspective, just like light and shadow, helps us to understand pictures, to make them closer to what we are used to seeing.

3-D models are used more and more in science and technology, where comprehension and understanding of complicated procedures is a major issue. Believing through seeing has become the basic tenet of communication in most human activities.

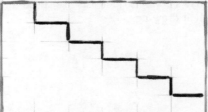 

The use of perspective in pegbar animation is a method of presenting three-dimensional objects and movements on a two-dimensional surface. To create this illusion, the size and speed of the objects are systematically reduced as they approach the vanishing point on the horizon line.

 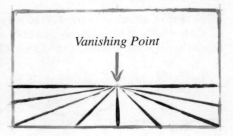

This change of size and speed is based on a natural law: the closer an object is, the bigger it looks and the faster it seems to move. On the other hand, the farther away it is, the smaller it looks and the slower it seems to move. For example, when you look out of a train window, trees close to the train seem to whiz by, while those further away seem to move much more slowly.

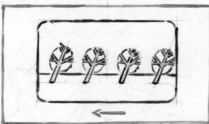 

A simple way to express perspective and the feeling of depth in a plane-view animation technique is to draw objects smaller and with thinner lines, the further away they are.

In the cut-out technique, where perspective moves are particularly time-consuming to make, a common trick is to have a character running out of field on one side and have him come in on the same side in a smaller shape. This is repeated, until he disappears.

0714_Breaking the Statics_Movement

Breaking statics and making drawings come alive is an old dream of all visual artists. The result of this desire can be observed in the drawings of the multi-legged boar in the cave of *Altamira* and the galloping horses in *Lascaux*. Later, Greek and Roman sculptors and painters rendered gods and athletes in full action or in a series of silhouette drawings. The painter *Marcel Duchamp (1887-1968)* and the illustrator *Grandville (Jean-Ignace-Isidore Gérard, 1803-1847)* each searched in his own way to break out of the frame. Today's comic strip artists use speed lines and colour blurs to suggest movement in their drawings.

Movement
The origin of life is movement. Catch a movement with your eyes and you get a slice of life which is idea generating. Movements can be associated with ideas. The movement of a snake, a cloud, of fire, of machines, of an explosion, of lightning or of a **flying bird...**

What kind of ideas and emotions are suggested by these movements?
Could the flight of a bird symbolize liberty? What happens if you speed up or slow down the same movement? Could it change liberty into loneliness?

Sequences_Scenes
To think and work in movement creates sequences. A sequence has a clear beginning and end; as a matter of fact, it is a short short-film.

Working in sequences is what really makes animation different from other visual arts. Animation is an art that takes place within a space and in a given time. Time and space are the raw materials the animator works with. To work with time and space is called timing. A **step in a dance** is like a scene within sequence.

Metamorphosis
In metamorphosis, there is the notion of change, transforming elements one into another; changing a fly into an elephant, a sheep into a wolf, and vice-versa, is quite normal in animation. Visual associations by morphing a pair of scissors into a crab, a pear into a light bulb, and **changing the charming prince into a frog**, is normal in fairy tales and animation too.

It is also normal in biology: the metamorphosing life of a butterfly, from the egg over the caterpillar to the chrysalis, or the life cycle of a frog, from eggs to tadpole and then frog.

Before and After

In Before and After situations, there is also the notion of change. What is important in animation is not so much the static pictures that form the film, but what is in between two pictures: the change that becomes the movement.

However, in certain situations, the *in-between the frames* element should be left to the imagination of the audience. The term *Before and After* is often used to describe two memorable situations: one before and one after a change: the **product to combat baldness** makes a miracle effect, a table set is neat and clean before people start eating, and messy and dirty after the party.

Before   *After*

Growing

Just like the sequence, growing has also a beginning and an end. Therefore it belongs also to the family of the very short short-films. Besides, in growing there is also the notion of birth and development. There are some fine examples in nature: the growing of a tree, a flower opening, the transition of a seed into a plant, the segmentation of a cel, from the egg to the chicken (never knew which was first), from an embryo to a baby, **from an egg to a salamander** or the extremely fast growth of the expanding balloon.

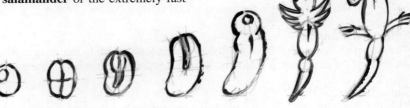

Evolution

In evolution there is also the notion of change. The evolution of human beings, from four-legged to two-legged creatures, from the wild to the civilised human and vice versa. The changes of the face and the body of a human being, from **a baby to an old person,** from birth to death. The evolution of Chinese characters, from the representational picture to the pictogram.

The change of landscapes: from the big plains to the urban cities and desertification, from the withdrawal of the glaciers to flooded islands; not to mention the evolution in architecture of a town, of a street, of a house, of an apartment, of a room, and so on.

Cycles

In contrast to the growth and evolution, cycles have no beginning and no end. Cyclical movements are super short short-films, as can be seen with the Internet. These short film loops are often associated with the natural phenomena of science and technique: **rolling waves in the ocean**, a water drop from the tap, a waving flag, smoke coming out of a chimney, twinkling stars, the turning hands of a clock, or the rolling wheel of a bicycle and most of human movements: walking legs, talking lips, winking eye, breathing lungs, beating heart...

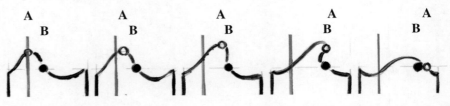

0715_Cinematographic Terms

During the first hundred years of cinema history, there have always been cross-fertilization between live action cinema and animated filmmaking. Although animation is at the origin of the cinematographic art, animators have adopted a number of rules and stereotypes commonly used in cinematographic language as well.

Set
Term for shooting area in stop-motion animation, also used in 3-D computer animation for background.

Tilt Shot Up
Camera angle that looks at the scene from a lower point of view than the subject.

Tilt Shot Down
Camera angle that looks at the scene from a higher point of view than the subject.

Shooting Angle
Camera's point of view represented and limited by the camera field.

Off-Screen (OS)
Often used to speed up an action and/or to make the economy of a expensive animation. The main action or characters are placed off-screen and their presence is only suggested by visual elements and sound effects.

Subjective Camera
The camera substitutes for the sight of a character, recording the images through the eyes of the character. Eventually, it becomes the point of view of the audience.

Time Jump
This is a jump into the future; a narrative technique that condenses time by deliberate omission of images and sounds, the logical or chronological actions that are not required for the understanding of the story.

Flashback
This is an insert into a story of a sequence or a scene that happens in the past or at a different place from the main action.

Sound-Off / Voice-Off
This is a cinematographic term used to describe a sound source which is not visible on the screen.

Dubbing
The dialogues and voice-off of a film that are re-recorded in another language.

Editing
Film editing is choosing and assembling the camera shots and the sound takes.

Jump Cut
The passing of the camera over the imaginary axis connecting two characters. The new shot from the opposite side of the axis is known as a Reverse Angle.

Reverse Angle
The camera field which is facing the shooting angle.

0716_Glossary of Image Transitions

Each change from one visual to another has a particular meaning, and each transition has to be indicated on the storyboard.

Metamorphosis
Metamorphosis is the gradual change and transformation from one form to another. This is certainly the most original picture transition, since it's only by means of projection that you can see the changes of the forms and the illusion of movement. Metamorphosis expresses an evolution in the sense of a development from one situation to another.

Cut
Instant change from one shot to another, but maintaining a continuous flow of action, like a comma in writing.

Jump Cut
In a shot with two characters there is a invisible line connecting both of them. The camera looks at this line at 90 degrees. The rule is that the camera is allowed to move 180° in front of this line. If the camera passes over the line in a cut, it is called a Jump Cut or Jumping the Line. In traditional filmmaking this rule is never broken.

Dissolve or Mix
Transitional change from one shot to another, indicates a minor change of location or a short lapse of time, like a full stop and a new paragraph in writing.

Fade-in / Fade-out
Beginning or finale of a shot, a scene, a sequence or of the film itself; it's the rising and falling curtain of a play, the end or the beginning of a chapter in a book.

Pan
Smooth change within a shot, with a continuous flow of action. The direction of a pan is described in terms of East, West, North or South. Diagonal pans from North-East to South-West would be indicated as NE to SW.

Zip Pan
An extremely fast pan between two shots, accomplished by moving the camera so quickly that the resulting image is blurred. Used as a transitional device to the succeeding shot without a cut.

Zoom-in / Zoom-out
Effect of traveling forward or backwards without moving the camera, obtained by using a zoom lens. The dramatic effect is identical to trucking.

Truck-in
Trucking is when the camera moves towards the subject without shifting off-centre. It's a continuous approach to draw attention to a part of the artwork, and increases dramatic effect.

Truck-out / Zoom-out
Trucking-out is when the camera retreats progressively from the subject in a straight-centre position. It reveals the relationship of the detail to the whole. It gives you the impression of diminishing strength, especially if done slowly. Change of camera position but not camera angle.

Off-centre Trucks and Zooms
A compound move is combined with a camera move to make an off-centre truck or zoom.

Animated Zoom / Animated Truck
Progressive changes in the sizes of the artwork gives the effect of a zoom.

Tilt-up / Tilt-down
Camera move pivoting vertically around the camera axes - up or down - showing a smooth change within a shot, with a continuous flow of action. Change of camera angle but not camera position.

Wipes
Optical transition effect whereby one shot is replaced with the following one. There are literally hundreds of possible wipes. Invent some for yourself !

Spin
Rotating a shot around its own centre point, changing from one shot to another or from one shot to black or vice versa.

Flip
One shot begins to revolve on its vertical or horizontal axis and a new shot is introduced with each half-rotation.

Iris-in / Iris-out
Changing a shot from a concentric opening, increasing in size, until the whole field can be seen. You can iris in or out from any section of the field and from one shot to another or from a shot to black or vice versa.

Pop-on / Pop-off
Instant appearance or disappearance of an image, character, or other object within a shot, without letting it enter or leave the frame.

Inlay / Multiple screen
Effect of inserting one picture source into another. The result can take many forms. It can be done with pop-ons, dissolves, overlays, super-impositions, or wipes.

Insert
Short for insertion. Close-up inserted between two larger shots of the same scene. It has the same tempo and feeling as the master scene.

Blue Box
Video effect that records an object in front of a blue (or green or red) screen and then superimposes it on another background recorded by another camera.

Overlay
Process of overlaying a foreground picture onto the background.

Continuity
Creation of a visual relationship between two shots in order to allow a fluid transition from one shot to another.

0717_ Drawings in Time_Sound Structures

Breaking the statics means going into movement. Movement in animation means drawing in time. Sound is a structure and a support to carry forms and shapes in time and space. Sound is also used to carry feelings, emotions, and messages to the audience.

Ideas, thoughts, and emotions are transported by **music**. You can listen to music to create inspirational drawings. These drawings will help you to generate new ideas. In return, your drawings or paintings can inspire a musician or composer to create music. Stories are told with music. Listen to music and imagine content and action in time and space and draw a **visual score.**

Prologue   *Act_01*   *Act_02*   *Act_03*   *Epilogue*

Structures for time are given by music and sounds. Listen to music, imagine the actions, and draw the dramatic outline of the film. This is the first step to get your hands on timing. Time is one of the raw materials that the animator has to deal with. Time is something abstract, invisible to our eyes; what we need is support to get our hands on the invisible. Sound can be used to make drawings in time, and to visualize the timing, very much like a **musical score.**

A sense for timing can be learned and developed just like the knowledge of colours, framing, or camera moves. In animation, the animator has complete control over time. The animator is the master of time; he can expand or squeeze time, he can twist and turn it, cut it into pieces - 24 pieces for every second - in order to fit it exactly to his needs. There is no good or bad timing in animation. All timing depends on the situation. What is good for one situation might be bad for another. The only valuable point of view is how it looks on projection. Does it fit the intention of the character or the object you moved ?

Good actors know how to communicate emotions and to anticipate the change in facial expressions. Animators have to slip into the skin of their character to get the right timing and to turn **motion into emotion.**

Meaningful movement means correct timing. In reality things do not just move like robots, they move in meaningful ways. The movement itself is not as important as the answer to the question of why this movement. What is the motor of the movement? Which thought, which feeling, which emotion, which action or reaction is the **motivation behind this move** ?

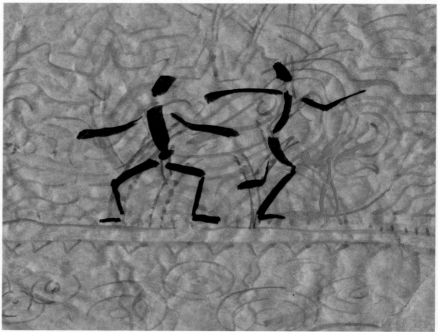

Sound structures can be found everywhere in daily life: the **cardiogram,** the **stock exchange index,** the **meteorological forecast,** the **diagram of a bird's song,**... Sound structures help the animator to find solutions to time and rhythm. It is not an exaggeration to say that half of the film's impact is on the soundtrack.

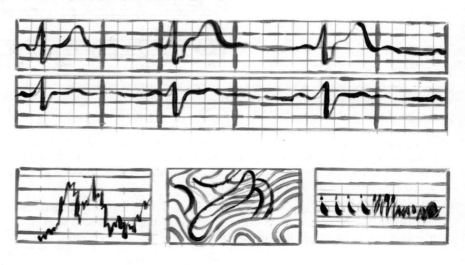

Animators like to look at their work as visual music. Images and sounds share the same elements of structure in time. Animation and music both have a basic mathematical foundation. They both move forward and at a given speed. Just as the composer creates the music note by note, the animator creates animation frame by frame.

0800_Characterisation
Development_Construction_Animation_Acting

Development

In character design, the vocabulary and the grammar of animation will be fully used to create and animate believable actors. Just as in live action films, the animator has to go through casting and research to find the unique character that will fit the film project.

Construction

A character is constructed from the inside to the outside. It's the form of a skeleton or armature that shapes the character, that gives it proportions and shows the limits and possibilities of its movement.

The body itself is constructed around this structure and gets its final shape, with more or less detail, according to the film design and the animation technique.

Animation

Turn-Arounds and Walking Cycles are basic exercises. Each character has its own way to move. It's part of the casting to find the right way for each one.

Acting

To bring your character to life and make it believable to an audience, you will have to blow life into drawings on paper or pieces of cardboard or clay. Acting is the most important and most difficult step in animation: from Motion to Emotion.

0801_Development
_Character Spectrum_Design

As soon as the idea of your film project takes shape you will feel the need for some characters to incarnate the story. You are now at the beginning of character development. They might be humans, animals, robots, and extraterrestrials or simply objects. In any case, you would like to make them believable characters and show that on the screen.

Each individual is different from others. Yet there are characteristics for each group of characters. Animated films are made to put the message across quickly. Therefore, the character must be easy to identify with. Think of the proportions of your figures. Go through the following questions and figure out what your characters will be.

Character Spectrum

Each character belongs to a family of characters. This classification is called the Character Spectrum. The range goes from the visual reality of drawings and beyond, to film and video, to visual abstraction of basic shapes and still further, to words and writing. Think about the position of your character in the spectrum: closer to reality or closer to abstraction ?

A character is not necessarily a human being. It can be an animal or any other fantasy object you would like to fill with life and to act for you.

Visual reality   *Visual abstraction*

Design Tools

A character must fit into your film design. There are two ways to accomplish this. Either you have a look around and collaborate with a designer who has already developed a particular style, or you set out to create your own. Don't forget, the character must be accepted by your sponsor/producer. Maybe this one has a partner who is a designer and would like... you never know!

The design depends a lot on what the character must do to communicate the content to the audience. Animation techniques and tools will influence the character design. Use different tools to express the same character. Choose the style that best fits to punch the content over to the audience.

| *Brush* | *Brush* | *Chalk* | *Pencil* | *Pen* |

Design Shapes

Which basic shape is best adapted to your character? Will it be round and cute? Will it be triangular and aggressive? Will it be square and good natured?

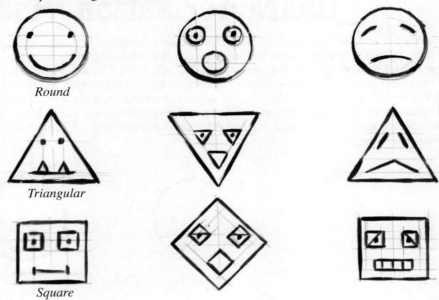

Design Family

To which family of shapes does your character belong? Or, is he or she a mix of several shapes? Will your character be in 2-D or 3-D?

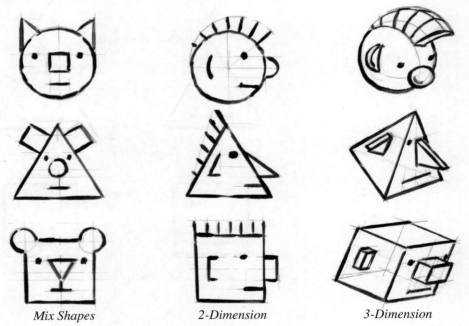

How old are they? Are they male or female? What kind of personality do they have? What is their profession? What is their nationality? What is their race? Are they like you? Are they like me? Are they like someone you know?

Exaggerate basic stereotypes. An old person is very old, a fat person is very fat, an angry person is very angry, and so on. Be a body language actor and slip into the skin of your characters and draw what you feel they are.

Don't forget the production aspect; the character design has to fit into your money and time budget. Adapt the style, reduce details to essentials; in short, make it simple but efficient.

0802_Development
_Characterisation_Head

Animated films are often made to put a message across quickly. Therefore, identification with a character must be fast and easy. The head, and particularly the eyes and mouth, are the most expressive parts of a character. The shape and form of the head helps the viewer to identify quickly with your character. If you try to avoid stereotypes, just remember that the audience must understand the message. Use round forms to create little children or cute figures. Strong and active heroes are constructed with triangular shapes. Older, down-to-earth characters are built with square shapes.

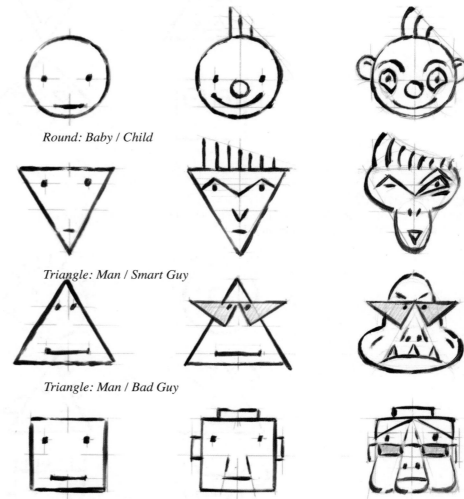

Round: Baby / Child

Triangle: Man / Smart Guy

Triangle: Man / Bad Guy

Square: Old Woman / Grandmother

An asymmetrical face is an interesting feature in character design. It gives the character a unique look and attracts the attention of the audience. Be careful with turn-arounds: there will be more work to do with asymmetrical faces.

Express the following characters by using simplified shapes and forms: rounds, triangles, and squares. Think of a colour that could go with each one of the actors.

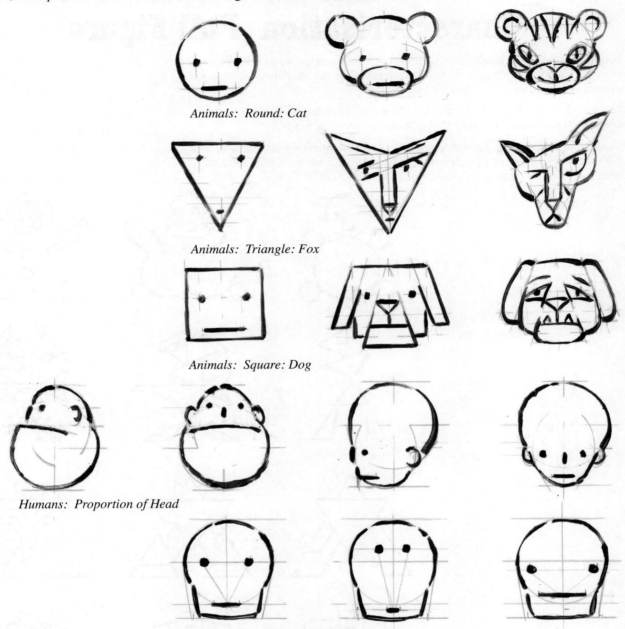

Animals: Round: Cat

Animals: Triangle: Fox

Animals: Square: Dog

Humans: Proportion of Head

Humans: Positions of Eyes and Mouth

Long before ethologists discovered and proved the influence of childlike features like a round head, low eye line, round cheeks and big eyes to attract the attention of animals and humans to care about their babies, sculptors and painters have used these forms to create the *cute* style. Animators use these forms to characterise innocence and communicate to audiences the feelings of empathy and sympathy for their characters.

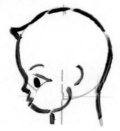   

0803_Development _Characterisation_Full Figure

Full figures, just like heads, are based on basic forms and shapes. Think of the proportions of your figures. Nervous characters will be tall and skinny, while good natured or lazy folks tend to be small and round.

Use simple body shapes to create characters with personality, adapted to things you want them to do. The same applies to hands, feet, and heads.

Make them simple with just enough lines to illustrate what they are doing or representing. A complicated figure can be very expensive in terms of time and energy invested. Every extra piece of clothing may take hours of work.

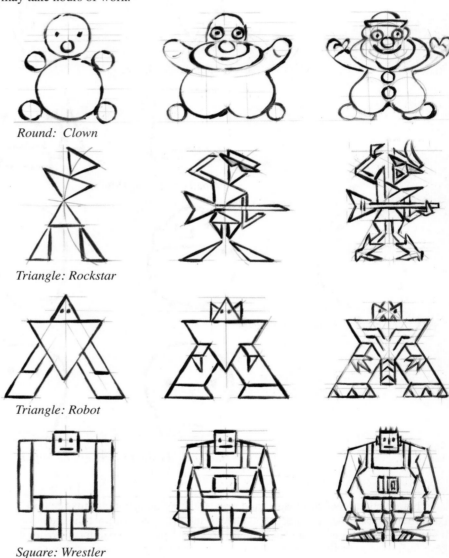

Round: Clown

Triangle: Rockstar

Triangle: Robot

Square: Wrestler

Express the following characters by using simplified shapes and forms: rounds, triangles, and squares. Think of a colour that could go with each one of the actors.

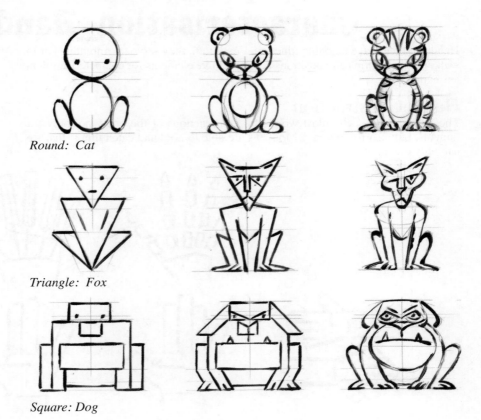

Round: Cat

Triangle: Fox

Square: Dog

Proportions

Television audiences are less attentive and they must understand quickly. Moreover, television and computer screens are smaller than movie screens. Much attention must therefore be given to the visual perception of forms, shapes, and colours.

Forms and shapes must be significant and comprehensive at first glance. On a television screen, the facial expression of a character with realistic proportions is difficult to read. In reality, the relationship of a human head to the body is 1:7. In animation, oversized heads, one sixth up to one third of the body, are a standard in character design for television. The head is the unit of measurement for the whole body. In animation, we express this as a *two, three* or *four head* character. If facial expression is the priority, the size of the head of a character can take up half of the body.

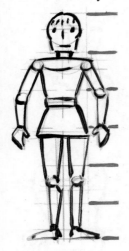 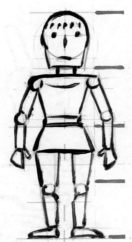 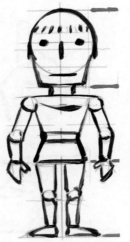 

Proportion: 1:6 *Proportion: 1:4* *Proportion: 1:3*
Three Head Figure *Proportion: 1:2*
Two Head Figure

0804_Development _Characterisation_Hands and Feet

Hands and feet have a double function. First of all, they serve to grab things or to walk, but their forms and positions are expressive elements for characterisation in animation.

Hand_Construction

The hand is one of the most wonderful constructions of the body, not only for humans, but also for animals. Monkeys are able to hold and catch things that we can only dream of.

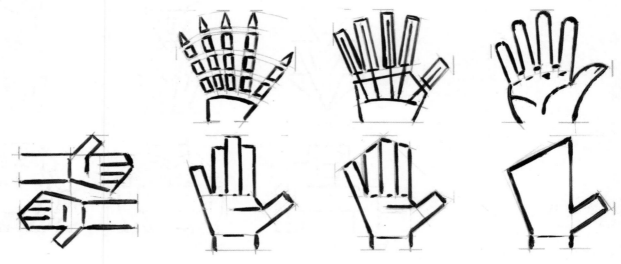

Hand_Positions

Beside this elementary function to grip and hold things, the position of the hand and fingers are an important tool in non-verbal communication. There are strong positions of hands and fingers that are universally and immediately recognised.

One finger in the air is a symbol that commands attention or accusation. Two fingers in the form of a V stand for Victory. The three fingers up is the symbol of a promise: *I swear!* The hand with five fingers flat up commands to stop. A raised fist is a powerful symbol for fighting and revolt. The horizontal hand with one finger pointed out stands for indicating a precise direction. One thumb up means, everything is under control, while the same thumb pointing down indicates disagreement. And, not to mention, all the positions of the fingers and hands that make more or less friendly signs to our fellow citizens.

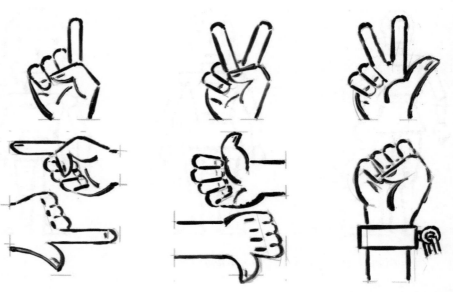

The hand is made to grip and hold things. Different tools demand different positions. Take some everyday objects in your hand and draw what you see.

Feet_Construction_Positions

The feet are, of course, just as important as the hands. First, they serve to stand upright and walk. The form and the position of the feet are paramount and tell all about the nature of the character. Big feet show the stability of the character, such that his or her feet are well on the ground, and it may even indicate a way of down to earth thinking. Little feet that hardly touch the ground have something delicate and fragile about them. They certainly represent a light-hearted character.

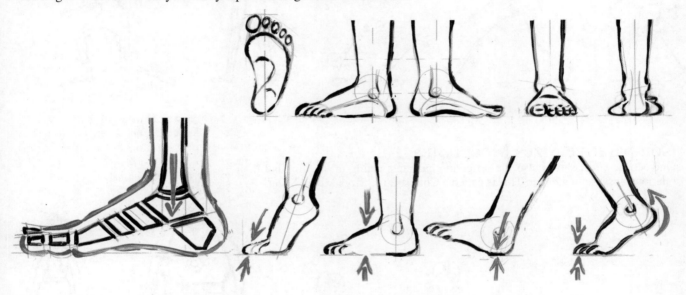

Footwear Varieties

Essential to the feet are, of course, the shoes, which in some way belong to the chapter on props and accessories (see: 0810_Props_Accessoires). The feet in sandals, in tennis shoes, in boots or in high heels,will indicate the nature of a character.

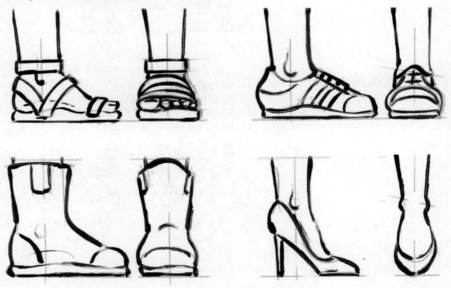

0805_Construction_Model Sheet

Model or Reference Sheet

In order to animate your character keeping with the original drawing, a Model Sheet (or Reference Sheet) is made for each character. The Model Sheet shows all the features of the character: the proportions and relationship between head, body, and members. This Model Sheet is the reference for all the animators throughout the production.

Construction is done from the inside out. Before you start drawing, you should have a clear idea of what your character will have to do and what will be the best anatomy for that job. Start by drawing the skeleton or armature. The next step is to put the body volumes around it and show the muscles. The flesh and skin is the last step before you put on clothes and accessories.

Comparative Sizes Model Sheet

One Model Sheet shows also the different characters acting in the film and their relationships one to another. This is called a Comparative Sizes Model Sheet.

Facial Expression Model Sheet

Your character is a personality. The characteristics of his or her personality show especially in facial expressions. Make up another Model Sheet that shows the character in a range of expressions that reveal his or her personality.

Turn Around Model Sheet

The character must be recognizable from every viewpoint. Visual problems in animating the character can be avoided if you show more than just the front and profile view of the character. The turn around model sheet gives information for different positions. At least five positions have to cover the 180 degrees of rotation and show the proportions and construction from every angle.

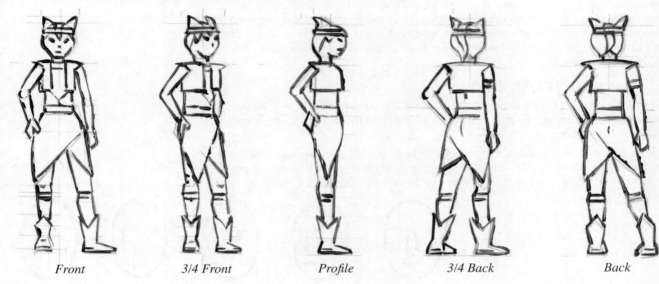

Front　　　*3/4 Front*　　　*Profile*　　　*3/4 Back*　　　*Back*

Characteristic Positions Model Sheet

The personality of the character shows also in the body expressions and positions. To makes the character immediately identifiable by the audience, the character will go into similar positions in similar situations. Make a model sheet that shows the character in a range of standard positions that reveals the personality.

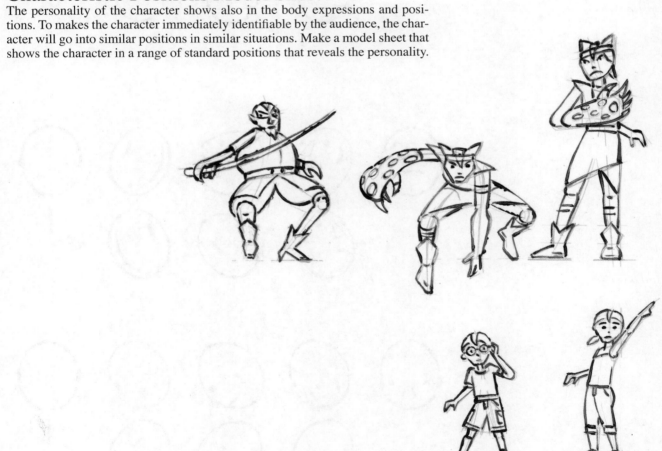

0806_Construction_Animation _Head Turn Around

A character has to be recognised from all points of view. Certain problems of animation can be avoided if the character's head is drawn from more angles than just frontal and profile. A 360 degree rotation gives all the information you need concerning the position and shape of the character's physique as well as his or her clothes and props. In 3-D modeling, turn-around is a standard function of any computer program.

Egghead Turn-Around

We live in a world of three dimensions. All our visual perception is based on three dimensions. For the animator, it is important right from the beginning to get into the world of volumes.

Using a simple form like a ball or an egg can best develop a feeling for volumes and movements of a head. Draw Guide Lines around the egg and indicate the position of eyes, nose and mouth. Turn the egg in various positions and draw what you see.

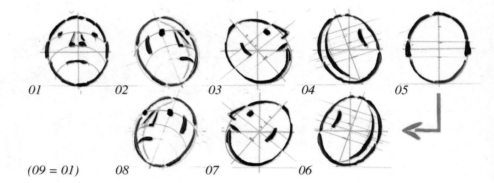

Horizontal   (09 = 01)

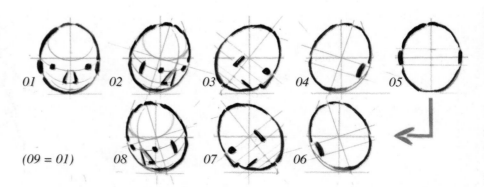

Up-Looking   (09 = 01)

Down-Looking   (09 = 01)

Model Head Turn-Around in 360°

Use the same procedure with the head of a model, whether plaster, clay, or your classmate's head. Turn the head in all points of the compass and draw what you see.

Most humans have asymmetrical faces. The turn-arounds, therefore, cannot be expressed only from front to back. For a 360 degree turn-around, more drawings are needed to show the head from front to back and to front again.

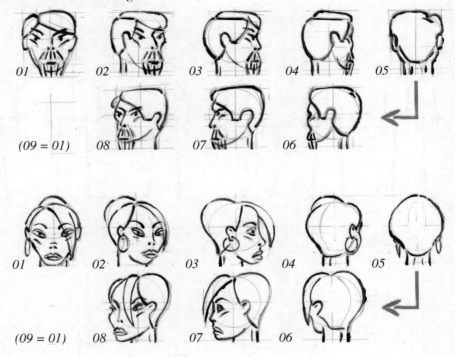

Turn-Arounds can be used for transitions from one head to another. By turning around 360° the head of a character can metamorphose. A cat becomes a woman... a crow turns into a man...

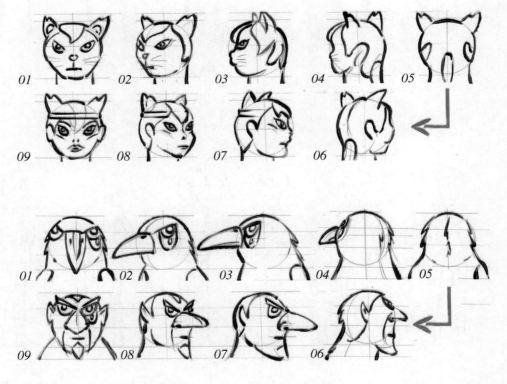

0807_Construction_Animation
_Full Figure Turn Around

An animated character is built from the inside out. Start with the skeleton and add the muscles, flesh, skin, and finally the clothes. Work out the position of the skeleton and construct basic body masses around it. Use a ball for the head, boxes for the body, and tubes for arms and legs.

Horizontal_Skeleton_Armature

01 02 03 04 05 06 07 08 (09 = 01)

Horizontal_Volume_Armature

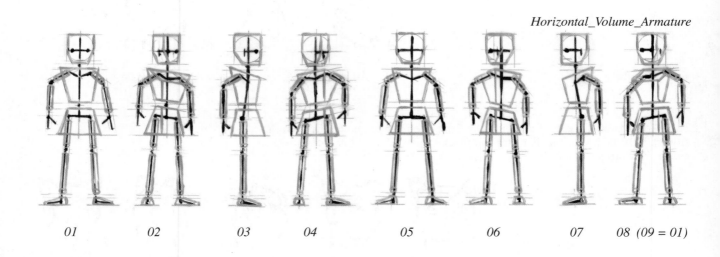

01 02 03 04 05 06 07 08 (09 = 01)

Horizontal_Skin

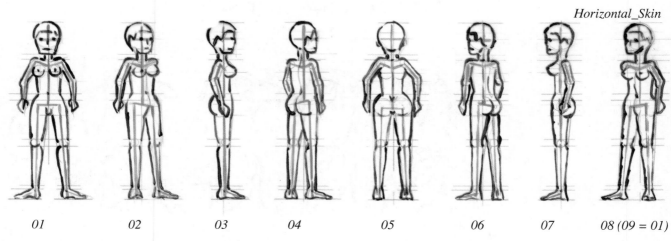

01 02 03 04 05 06 07 08 (09 = 01)

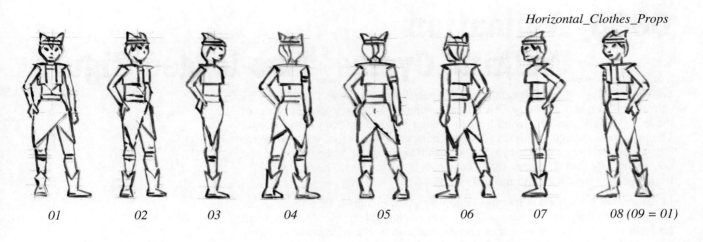

01   *02*   *03*   *04*   *05*   *06*   *07*   *08 (09 = 01)*

Down-Looking

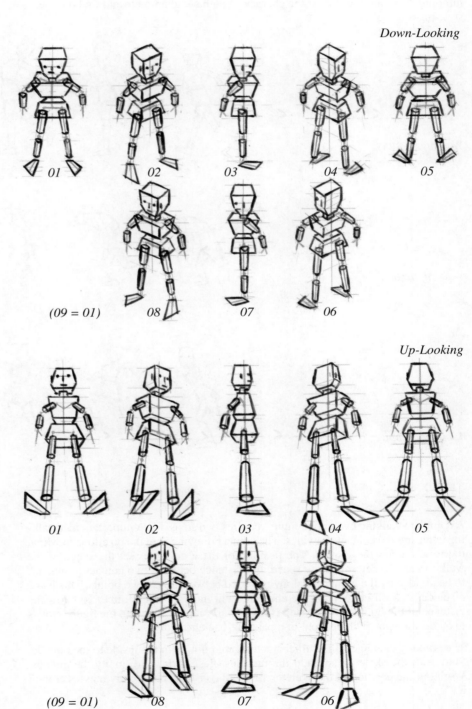

01   *02*   *03*   *04*   *05*

(09 = 01)   *08*   *07*   *06*

Up-Looking

01   *02*   *03*   *04*   *05*

(09 = 01)   *08*   *07*   *06*

0808_Animation _Walking Cycles_Two-legged Figure

Walking involves losing and catching one's balance all the time. This is done by shifting the weight of the body forward and raising the left foot to the high point of the arc. The right arm will swing back to counter-balance the body shift forward. The left arm is swinging forward for added balance. The left foot will then touch the ground and the cycle begins again with shifting the body weight forward and raising the right foot. The arms swing conversely with the legs. The right arm is in front when the right leg is behind and vice verse.

In reality, not everybody walks the same way. As a matter of fact, there are as many ways to walk as there are people living on this planet. An old person will walk slowly, a business man will be speedy, and a little schoolgirl will be happily jumping. Slip into the skin of the character you have to animate and find out their style of walking.

Walking proudly

Walking tired

Jumping happily

A complete walking cycle for a figure requires two steps. Most important in a walking cycle are the contact drawings. The contact drawings are the positions in which the foot touches the ground. The position of these drawings set the speed of the walk or run. To determine the speed, the distance between two contact points has to be divided by the number of drawings used between these two points. This is the distance (in millimetres) that the character will move on each frame. To know the distance of the figure for each step is particularly important when the figure moves in an on-the-spot cycle in front of a panning-background.

The walking characters, like all characters, are built from the inside to the outside. Start with the skeleton and add the muscles, flesh, skin, and finally the clothes. Work out the position of the skeleton first and construct basic body masses around it.

01

02

03

04

05

06

07

08

09

10

11

12 (13 = 01)

01 02 03 04 05

06 07 08 09 10 (11 = 01)

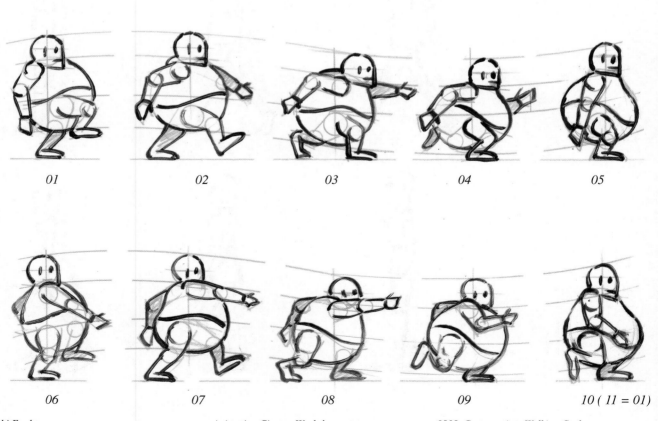

01 02 03 04 05

06 07 08 09 10 (11 = 01)

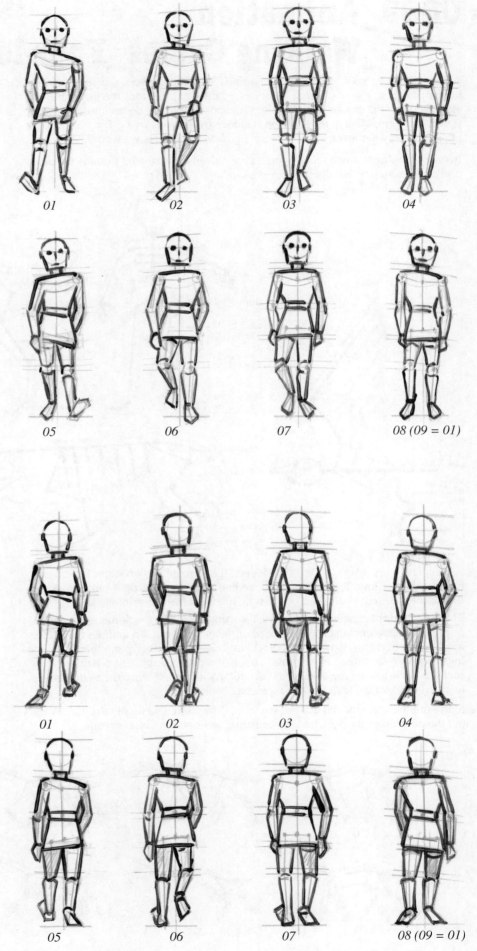

01   02   03   04

05   06   07   08 (09 = 01)

01   02   03   04

05   06   07   08 (09 = 01)

0809_Animation
_Walking Cycles_Four-legged Figure

Although the number of bones in an animal skeleton is about the same as in a human skeleton, the position of them is very different. Besides the fact that most animals touch the ground with four legs, the position of the bones inside the body is very different. Most of the skeleton is hidden by the body mass. The visible parts are in fact only the lower legs, feet, and nails. Most animals walk on their nails.

In order to animate anatomically correct animals, it is paramount to study the position and function of each part of the skeleton.

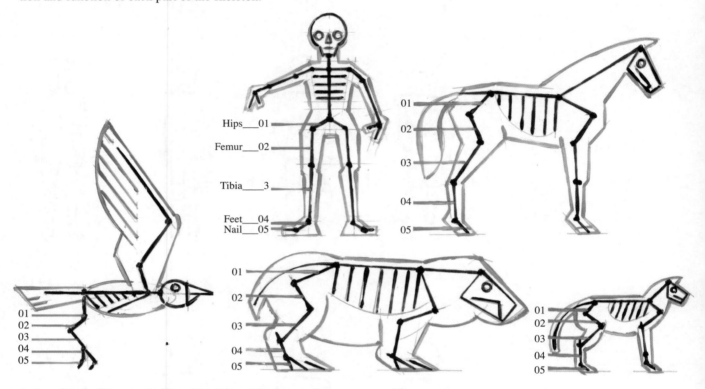

Hips___01
Femur___02
Tibia____3
Feet___04
Nail___05

A complete walking cycle for a four-legged figure requires two steps. For an animal's walk, the hind legs are usually one half step ahead of the front legs. Most important is the equal distance covered by hind and front legs in one step.

The contact drawings are the positions in which the feet touch the ground. The position of these drawings set the speed of the walk or run. To find out the speed, the distance between two contact points has to be divided by the number of drawings used between these two points. This is the distance the figure will move in each frame. Knowing the distance is particularly important when the figure moves in an on-the-spot cycle in front of a panning background.

Start with the skeleton and add the muscles, flesh, skin, and finally the hair. Work out the position of the skeleton and construct basic body masses around it.

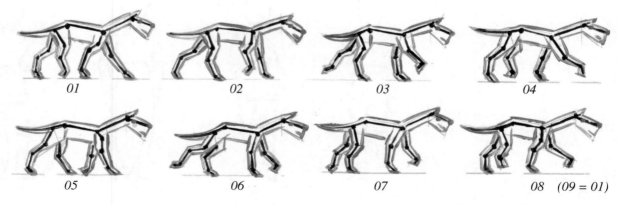

01   *02*   *03*   *04*

05   *06*   *07*   *08*   *(09 = 01)*

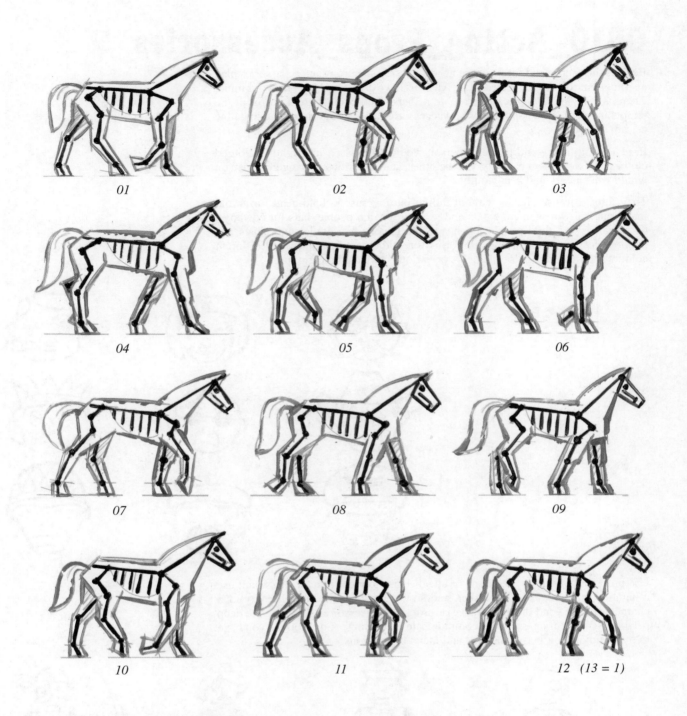

01   *02*   *03*

04   *05*   *06*

07   *08*   *09*

10   *11*   *12 (13 = 1)*

_Flying Bird Cycle

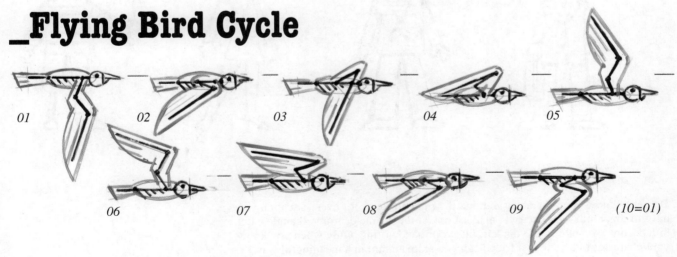

01   *02*   *03*   *04*   *05*

06   *07*   *08*   *09*   (10=01)

0810_Acting_Props_Accessories

Besides the shapes and forms of the head and body, the props and accessories play an important role in characterisation. All of us have pictures of people in our mind. There is a saying: *Clothes make people !* Shapes and colours are a mirror of the temperament of the person. Props and accessories are a visual shorthand to define certain characteristics.

In general, a happy and peaceful person would be dressed in brightly coloured clothes and wear them casually. On the other hand, a serious or dangerous person would wear a dark and heavy outfit.

The secret is to use cliches without falling into overuse: a bald head for an old man, long hair for women, cigars and jewelry for rich people, hats for cowboys, dark glasses for blind people, eggheads and glasses for intellectuals, flags and national costumes for patriots, uniforms for soldiers and postmen and different colours and face shapes for members of various human ethnic groups.

Use props such as a mobile phone or attache case to identify a businessman; use a hammer and shovel for a worker, and so on. However, the real identity of a character lies beyond the appearance of props and accessoires. To show the deep personality of your character, to communicate his feelings and emotions you have to make full use of body language and facial expressions.

Do get to know your character and find the right attitudes for every situation you have to draw him over and over again. Look at the character from all angles. Let him become something of yourself, like your handwriting. Only when you know your character like your best friend can you animate him in a meaningful way.

0811_Acting_Positions_Attitudes

Today's audiences are less attentive and they must understand quickly. Moreover, television and computer screens are smaller than movie screens. Much attention must therefore be given to the visual perception of forms, shapes, and colours.

Forms and shapes must be significant and comprehensive at first glance if the message is to be put across in a quick, clear, and unmistakable way. Get inspiration from good roadside pictograms that enable quick identification of objects and activities.

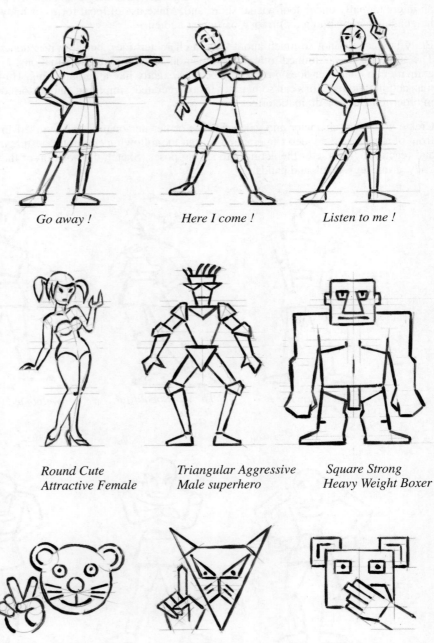

Go away !   *Here I come !*   *Listen to me !*

Round Cute   *Triangular Aggressive*   *Square Strong*
Attractive Female   *Male superhero*   *Heavy Weight Boxer*

Hi, there !   *Watch it !*   ***Oooops !***

0812_Acting_Body Language

Emotions are not only expressed by the movement of eyes and mouth, but also through the shape and position of the face and body. It's the combined use of facial expressions and body positions that brings your character to life. And, they make the audience forget that they're only watching a piece of clay or some paint on paper.

Body language is a form of nonverbal communication. Although some people, such as Italians, have a more extensive body language vocabulary than others, it is an internationally understood visual shorthand. Make use of local forms of body language when planning a film for a particular audience.

Body language is not so much about what a character does, but how it is done. The audience is conditioned to look at human characters in human situations. In animation, a character does not need to behave exactly like a human being. Human actions and reactions can sometimes be exaggerated, simplified, and distorted in order to achieve a dramatic effect.

Create your own character and get inside his or her personality. Put yourself in front of a mirror, or a video camera, and act out the following emotions, gestures, and reactions. Then, edit the acting into strong poses. Sketch the position of the body, arms, legs, head, and hands.

I'm the owner !

The most beautiful.. it's me !

Welcome !

What are you talking about ?

I'm out of cash !

I dare you to say that again !

What happened here ?

I'm innocent !

What you want ?   *He has taken my toy !*   *Stop here !*   *Look at me !*

How come ?   *Let's dance !*   *What the hell !*

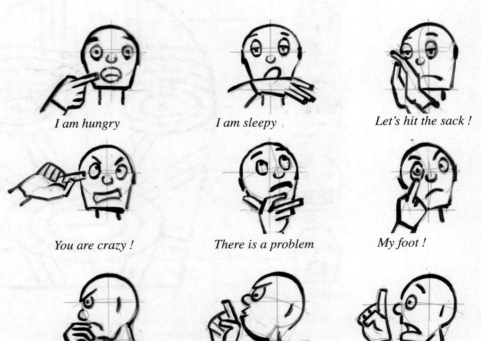

I am hungry   *I am sleepy*   *Let's hit the sack !*

You are crazy !   *There is a problem*   *My foot !*

Ha... ha... ha...   *Something's fishy*   *Silence - please !*   *Listen to me*

0813_Acting_Facial Expressions

The face of a human being is the most expressive part of the body. Human feelings are written on the face and it's on the face that you can read what's going on inside the head, even on a poker-face! It's partly through facial expressions that thoughts and ideas are communicated in a nonverbal way.

A bit more than a century ago *Charles Darwin* (1809-1882) told us that facial expressions of human emotions are universal. The imperfection of his research made it easy for his opponents to assert that facial expressions are modeled by civilisation and culture. Universality or specific cultural heritages - that was the question. New research and experiments seem to give right and honour to *Darwin:* in western civilisations, just as in the untouched oral societies of New Guinea, human beings feel and express emotions in much the same way. Facial expressions are therefore an international language and can be developed, as comedians, mimes, clowns, and the great comics of the silent movies have done.

The head is made only out of two pieces, the skull and the jaw. The jaw moves up and down on a hinge. Besides opening and closing the mouth, don't expect more expressions from the rigid skull.

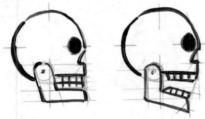  

Facial expressions are made by the muscles and the skin of the head.

Every facial muscle has its own function and allows one to move anything from the mouth for speaking to raising eyebrows or opening and closing the eyes. Special training will even allow one to move the ears !

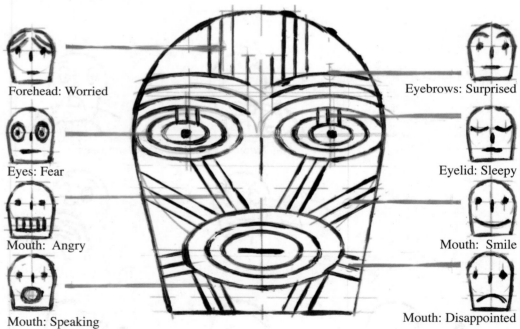

Forehead: Worried

Eyes: Fear

Mouth: Angry

Mouth: Speaking

Eyebrows: Surprised

Eyelid: Sleepy

Mouth: Smile

Mouth: Disappointed

To get all the human feelings of your character onto the screen, you must slip into the character's skin. Feel with it, just like a live actor. Sit in front of the mirror and move your eyeballs, eyebrows, mouth and ears.

Create your own character and always use the same one for this exercise. Go through the following expressions and reduce what you see in the mirror to basic drawings.

Smiling

Lighthearted

Pleased

Thoughtful

Happy

Laughing

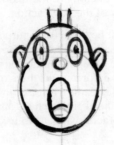

Frightened

Shocked

Surprised or puzzled

Shy

Winking

Coy and smart

Knocked out

Sad or tired

Ashamed

Sceptical

Determined

Impatient

Angry

Mad

Yelling

Crying

Worried

Fearful

0814_Acting_from Motion to Emotion

A good animator is good at drawing, good at acting, maybe a good musician and even better, a captivating storyteller. Character animation is the interdisciplinary combination of craftsmanship, acting, and timing. The use of time and space, together with music shows the close relationship between dance and animation.

A good actor never acts naturally. To appear natural the acting must be unnatural. That means that all actions that don't belong to the main action have to be eliminated in order not to disturb the flow of the main action.

Every movement of a character must be there for a purpose. The movements and actions originated by a character are the result of his thoughts. The driving force behind every action are therefore the thoughts of the character. The thought is the seed of the action: we think of things before we act them out. The eyes are the windows to the thoughts and therefore the leading force of the action. The character's eyes are anticipating the move of the head and the head anticipates the move of the body and the main action. If the character happens to have no eyes, the head will be first to start and lead the action.

The features of the character must be simple enough to allow a maximum of body and facial expressions. The key position must be a strong and expressive pose and the hold must be just long enough to transmit the message to the audience. Remember also, most importantly: animate only one thing at the time!

Sir Isaac Newton's law of motion *(see: 0609_Newton's Law of Motion)* is a wonderfully basic acting principle and can be easily applied to animation. There are not only physical forces which lead to actions, but also psychological states of mind.

Look - there's Hook !

Your character needs to have an objective

Newton's Law of Motion: **Lex Prima**

A body continues in a state of rest or uniform motion unless acted upon by a force.

To change the state of rest or motion of your character, a motivation and an objective are needed. Motivations and objectives are born out of ideas. To produce an idea, your character must think. Thinking leads to emotion, and motivation leads to movement.

If you hear footsteps behind you in the dark, you will start to think and get emotions. The emotional thoughts will lead to movement and action. What will be the possibles actions?

Here storytelling begins.
You build up an action and
you show the resolution.
Or you let the audience find out.
Which ever way you choose,
you must know the answer.
If you don't know it
the audience will know it -
and maybe you don't like it !

State of motion   Action   Reaction   Questions... Answers...?

A character will stay in bed as long as he isn't motivated to get up. Put yourself in the skin of your character and imagine the different motivations to get yourself out of bed. What will be the force to get you up?

State of rest   Action   Reaction   Questions...   Answers...?

A long distant runner will not stop until some motivation or objective acts upon him to make him slow down and come to a rest. Put yourself in the skin of the character and imagine the different forces that will eventually stop him.

Action

Reaction
Tired - Give up !

Reaction
Happy - Arrival !

Put yourself in the skin of the character and imagine the different forces that will act on you.

Newton's Law of Motion: **Lex Secunda**

The rate of change of the movement of a body in a given direction is proportional to the resulting force applied to it in that direction.

This law applies not only for physical forces, but it also works in psychological situations. Whatever action or thinking your character undertakes, the amount of energy that goes into the movement will be in a direct relationship to the force that was at the origin of the change. An obstacle can slow down or stimulate the action. Every character's movement needs to have a motivation and an objective. An action without an initial thought is impossible, or else it will be a mechanical, robotic movement.

The louder the mobile phone rings in your pocket, and the longer you take to reply, the more angry the people around you will react.

Action   *Reaction*

The kind of running is not the same if the character is running for fun on a sunny afternoon in the park or if he is running for his life with a bulldog behind him.

Running for pleasure !   *Running for life !*

Waving your arms to say goodbye to an old friend on the platform of a train station is not the same as waving your arms to ask for help when you are surrounded by sharks in the sea.

Bye... bye...   *Help !*

Put yourself in the skin of the character and imagine the different forces that will act on you.

Newton's Law of Motion: **Lex Tertia**
For every action, there is an equal and opposite reaction.

Acting is reacting. Every action is announced by anticipation. Before you speak, you will move your head, clear your throat, or hit the microphone with your hands.

Before you release the arrow towards the target, you will pull the string of the bow in the opposite direction. To check the result of the action, you will bend again in the direction of the target.

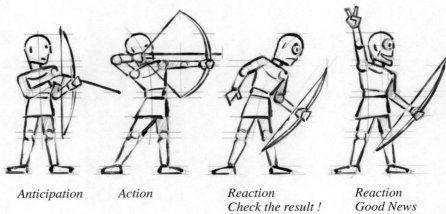

Anticipation   *Action*   *Reaction*   *Reaction*
Check the result !   *Good News*

Before you turn your head, your eyeballs will move in anticipation. According to what you see, there will be a reaction.

Anticipation   *Reaction*   *Reaction*
Bad News   *Good News*

At the end of the action, there is the reaction. The more money you win or lose at poker, the more or less violent will be your reaction.

Anticipation   *Reaction*   *Reaction*
Bad News   *Good News*

Put yourself in the skin of the character and imagine the different forces that will act on you.

This page is for your own drawings.

0900_Pre-Production_Content_Story

The techniques and the language of animation are no more than means to transport the most important thing: the Content.

And an audience not only wants to see a good story – they also want the story to be well told.

A clever way to tell the story helps to transmit the message, but it could never replace the content of the story.

This chapter will tell you how to *wrap-up* the content, that is, how to get the message across on the screen so it will be accepted by an audience. Acceptance does not mean that the content will be understood in the same way by all audiences. A good and efficient film can be understood in different ways by different audiences.

In a personal, **artistic film**, the filmmaker expresses his or her own feelings and emotions. In this case, the filmmaker's first concern is not to *punch the message home*. The filmmaker is occupied by a personal subject and works in a poetic and artistic way without being concerned with questions about target audiences.

In **commissioned films** where the content is given by a customer, you have to deal with precise messages. This is the case in pedagogical or commercial films. The message has to be transmitted to the audience in a unmistakable, direct, and instantly recognizable way.

Filmmaking can also be used as an **educational tool**. It's through making the film that filmmakers learn the various aspects of the subject of the film's content. The film itself becomes less important than the making of it. These films are finally only intended for those who made them.

The most important thing: The Content

0901_Improvised and Planned Animation

There are basically two ways of working with animation: improvised and planned. Most commercial work is done using planned animation while most experimental filmmaking is done with improvised animation. There is no right or wrong way to do it. Besides, every improvised animation needs some planning and in every planned animation there is some improvisation.

Improvised animation starts very much in the same way that someone writes a letter. The writer/animator has a basic idea, some content he or she would like to communicate. An original idea comes from something the author has experienced, from a feeling, an image, a sound or a movement.

Improvised animation starts without a precise structure of content and time. The animator will explore the idea visually through animating. One picture will bring up the next one. The work will evolve until it comes to the point when the animator considers the work to be finished. In improvised animation, the procedure of making the film is often more important than the final result. This is particularly the case when the filmmaking is to be used as an educational tool. Most improvised animation is done with direct animation techniques, where the artwork is animated directly under or in front of the camera.

In pegbar animation, the drawing on paper or straight to a computer screen technique is the most suitable to explore the possibilities of improvised animation.

Planned animation needs, like improvised animation, an idea to start with. In addition, the animator has a precise vision of what the finished work will be. The film on the screen should be as close as possible to this vision. The animator needs control over the film from the idea to the screen. In planned animation, the final product is more important than the process of making the film. Pre-visualization is therefore a must for this procedure. It shows and communicates the way the film will be made, first to the animator himself, but also to the team, the producer and sponsors. The basic idea will be clarified by evaluating and selecting. This procedure is continuous with a concept and a written treatment. The treatment will become the script for the future film. Scriptwriting will strengthen the story structure and the breakdown will clarify transitions from one scene to another.

The character and background design should be approved. The timing and soundtrack are established. The storyboard and the resulting animatic both show the film before a single frame has been animated. In planned animation, the method of pegbar animation with key drawings and an exposure sheet is the most suitable technique.

0902_Ideas_Creative Impulse _Image and Sound

An idea is a thought or a concept formed by experiences. The word *idea* comes from the Latin word, *ide*, meaning *to see*. An idea is a mental image - an organized picture created out of the chaos of experience. Humans are idea-makers by instinct. Ideas can come out of the blue. But they can also be developed.

People develop ideas because they need to communicate and share their thoughts and feelings with others. Ideas can be accepted or rejected. Thoughts and feelings have developed ideas: for example, led people to form philosophical ideas.

Creative Impulse
In search of creative impulses you could look at ideas expressed in other media. Look at them from an animator's point of view and adapt sounds and visuals of different media to animation.
The theatre, circus, puppet show, mimes, magic acts, music, dances, radio, books, comic strips, newspapers and even garbage cans are possible sources for creative impulses.

Generating Ideas with Images and Writings
Go to libraries, galleries, and museums to see pictures. Go to concerts or play for yourself on a guitar or piano for music and sounds. Go to the zoo, circus, and ballets to observe the movements of animals and humans. Go to the theatre and read books to develop characters. Read novels, folk-tales, or poems for narrative structures.

Generating Ideas with Sound and Music
Music is a universal language. Ideas and stories are communicated with sound and music. Music is also idea-generating. An idea can be born straight from a sound track, without passing through written words. Take any piece of music, close your eyes, listen to it intensely and you will see pictures. Shapes, forms, and colours will come into your mind. You will make your own interior cinema. Take a brush, ink and plenty of paper. Listen over and over again to the music and draw what you feel and see in your mind. These musically created drawings are inspirational drawings for content - whether natural or urban landscapes, or even technical content.

Is the First Idea the Best One ?
A good idea can be killed if you work for too long on it, or if there are too many commentators on it. Sometimes you feel that the basic idea is good, but somehow you got stuck in the middle of it, or you don't know how to end the story. Try to look at your project from the outside. Step back and have a look from different angles.

By changing the angle of your observation, your idea might take another and stronger direction.

Tricks-of-the-Trade

Exchanging: Human beings can become animals or mechanical objects, but still have human behaviour.

Extensions: Well known stories like *Little Red Riding Hood,* can be developed further, put in a different context, or serve as the beginning or end of a new story.

Contexts: A simple plot is taken out of its original context and placed in a new one. For example the story of *William Tell* becomes an aboriginal liberation plot.

Transfers: Well known characters are transferred into other situations: *Snow-White* finds seven extra-terrestrials behind seven planets in a science-fiction land.

Reversals: Stereotyped situations are reversed: The director becomes the worker and vice-verse, the servant becomes the lady.

Switching: The main character of a plot is put into another story: *Robin Hood* becomes an Urban Fighter.

Combination: Taking parts of different existing stories and mixing them up into a new and unique story.

Warning
Deep knowledge of your own idea is needed to create a story.

***The Tricks-of-the-Trade** are meant to kick you off when you are grounded. Use these hints carefully and make sure they don't become the main plot. You risk falling into clichés for which the audience will not forgive you.*

0903_Storytelling_Development

There is a saying that *When your heart is full, your mouth will overflow*. You will tell a story because you are moved by an idea and you need to share and to communicate the content of it. To communicate your idea you will develop a story. All great teachers like *Lao-Tzu* told stories to promote their ideas and often using metaphors. Storytelling is the art of communicating your ideas in a way that will catch the attention of an audience. The audience should remember your story and more important, they can tell the story to others and thus communicate and promote your idea.

To tell a story in an efficient way you need the skill of **Characterisation** and the knowledge of how to wrap up the **Content** in a way that will be understood by an audience. You want your audience to identify with the character and the story to become the story of their own life. For an audience there is nothing more important and interesting than their own story. People want to recognize themselves in the story, to be the hero or realize that after all they are the bad guy.

The tools like *Story Structure*, *Character Functions* and *Scriptwriting* can help to develop the story but without your deep knowledge of the content you will never make a believable story.

In literature great storytellers like *Aesop* in his *Fables* and *Geoffrey Chaucer* in *The Canterbury Tales* knew what they were writing about. They knew how to develop characters and tell stories in a universal and believable way that moves readers over the centuries.

In animation storytelling is visual storytelling. There are no limits. Animators can tell stories without words, without human characters. Animation can tell a heart touching story about happiness on a sunny spring morning or a sad story about a rainy blue Monday by using colours, shapes and music.

Whatever structure you use for your storytelling, the classical straight forward three acts or a non-linear puzzle of actions that will form a story at the end, you cannot tell a story without a change of values. Changes are chances as they say, but not necessarily for everybody. Not all stories have a happy end and some of the strongest stories end in a catastrophe. But, whatever ending your story will have, there must be a change and it must be surprising.

To be sure your story will work you need to know the beginning and the ending. Whatever happens in-between can be worked out. But you will never tell a good story without knowing how to start and how to end.

In the beginning of all film projects there is the question: how to get out of the dark tunnel into the bright and clear light that leads to the desired, divine sparkle: **The Idea !**

And then, when you have the idea, how to transport it to the audience in a way they will understand? Different arts give form to ideas and feelings in a particular media. A painter creates an image, a poet organizes words, a musician composes sounds, a dancer choreographs movement, a sculptor shapes and forms clay and a storyteller writes stories. Different artistic media are like different languages; each requires its own method of expression. An animator uses the language of animation, which is a unique visual language, making full use of images, sounds, movements and storytelling.

When you work on a subject, try to think and regularly note your ideas. Put the subject in a corner of your brain and think about it before you go to sleep. Through associative thinking, a new idea can be linked to the subjects. Think of your idea like that of a baby with which you are pregnant. Take care of him up to the day of his birth.

From Sketchbook to Portfolio

Ideas are everywhere. To put your hands on ideas and to find the good ones for the story you have to observe. Open your eyes and find the environment that fits best for your inspiration. A quiet place is not necessarily the best place for thinking. Some creators need the busy atmosphere of a coffee house or a journey on a train. Other persons prefer the countryside or their bathroom. Observe with your eyes, but do not forget that inspiration also comes through hearing, smelling and touching. Take an object in your hand, close your eyes and feel the shape and the structure of it. Does it tell a story?

Collect all ideas. Create an idea bank. Record your observations and put them in writing and drawing in your sketchbook or scratchpad. Pin up in your room all the collected items; paper clippings, photos, letters, postcards, train tickets... Make an exhibition of the objects related to your project. Live with them, keep them around like your friends and members of a family.

The next step is to evaluate and select your ideas. You know what you need first of all: the beginning and the end of your story. Look critically at your ideas and decide what will be the leading idea and what could make it confusing. Be careful in this step of the process and never throw away any idea. A useless idea can hide a useful one. What looks confusing at first sight makes your project maybe more complicated, but also more interesting and shows your idea from a different point of view.

Selecting also means organizing. Put your ideas in chronological order to bring out the leading idea, the driving force of the story. Think about the story structure and remember that a story needs a change of value. You should consult experts in fields you do not know much about it, but do not forget you make the film, not the expert. You may ask friends to help you in the selection. However, this is a dangerous game, because you are at risk of having too many opinions – too many cooks spoil the soup! Respect your advisers, but keep them at a distance. Talk about your project – that is the best way to protect your original idea – and see how people react.

Somehow you have to find a way to communicate your idea to people who are likely to help your project to get off the ground. These people, called sponsors, might be a producer, a television station, a government institution, a foundation, a distributer or an investor. You have to convince a lot of people to get all the money you need to make the film. But you are the first one you have to convince about your project. It's only when you identify entirely with the project that you can sell it to others.

There are many ways to communicate your project. The classic one is the printed portfolio. The portfolio must be serious and attractive at the same time. It should be appealing at first sight. The title is an important part of this presentation. Even a working title should be significant and give information about the project content. A two-line-pitch is like a subtitle and tells in a few words the whole story. This element is a must and should make the reader curious to know more about the project. Besides, it is a good exercise for you to learn how to communicate your idea in the form of a shortcut. Most sponsors will ask you for a treatment. The treatment is the written concept of the whole story that shows clearly what the film is about. Pictures are another must for a convincing presentation. Sketches, character model-sheets, film design and background studies tell more than words and express the mood and atmosphere of the project. Information about the animation technique may also interest the potential sponsors as well as the budget and financial planning.

At this point you will have made an important step from developing an idea to a first presentation. The next step will be a pre-visualisation of your project in whatever form you chose: a portfolio, a ppt-presentation, a storyboard, an animatic, a teaser or even a pilot film.

0904_Pre-Visualisation

Commercial animated filmmaking is an expensive business. Long feature films and TV series require a solid financial base before you can go into production. To convince producers and TV stations to invest in the project, filmmakers are more and more forced to show the film even before a single frame has been recorded. Pre-visualisation is used to get a feeling for the finished film, to see the background and character design, and to get into the story; in short, to see the film before it is on the screen.

Pre-Visualisation means developing the film project by using all the elements of Pre-Production. First you have to define the target audience and the objectives, a well as the cinematographic form. Without a leading idea, an attractive script and a solid story structure, you will not be able to present a convincing storyboard. The work flow and the production procedures should be clear, as well as the production planning and the budget.

Presentation of the pre-visualisation depends on the audience to whom you will have to *sell* the project. It can be a portfolio, a power-point presentation, an animatic storyboard, a short trailer, or all of these. Most important for the presentation is that you are convinced of the project. Your engagement and conviction, together with a professional pre-visualisation, is paramount in order to convince people to invest money in your film.

Don't forget that the first impression of your project is the most important. You will never get a scond chance to make a first impression !

0905_Objectives and Targets

At the beginning of any film project there is a good deal of uncertainty. To make a good film you have to light up that darkness with some clear thinking. Define the objectives clearly and analyse your task step by step.

Deciding Whether or Not to Use Animation
Can the same message be expressed through live action? Is there a need to make the point quickly and precisely? Can you make use of the *impossible* possibilities of animation? This includes the possibilities of showing the invisible, turning physical laws upside down, making an elephant fly and a bird swim like a fish...

Subject, Content and Story
What does the film have to say? What is the subject? Which is the best part of the content to be developed into a story? Make a list of different suggestions and write a statement about the film's content.

Audience and Market
Who would be interested to see such a film? Who are the people your film will be made for? What do you know about them?

Purpose
What do you want the target audience to know or to feel after viewing the film?

Identification
How do you want the target audience to identify themselves within the film?

Distribution Format
How and where will this film be shown and who will distribute it? Is it for theatrical release, Film festivals, DVD, or a Web Showcase? The forecast distribution will influence the technical format and the cinematographic form.

Time Factor
How many seconds or minutes is the film supposed to run? Can the message be expressed and assimilated in the given time?

Economic Factors
What is the cost/time relationship, including the cost of materials and labour ? What is the budget? Adapt the animation technique to the available time and money. Perhaps you have to shorten your project, simplify the design, or reduce the number of characters.

Working Schedule and the Deadline
Can the film be made within the given deadline and budget? Perhaps you need to change the technique. Break down your work into a production line, from idea to screen. Make a work flow chart and stick to it.

0906_Cinematographic Forms

How will you, as a filmmaker, present the subject, considering target audience, purpose, and identification?
You will have to chose from among the following spectrum of possibilities:

TV spot or **Advertising commercial** = 15 to 30 seconds.
Music clip = 1 to 3 minutes.
Internet showcase = 1 to 2 minutes.
Public relations film = 10 to 20 minutes.
Industrial film = 20 to 30 minutes.
Educational film = 5 to 20 minutes.
Scientific film = 5 to 50 minutes.
Entertainment short film = 3 to 7 minutes.
TV series = 13, 26, 52 or more episodes of 5, 13 or 26 minutes.
TV-special = 26 minutes.
Feature film = at least 70 minutes.
Experimental film = anything from 5 seconds to 5 hours!

0907_Story Ranges

Each story belongs in a way to a family of stories. This classification shows the possible ranges of stories. Most short animation films belong to the **01_Mini-Story** group. Nearly all animated feature films are in the **02_Maxi-Story** group. Experimental films are naturally part of the **03_Anti-Story** family. The **04_Multi-Story** is a mix of **01_02**. The **05_Non-Story** group are action films with plenty of special effects but no value changes.

01_Mini-Story
Minimalism
Passive / Multi Protagonist
Open Ending

03_Anti-Story
Anti-Structure
Inconsistent Realities
Nonlinear Time
Hazard

Value Changes

04_Multi-Story
Variations of
Mini and Maxi Stories

02_Maxi-Story
Classical Design
Active / Single Protagonist
External Conflict
Linear Time
Closing Ending

05_Non-Story
Actions
No Value Changes

0908_Visual Unities

In classical animation, the visual unities of the film are considered on five levels:

Film and Acts
01_Acts
On the number and the lengths of the **acts** depends the rhythm of the film.
For example: 1 - 2 - 3 acts.
The basic structure of a film has **three acts**: Establishing, Action and Resolution.

Acts and Sequences
02_Sequences
On the number and the lengths of the **sequences** depends the rhythm of the act.
For example: 1 - 2 - 3 – 4 - 5 - 6 - 7 sequences.
A **sequence** is a series of scenes or shots presenting a subject, intention, or place that forms a complete dramatic action.

Sequences and Scenes
03_Scenes
On the number and the lengths of the **scenes** depends the rhythm of the sequence.
For example: 1 - 2 - 3 – 4 - 5 scenes.
A **scene** is a series of images representing one continuous action, recorded by a camera without any interruption on the same background. In a scene, besides the steady shot, there can be camera moves, a change of camera angle, change of focus, change of light and colour.

Scenes and Shots
04_Shots
On the number and the lengths of the **shots** depends the rhythm of the scene.
For example: 1 - 2 - 3 shots.
A **shot** has its own rhythm of action including movements of the characters or objects. The longest possible shot is the sequence-in-one-shot.

Shots and Frames
05_Frames
On the number of **frames** depends the length and rhythm of the shot.
For example: 2 seconds = 50 frames
A **frame** is the smallest visual unity of the film: 25 frames for one second of film.

0909_Story Structures

Time is the fourth dimension for a filmmaker and animator. Storytelling and Story Structures happen in time and in dramatic intensity. The audience will follow your story action by action. The individual actions or scenes have to be connected to one another. This linear structure, or chain of actions, has not changed since *Aesop* told his fables in 500 BC.

Like all rules, you surely would like to break it. *Gao Xing Jiang*, in his book *Soul Mountain*, did it in the most talented way. If you work for the Game industry, you have to break the linear structure anyway, since the story structure is necessarily interactive and therefore nonlinear.

However, before breaking a rule efficiently, you better know the rule.

Traditional storytelling, like animation, is subject to the passing of time. This is why in every story there is a **Before** and an **After**. To get from one point to the next, there is a **Whilst**. In other words, every plot has a **Beginning**, a **Middle**, and an **End**. The classic formula *Aristotle* developed as a narrative structure in the 4th century BC remains the same: the three-act structure of Establishing, Action and Resolution.

Before_The Prologue
The initial situation shows the existing state, stable and balanced, before something happens that will break this balance, modify the situation and kick off the story. The characters, their situations, and their environment have to be established in this part of the story.

Beginning_Establishing_Act 1
The provocation, or story kick-off, introduces a new element that will modify the established situation. A new desire will raise questions and create an unbalanced situation. Unexpected problems appear and conflicts burst out.

Middle_Action_Act 2
The action and evaluation part is the heart of the film. This includes a series of actions or researches in order to find a solution to the problems and provocations launched in the first act. The conflict will be developed. Catastrophes, deceptions, suspense, discoveries, true and false answers, great hardship and the final showdown will lead to the story climax at the end of the second act.

End_Resolution_Act 3
The resolution brings up a solution that will lead to the final situation. The way out of the problem can be violent or dramatic but it is always surprising. It is the final turning point of the story, the point of no return. The conclusion and the solution to the problem contain the message of what you want your audience to believe in.

After_Epilogue
The final situation is the state when a new balance is reached. At this point, changes in the characters' situations and/or their environment that transpired during the film should be clear to the target audience. A new life will open the door to new destinies, new questions, a new beginning and eventually a new story.

*A content
needs a story.*

*A story
needs a structure.*

*A structure
needs a change.*

To construct a linear story that will be understood by an audience you need these five basic structural elements: **Prologue, Establishing, Action, Resolution,** and **Epilogue.**

Mini-plots, **Maxi-plots** and **Multi-plots** follow the story structures. **Anti-plots** and **Non-plots** don't need any structure.

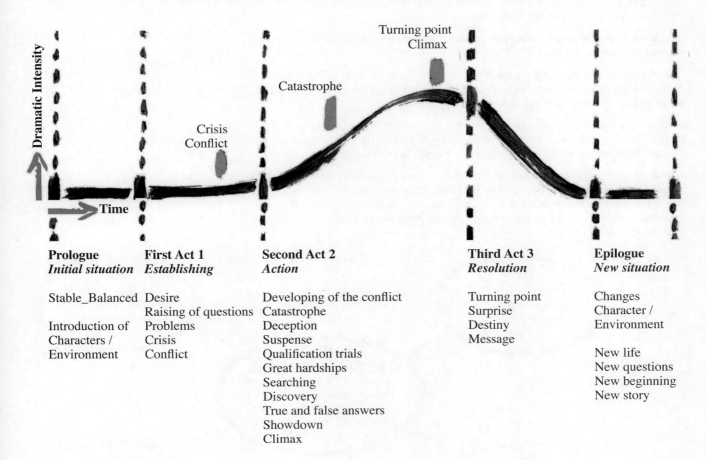

Prologue *Initial situation*	**First Act 1** *Establishing*	**Second Act 2** *Action*	**Third Act 3** *Resolution*	**Epilogue** *New situation*
Stable_Balanced	Desire	Developing of the conflict	Turning point	Changes
	Raising of questions	Catastrophe	Surprise	Character /
Introduction of	Problems	Deception	Destiny	Environment
Characters /	Crisis	Suspense	Message	
Environment	Conflict	Qualification trials		New life
		Great hardships		New questions
		Searching		New beginning
		Discovery		New story
		True and false answers		
		Showdown		
		Climax		

0910_Characters and their Functions

A fictional character is any person who appears in a work of fiction. In addition to humans, characters can be aliens, animals, gods or objects. The characters and their functions are part of the story structure.

The basic function of all characters is that they carry to the audience the most important part of the film: the Content.

The characters are messengers, speakers of what you have to say. The quality of the characterisation and the clarity of their motivation helps the audience to understand what you want them to know.

Moreover, the characters are powerful tools that enable the audience to identify themselves with the plot, to believe in the story, and make them forget that the actors are only pieces of clay or cardboard or a brush line on paper.

Based on the functions established by *Vladimir Propp* regarding action spheres, *Algirdas-Julien Greimas* proposed in 1966 his actant-theory in which each actor has a force with clearly defined aims and place in the story structure. The five principle functions of the actants turn all around their desire to obtain something or to be separated from it.

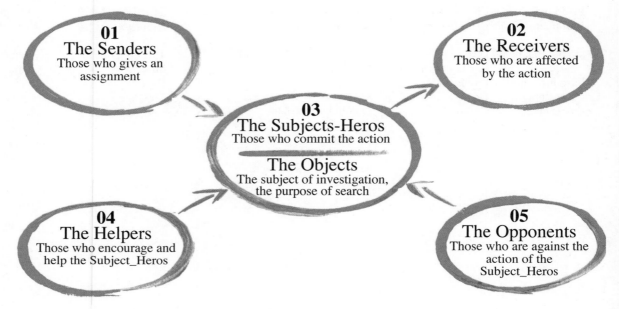

01
The Senders
Those who gives an
assignment

02
The Receivers
Those who are affected
by the action

03
The Subjects-Heros
Those who commit the action

The Objects
The subject of investigation,
the purpose of search

04
The Helpers
Those who encourage and
help the Subject_Heros

05
The Opponents
Those who are against the
action of the
Subject_Heros

01_The Senders
Those who give an assignment

The Senders are at the origin of the actions, since they provoke change and establish a contract with the subject (Heroes). They formulate the object (the Subject and Purpose of action) and give an assignment to the heroes. They don't necessarily physically appear in the film. They can play the function of a hidden power and be part of the back-story. Nevertheless, without the Senders, there will be no story, no film.

02_The Receivers
Those who are affected by the action

The Receivers are secondary characters in terms of action, but still very important, since the whole plot is built up to help them to change their conditions. If they don't die during the action, they often have the role of the survivors, able to establish a new situation. But even when dead, the Receivers will teach the audience from their experiences and transmit knowledge which could lead to another story. They might as well become the new generation of Senders and be at the origin of a new plot.

03_The Subjects-Heroes
Those who commit the action

Heroes are traditionally the main characters who have been chosen by the Senders to commit the action that will change the life of the receivers and maybe their own lives as well. Heroes feel that they fulfill an existential task. They are ready to suffer great hardship, or undergo several trials in order to become qualified and continue right to the final showdown. They will fight for and believe in the Object, and make it their personal mission. Another mission is to transmit their commitments to the audience and help the audience to identify with them.

The Objects
The subject of investigation, the purpose for searching

Objects are formulated by the senders and the heroes make a mission out of them. The Object can be a human or animal being that has to be found or maybe a mysterious thing or idea which has to be conquered or saved. In search of the Object, the Heroes have to fight and suffer. For the sake of the Object, Heroes will undergo any number of trials and will risk their lives in order to fulfill the mission, and to save, more important than their lives, their honour.

04_The Helpers
Those who encourage and help the subjects/heroes

Helpers are the good and stimulating forces that the heroes will encounter on their road in search of the object. The Helpers, who represent the forces of justice, give good advice, and encourage and help the heroes to overcome the many trials to which the Heroes are challenged. Good Helpers react well in the face of adversity and never let the heroes down. A false Helper is an Opponent.

05_The Opponents
Those who are against the action of the subject/heroes

These are the evil forces representing the conservative power of those who don't accept the changes of the initial situation. Their job is to get in the way of the heroes and stop their actions. They will create and build up as many obstacles and problems as possible to challenge the Heroes and their Helpers. The Opponents are in a constant battle with the Helpers.

A character in a story can have several functions or several characters can have the same function. And, one who has a function must be qualified to exercise it.

To blow life into a character, to create and animate believable actors, the animator must give them a visual and psychological identity. Just as in live action films, the animator makes a *casting* and researches the unique character that will fit the film project.

0911_Scriptwriting_Controlling idea _Pitch_Synopsis_Music Score

Even if the basic purpose of storytelling is to entertain, there can be other values added: to inform, to educate, to communicate political, social or religious issues, and so on. In all these cases, the events told in a script will stand for a value.

Scriptwriting for animation can be reduced to a few lines to describe the outline of the action and give some indications about continuity and sound effects. For all animated films where the visual part is paramount, this short-cut scriptwriting approach is the right one.

However, scriptwriting for animation is a field that has seen very much development in recent years. This is partly due to the fact that the content and purpose of the future film have to be communicated to more and more people, including to people who will give you the money to make the film! Moreover, in narrative film structures, the words, and therefore the script and dialogues, are important parts of the whole film, often equivalent to the visual part.

The first draft of a script is always written before the synopsis and the pitch. In reality, it is a constant Work-in-Progress, a back and forth between the writing of the various versions of the script and the different versions of synopses and pitches. In the portfolio presentation, the pitch is, however, always first, followed by the Synopsis and Script

Controlling Idea
The controlling idea is the expression of this value. Storytelling has to serve this main purpose.

Example of the Controlling Idea for the film: **The Big Game**
The Hunter Hunted

Two-Line Pitch
The Pitch is the expression of the leading, controlling idea (the content or object) developed by evaluating and selecting the ideas, which is the seed for the whole procedure. A good way to check the value of the controlling idea is to express it in a two-line sentence. The purpose of the Two-Line Pitch is to communicate in a shorthand style the basic idea of the film and to check if the idea appeals to a potential audience.

Example of the Two-Line Pitch for the film : **The Big Game**
There is peace and harmony in the deep forest, a paradise on earth, until a hunter decides to go out for the big game. The result of the hunting is more than he ever dared to dream of, but the happy ending is not to everyone's taste.

Synopsis
The Synopsis develops the controlling idea in the form of a short text. The writing of the synopsis will strengthen the story structure, and clarify the content and continuity within the film. Later on, the Synopsis will become the script for the future film.

Example of the Synopsis for the film : **The Big Game**
A hunter and his dog sleep in a blockhouse. The hunter dreams about a nice and crispy roasted rabbit. The following morning, in the forest, the birds sing, an old boar is snoring, and a rabbit pops out of the high grass. It's a paradise on earth. The hunter and the dog, ready for the Big Game, walk through the forest. The dog sniffs on the ground while the hunter sings a happy song. On top of the cliff a strange sound stops them. The hunter takes his gun and aims carefully. Silence... The hunter fires and the dog runs off to get the game. The hunter, expecting the dog to bring the game, calls the dog. Sounds of crackling wood, footsteps getting closer… Instead of the dog, out of the high grass comes the old boar holding the knocked out dog between his teeth. The hunter faints and falls backwards over the cliff.
The hunter, with his head, leg and arm plastered, lies in a hospital bed. His dog, also badly wounded, accompanies him.The hunter has a nightmare: His dog is served on a plate as a nice and crispy roasted dish. Popping up behind the roasted dog: the Rabbit! He holds up a delicious carrot and suggests becoming vegetarian!

Script

Scriptwriting in planned animation, is used to communicate the concept and treatment to the team, the producer and the sponsors in the form of a written text.

A basic script will give you clear and detailed information about the content, the film structure, the actions, and the dialogues. In most cases, several versions of the script will be produced. Re-writing is a procedure where each new version represents more value in relationship to the former one. Scriptwriter, director and producer have to absolutely agree on the final version. A carefully prepared script will save a lot of money, time and labour when it comes to storyboarding.

Example of a Script structure for the film : **The Big Game**

Before: Prologue and Initial Situation
In the deep forest, within a hunter's blockhouse, a hunter and his dog sleep. The hunter has a sweet dream: A bunch of rabbits are jumping over his head and one of the rabbits jumps into a plate and becomes a nice and tasty roasted dish.

Act 1: Beginning_Establishing
In the morning, in front of the blockhouse, the hunter strokes the head of his dog. In the forest, the birds sing, while under the deep thicket, a boar is snoring and a rabbit shows his head out of the high grass. It's a paradise on earth.

Act 2: Middle Action
The hunter together with the dog, walk through the forest. The dog sniffs on the ground and a squirrel jumps from branch to branch. Happy, the hunter sings a song: With arrow and bow...On the top of the cliff, a strange sound stops them. The hunter looks closer and aims carefully. Silence... The hunter fires and the dog runs off to get the game. The hunter observes the bush, expecting the dog to bring the game. The hunter changes his expression from expectation to surprise...

Act 3: Ending_Resolution
Over the sound of crackling wood, footsteps are getting closer... Out of the high grass comes the old boar holding the knocked out dog between his teeth. The hunter faints and falls backwards over the cliff.

After: Epilogue_Final Situation
The hunter and his dog, badly wounded, lies in a hospital bed. The hunter has a nightmare: his dog is jumping over his head and finally jumps onto a plate and becomes a roasted dish. Popping up behind the roasted dog: the rabbit! He holds up a delicious carrot and makes a suggestion to the hunter: For safety reasons - go vegetarian!

Music Score

Musicians and music composers have to be associated at the very beginning of the film project. There are two ways: You may use a existing score and aquire the musical rights for your film or you ask a composer to make an original film score. In any case the song and especially the lyrics are important parts of the scriptwriting.

Example of Music Score for the film: **The Big Game** Song: With Arrow and Bow
Original score by Bernhard A. Weber 1804   Original text by Friedrich Schiller 1803

With his bow and a - rrow   through mou-ntain and valley____   walks the hun - ter

free - ly   in the mor - ning sun   Tra la la, la la la, la la la____   tra

la la la   la la___ tra la la la la la, la la la_____   tra la la la la la la la____

Music Score
With arrow and bow...
Score by Bernard A. Weber
and
Text by Friedrich von Schiller

0912_Breakdown_Dialogues _Maps of situation

The final script, in order to be used for the storyboard, will need to be broken down into sequences, scenes, and shots. This breakdown will contain information about the actions, sound design, dialogues, and/or voice over, as well as an approximate timing for each shot. The shots will be numbered in chronological order by sequences, scenes, and shots. Each shot will have the indication of its fieldsize and eventually camera and compound movements.

The following is an example of a breakdown for a story according to the classic formula of the three-act structure: **Beginning**/Establishing - **Middle**/Action - **Ending**/Resolution, including a **Prologue** and **Epilogue**.

Breakdown

Example: The Big Game

Prologue_Initial situation

Pro_01
Action_Medium Shot
Hunter and his dog sleeping in his blockhouse.
Sound
Hunter and dog snoring

Pro_02
Action_Medium Close up
Zoom-in to Medium close up
The hunter has a dream: A joyful bunch of rabbits are jumping over his head
Sound
Hunting horn

Pro_03
Action_Close up
Zoom-in to Close up
The hunter's dream: cont.
One Rabbit jumps into a plate and becomes nice and tasty roasted dish.
Dissolve to scene Act_01_01

Act 01_Establishing

Act_01_01
Action_Long shot
A dog barks and looks in the direction of the sound of his master's voice.
Dog runs off. Pan following the dog
The dog arrives in front of his master, the hunter, next to the blockhouse.
Sound
Forest ambiance, dog barking
Dialogue
Hunter off
Com'on... Doggy... Com'on...

Act_01_02
Action_Medium Close up
Tenderly the hunter strokes the head of his dog.
Sound
Continuity
Dialogue
Hunter to his dog
Good Doggy... it's time for the big game...
Dissolve to 01_03

Act_01_03
Action_Long shot: Pan_W-E
Film Title _Main credits
The Big Game

Pan across the deep forest.
A sunny spring morning. Birds fly in the sky. In the thicket sleeps peacefully an old boar and a rabbit shows his head out of the grass.
Everything is peace and in harmony.
Sound
Forest ambiance, sound of birds, snoring of the boar

Act 02_Action

Act_02_01
Action_Medium shot
The hunter gets up and points out into the forest to encourage his dog.
Dialogue
Hunter to his dog
Let's go... It's time for the big game...

Act_02_02
Action_Long shot_Pan W-E
Hunter walks through the forest and out of frame A squirrel jumps from branch to branch. It's a paradise on earth !
Sound
Forest ambiance Footsteps on the leaves
Dialogue
The hunter sings
With arrow and bow...
Music
Score: Bernard A. Weber (1804)
Text: Friedrich von Schiller (1803)

Act_02_03
Action_Medium shot
Hunter and dog on top of the cliff. Hunter and dog stop
Sound
Strange noise
Music
Song fade out

Act_02_04
Action_Close up
Hunter takes a closer look and gets his gun ready

Act_02_05
Action_Close up
The dog takes a closer look and barks

Act_02_06
Action_Close up
The Rabbit looks in the direction of the barking dog and disappears.
Sound
Dog barks, footsteps in the leaves

Act_02_07

Action_Medium Shot

The hunter takes his gun and aims carefully...   The dog is highly excited.
The hunter fires....   The dog runs off screen

Sound

Silence – then gun shot
Dog barking - then sound of battle

Dialogue

Hunter encourages his dog:
Good doggy - good game.

Act_02_08

Action_Medium close up

The hunter, expecting the dog to bring the game, looks into the bush
Hunter changing expression from expectation to surprise.

Sound

Silence - then sound of breaking branches

Dialogue

Hunter calls his dog:
Doggy... com'on... bring back...

Act 03_Resolution

Act_03_01

Action_Medium shot

Out of the thicket comes the old boar:
Smiling, he holds in between his teeth the knocked out dog

Sound

Sound of crackling wood, footsteps getting closer

Act_03_02

Action_Close-up

Boar enters the frame with the dog in is mouth
Pan W-E to the hunter who has a shock and falls backwards over from the cliff,
out of frame.

Sound_Music

Dramatic apotheosis

Dialogue

Cry of hunter, fading out as he falls

Disolve to Epi_01

Epilogue_Final situation

Epi_01

Action_Medium Shot

Hunter in a hospital bed. His head, arm and leg are heavy bandaged after falling
from the cliff.
He strokes the head of his dog which is also in a bad shape

Epi_02

Action_Zoom in to Medium close up

Hunter has a strange dream:
His dog is jumping over his head over and over again...

Epi_03

Action_Close up

The hunter's dream turns into a nightmare: The dog jumps into a plate and be-
comes nice and tasty roast dish.
Popping up behind the roasted dog: The Rabbit !
He holds up a delicious carrot and makes a safety suggestion to the hunter.

Dialogue

Rabbit

Dear friend - for safety reason - how about going vegetarian ?

Music

Hunter's Song : *With arrow and bow…*

Credits-Ends

Maps of situations

Throughout the procedure of writing the script, it is critically important to know where the actions take place. You should be able to follow the character's actions step by step, from location to location.

This can be done with a simple top-view sketch, indicating the important locations and showing the path of action

Map of situations
Framings

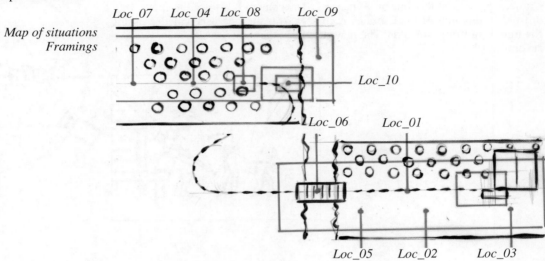

For more information, especially if you work with a team, the map can be a 2 or 3-D layout showing more details concering the backgrounds.

In both cases the maps are used to clarify the continuty of action for the scriptwriter and as a communcation tool for the storyboarder, layouter as well as for the director and producer.

Interior of Blockhouse
Interior of Hospital

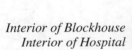

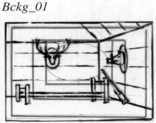

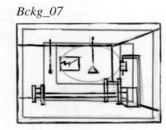

Outside Backgrounds
and Framings

0913_180 Degree Rule_Continuity

A continual problem with storyboarding involves the issue of *crossing the line*. In the example of the scenes between the hunter and the dog, the establishing shot shows the hunter on the right side of the frame, in front of the dog, which is on the left side. The red line is the imaginary axis connecting the two characters. **Camera A** looks at this line at 90 degrees. The camera is allowed to move 180° in front of this line. If the **Camera A** passes over the line it is called **crossing the line** or **jumping the axis**. The new shot from the opposite side is known as a **reverse angle.**

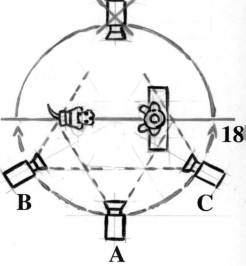

In a continuous shot from the dog's point of view, **Camera B**, the hunter is still on the right and the dog on the left side. In a shot from the hunter's point of view, **Camera C**, the dog will remain on the left side and the hunter on the right. Shifting the camera to the other side of the line in a cut, in order that the dog will be on the right and the hunter on the left side, will confuse the viewer and break the flow of action.

The 180 degree rule enables the audience to visually connect with what happens between two scenes. In an example of an action scene, such as a character running across the screen and out of frame on the right side of the screen he should enter from the left side in the next shot. Leaving the screen on the right side and entering the character from the right side in the next shot will create a disorientation. The audience may think of another character running in the opposite direction.

In classical professional productions the application of the 180 degree rule is a must for continuity editing. This rule is never broken.
But, of course, rules are made to be broken ! Many filmmakers purposely break the 180° rule to draw attention to an unusual situation - like in horror films - and to create confusion in the viewers' minds.

0914_Storyboarding

There are two kinds of storyboards.

The **Presentation storyboard**, used in commercial filmmaking, is a selling instrument. With this Storyboard you will have to convince the sponsor to produce the film. The Storyboard will therefore look like the film. It will give precise information and answer all the questions your client wants to know about the finished film: graphic style, character and background design, framing, colours, timing, etc.

The **Communication storyboard** is a tool for the whole team working on the film. In this case it will not necessarily express the final style of the film. Details of background and character design and colours and graphic design will be presented separately. The Storyboard will however be very clear about the flow of actions, timing, framing, and camera angles. This Storyboard is the last step before Layout and Posing.

In any case, the Storyboard is clearly a step from words to visuals. Storyboarding starts when your script and action-breakdown are accepted. That means the content, the target audience, and the objectives of the film are clearly defined. You have an outline of the action and you have knowledge about the characters and the background. Final story structures, production procedures and picture changes will be influenced by the Storyboard, so they do not need to be too detailed at this stage of production. It helps, of course, if you have already given some thought to it. The final Storyboard will carry all the information you need to produce the film.

From visual thinking to timing, the Storyboard uses all the elements of the language of animation to put the message across.

The final storyboard is the pictorial expression of the script and breakdown. It shows the film's content in visual writing. Visual language is not just illustrating the facts mentioned in the script, but transposing the written words into a pictorial message. The final Storyboard may include indications of graphic style, colours, movements, sounds, and timing.

When drawing the Storyboard you should eliminate all written words, except for titles and credits. The Storyboard is not a comic book with bubbles. Express the dialogue, if any, in non-verbal communication using facial expressions and body language, reinforced with sound effects. Learn non-verbal communication from the great actors of the silent movies, from mimes and good circus artists.

In the process of storyboarding, you pass from individual drawings – illustrations and background research - to a continuous flow of pictures. The Storyboard must express the flow of the action in your film, the visual continuity and the coordination of individual actions. It shows all important actions and events as well as the camera moves and changes from one visual to another. You should indicate all information on special effects, titles and the exact timing.

To get precise timing you should act out the whole Storyboard. With the help of a stop watch or tape recorder, go through each scene telling the action while looking at the storyboard. Put yourself *into the film*, acting out every movement, and make several takes to get an average timing.

All the factual errors, lack of continuity, and lack of clear thinking should be eliminated on the Storyboard - not at the editing table. Working with a good storyboard will save time and effort, avoid mistakes, and improve the quality of the finished film.

  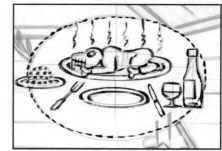

Pro_01   00:05_00:**05**   Bckg 01

Action_Medium
Hunter and dog sleeping in the block-house

Pro_02   00:09_00:**09**   Bckg 01

Action_Medium Close up
Zoom in to Medium close up

The hunter has a sweet dream:
A joyful bunch of rabbits are jumping over his head

Pro_03   00:15_00:**06**   Bckg 01

Action_Close up
Zoom in to Close up

The hunter's dream: cont:
The rabbit jumps into a plate and be-comes nice and tasty roasted rabbit

Disolve to scene 01_01

Sound
Hunter snoring

Sound
Music Hunting horn

Sound
Continuity

Prologue

Act_01_01   00:24_00:**09**   Bckg 02   Pan W-E

Action_Long shot
A dog barks and looks enthusiastically in the direction of the sound of his master's voice

Dog runs off
Pan following the dog

Action_Continuity
The dog arrives in front of his master, the hunter, at the blockhouse

Act_01_02   00:30_00:**06**   Bckg 02

Action_Medium Close up
Tenderly the hunter strokes the head of his dog

Disolve to 01_03

Sound
Forest atmosphere
Dog barking, in the direction of his master's voice

Sound
Forest atmosphere

Sound
Continuity

Dialogue
Hunter off
Com'on... Doggy... com'on...

Dialogue
Hunter to his dog
Good Doggy... it's time for the big game...

First Act_01_Establishing

Act_01_03   00:42_00:**12**   Bckg 03

Action_Long shot: Pan_W-E
A sunny sping morning. Birds fly in the sky
Pan across the deep forest

cont

In the thicket sleeps peacefully an old boar

Film Title _Main credits
The Big Game

Action:End of Pan: The forest ends abruptly with a cliff
A rabbit shows his head out of the grass.

Everything is peace and harmony

Sound
Forest atmosphere, Sound of birds

Sound
Happy snoring of the boar

Sound
Continuity of forest atmosphere

Second Act 02_Action

Act_02_01   00:48_00:**06**   Bckg 02

Action_Medium shot
The hunter gets up and points off into the forest to encourage his dog

Act_02_02   00:58_00:**10**   Bckg 04

Action_Long shot_Pan W-E
Hunter walks through the forest

cont Pan W-E

Hunter and dog walk out out of frame.
A squirrel jumps from branch to branch

It's paradise on earth

Sound
Forest atmosphere

Sound
Cont. Forest atmosphere
Footsteps on the leaves

Sound
Cont. Forest atmosphere

Dialogue
Hunter to his dog
Let's go... it's time to hunt...

Dialogue
The hunter sings
With arrow and bow…

Music
Score: Bernard A. Weber (1804)
Text: Friedrich Schiller (1803)

Act_02_03   01:02_00:**04**   Bckg 05

Action_Medium shot
Hunter and dog on top of the cliff.
Strange noise. Hunter and dog stop

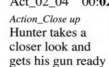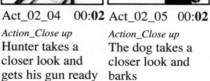

Act_02_04 00:**02** **Act_02_05** 00:**02**

Action_Close up
Hunter takes a
closer look and
gets his gun ready

Action_Close up
The dog takes a
closer look and
barks

Act_02_06   01:16_00:**04**   Bckg 05

Action_Close up
The rabbit looks in the direction of the
barking dog and disappears

Sound
Strange noise
Music
Song fades out

Sound
Dog barks, footsteps in the leaves

Act_02_07   01:16_00:**06**   Bckg 05

Action_Medium
The hunter takes his gun and aims
carefully...
The dog is highly excited

The Hunter fires....

cont

Action_Continuity
Immediately after the gun shot
the dog runs off screen

Act_02_08   01:20_00:**04**   Bckg 05

Action_Medium close up
The hunter observes the bush,
expecting the dog bringing the game

Hunter changing expression from
expectation to surprise

Sound
Silence – then gun shot

Sound
Dog barking - then sound of battle

Sound
Silence - then sound of breaking
branches

Dialogue
Hunter encourages his dog:
Good doggy - good game...

Dialogue
Hunter calls his dog:
Doggy... com'on... bring back...

Act_03_01 01:24_00:**04** Bckg 06	Act_03_02 01:32_00:**08** Bckg 05	cont
Action_Medium Close-up	*Action_Medium shot*	*Action_cont*
Out of the thicket comes the old boar, smiling, he holds in between his teeth the knocked out dog	Boar enters the frame with the dog in is mouth Pan W-E	The hunter has a shock and falls backwards over the cliff Hunter falls out of frame.

Sound	*Sound_Music*	
Sound of crackling wood, footsteps, getting closer	Dramatic apotheosis	

		Dilalogue
		Cry of hunter, fading out as he falls Dissolve to Epi_01

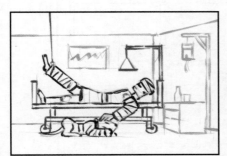

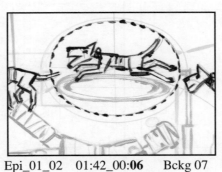

Epi_01_01 01:36_00:**04** Bckg 07	Epi_01_02 01:42_00:**06** Bckg 07	Epi_01_03 02:00_00:**18** Bckg 07
Action_Medium	*Action_Zoom in to Medium close up*	*Action_Close up*
Hunter in a hospital bed. His head, arm and leg are heavy bandaged after falling from the cliff He strokes the head of his dog which is also heavily bandaged	Hunter has a strange dream His dog is jumping over his head over and over again...	The hunter's dream turns into a nightmare: The dog jumps into a plate and becomes nice and tasty roast dish Popping up: The Rabbit ! He holds up a delicious carrot and makes a safety suggestion to the hunter

		After Dialogue *Music*
		Hunter's song *With arrow and bow…*

		Dialogue
		Rabbit *Dear friends - for safety reason - how about going vegetarian ?* **Credits-Ends**

Example of Storyboard Formats

Storyboard models are as numerous as animators. According to the film project, the storyboard can emphasize more on pictures or more on text. The paper format can range from A4 to A3 or any other format of your choice.

The proposed model for *The Big Game* holds basically six shots on one page. It offers the possibility of indicating the shot number, the length of each shot, the field size and the background number. There is space for the description of the action, for the sound track, and the dialogue/voice over.

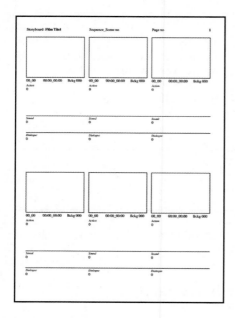

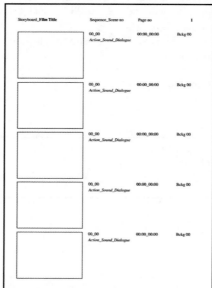

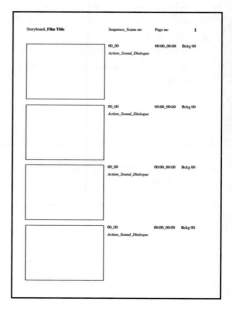

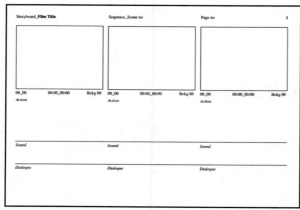

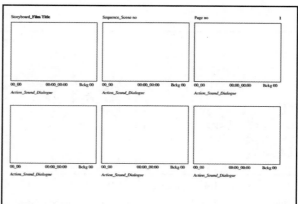

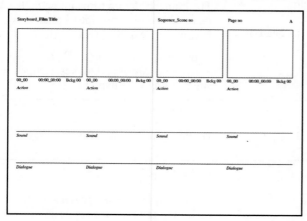

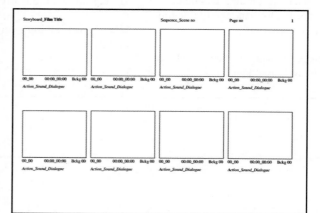

Storyboard

Sequence / Scene No

Page No

Action

Action

Action

Sound / Music

Sound / Music

Sound / Music

Dialogue

Dialogue

Dialogue

Action

Action

Action

Sound / Music

Sound / Music

Sound / Music

Dialogue

Dialogue

Dialogue

Page no

Sequence_Scene no

Storyboard

Action_Sound_Dialogue

Action_Sound_Dialogue

Action_Sound_Dialogue

Action_Sound_Dialogue

Action_Sound_Dialogue

Action_Sound_Dialogue

0915_Animatics_Time Visualisation

An Animatic is the pre-visualisation of the finished film. A series of pictures - usually the pictures from the storyboard - are recorded to film or video tape, or captured and scanned using a computer program. Each image will be recorded with the length of time it represents in the film. By playing it back in real time, you will get a feeling for the timing of the finished film.

The length of each picture will be set according to the indication in the storyboard. Another possibility is to edit the pictures according to a soundtrack. If your project is based on sound, you can import the soundtrack into the computer and match the length of the storyboard pictures to the track. In case you have no idea about the timing of your project, you can record each picture for three seconds and shift around the length to adjust to what you feel is the right timing.

The Animatic is the last step in pre-production. It is also the last chance before making artwork and animation to change not only the timing but also the field size and composition. Scenes that seemed correct on the storyboard may lack continuity when they are presented in time and space.

As your film progresses, the animatic pictures are replaced first with line-test files and later with the finished animation. During the process of production, the animatic will at each moment show the work in progress of your film.

Time Visualisation

Another way to visualise the time line of the film and get an idea about its dramatic line is to draw a graphic which represents the length of each scene and each sequence in chronological and proportional order.

This graphic gives an overall view of the film's structure in time.

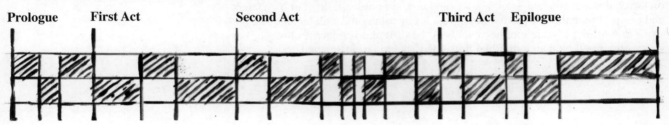

Prologue   **First Act**   **Second Act**   **Third Act**   **Epilogue**

Combined with dramatic intensity this graphic allows one to have a good idea of the finished film

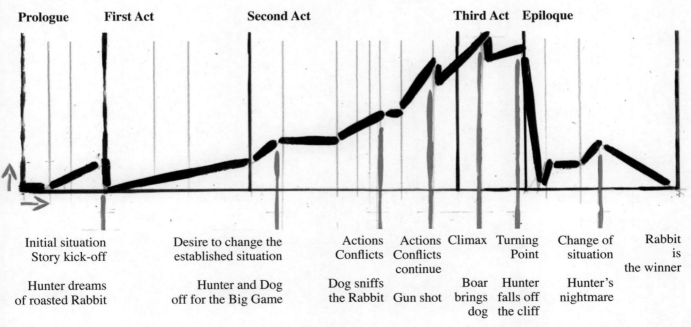

Prologue   **First Act**   **Second Act**   **Third Act**   **Epiloque**

| Initial situation Story kick-off | Desire to change the established situation | Actions Conflicts | Actions Conflicts continue | Climax | Turning Point | Change of situation | Rabbit is the winner |

| Hunter dreams of roasted Rabbit | Hunter and Dog off for the Big Game | Dog sniffs the Rabbit | Gun shot | Boar brings dog | Hunter falls off the cliff | Hunter's nightmare | |

0916_Production Flow Charts

Before your animation project goes into production you have to think about the animation technique and the production procedure that leads to the final result.

Classical Pegbar Animation

This is the classical animated drawing technique with traditional tracing and painting onto paper or cels and recorded digitally into a computer or analogue on film stock.

Stop-Motion_Model Animation

Stop-motion animation requires the making of movable puppets and the construction of a three-dimensional set. This is a direct animation technique, and the recording can be done either with digital support or onto film stock.

2-D Computer Assisted Animation

This is the combination of the classical animated drawing technique assisted by computer program for scanning and colouring of characters and backgrounds. Recorded digitally, this technique has become the standard for all 2-D animation.

3-D Computer Animation

3-D computer animation, using virtual actors animated by key-frames or by motion capture is the new standard for TV serials. The animated characters can be combined with 2-D or 3-D backgrounds.

The choice of technique depends on the content and purpose of the film as well as on the equipment and budget you have - and last, but not least, on your own talent and desire. Pre- and Post-production have a lot in common for all techniques, the work flow of the Production, however, will be different for each technique. For every film production an individual flow chart should be established.

Flow Chart for
Classical Pegbar Animation
recorded to filmstock or digital disk/tape

Flow Chart for
Stop-Motion_Model Animation
recorded to filmstock or digital disk/tape

100	**Pre-Production**
101	Research, Development
102	Treatment, Script
103	Character and Props design
104	Background design
105	Script breakdown, Storyboard
106	Animatic
107	Portfolio, Planning, Budget
108	Sound research, Voice casting
109	Recording music, Voice dummy
110	Continuity checking
200	**Production**
201	Recording, Sound-Voice
202	Lip sync exposure sheet
203	Layout background
204	Layout-Posing, Character, Exposure sheet
205	Background tracing on paper
206	Animation keys, In-Betweens on paper
207	Pencil test, Check animation
208	Animation tracing onto cels
209	Animation ink and paint
210	Background paint
211	Recording to film or digital tape
212	Extras recording
213	Music composition
214	Music, Voice recording
215	Final quality check
300	**Post-Production**
301	Film laboratory, Processing, Prints
302	Edit picture
303	Test screening, Legal review
304	Negative cutting, Colour correction
305	Credits, Main and ends
306	Final sound recording, Score, Songs, Voices
307	Edit sound and picture
308	Sound tracks mixed
309	Film transfer to videotape, DVD
310	Lab makes final print
311	Print projected to audience

100	**Pre-Production**
101	Research_Development
102	Treatment_Script
103	Character and Props design
104	Set design
105	Script breakdown, Storyboard
106	Animatic
107	Portfolio, Planning, Budget
108	Sound research, Voice casting
109	Recording music, Voice dummy
110	Continuity checking
200	**Production**
201	Recording, Sound-Voice
202	Lip sync exposure sheet
203	Layout set
204	Puppets, Models construction
205	Set construction
206	Animation puppets on set
207	Line test, Check animation
208	Final model design
209	Set colour and lighting
210	Animation models on set
211	Recording to film or digital tape
212	Extras recording
213	Music composition
214	Music, Voice recording
215	Final quality check
300	**Post-Production**
301	Film laboratory, Processing, Prints
302	Edit picture
303	Test screening, Legal review
304	Negative cutting, Colour correction
305	Credits, Main and ends
306	Final sound recording, Score, Songs, Voices
307	Edit sound and picture
308	Sound tracks mixed
309	Film transfer to videotape, DVD
310	Lab makes final print
311	Print projected to audience

Flow Chart for
2-D Computer Assisted Animation
Digital recording

100	**Pre-Production**
101	Research, Development
102	Treatment, Script
103	Character and Props design
104	Background design
105	Script breakdown, Storyboard
106	Animatic
107	Portfolio, Planning, Budget
108	Sound research, Voice casting
109	Recording music, Voice dummy
110	Continuity checking

200	**Production**
201	Recording, Sound-Voice
202	Lip sync exposure sheet
203	Layout background
204	Layout-Posing, Character, Exposure sheet
205	Background tracing on paper
206	Animation keys, In-Betweens on paper
207	Pencil test, Check animation
208	Animation scan
209	Animation computer ink and iaint
210	Background scan, Computer paint
211	Compositing of animation-background
212	Rendering composite
213	Music composition
214	Music, Voice recording
215	Final quality check

300	**Post-Production**
301	Transfers to digital video
302	Edit picture
303	Test screening, Legal review
304	Colour correction
305	Credits, Main and ends
306	Final sound recording, Score, Songs, Voices
307	Edit sound and picture
308	Sound tracks mixed
309	Transfer digital to DVD
310	Transfer digital to film
311	Print projected to audience

Flow Chart for
3-D Computer Animation
Digital recording

100	**Pre-Production**
101	Research_Development
102	Treatment_Script
103	Character and Props design
104	Set design
105	Script breakdown, Storyboard
106	Animatic
107	Portfolio, Planning, Budget
108	Sound research, Voice casting
109	Recording music, Voice dummy
110	Continuity checking

200	**Production**
201	Recording, Sound-Voice
202	Lip sync exposure sheet
203	Layout set
204	3-D Characters and Props modelling
205	3-D Background, Environment modelling
206	Rigging of characters and props
207	Test animation, Check animation
208	Texture, Colours of characters, Props
209	Final model, Final location
210	Background, Environment texture and colour
211	Final animation, Lighting and effects
212	Rendering composite
213	Music composition
214	Music, Voice recording
215	Final quality check

300	**Post-Production**
301	Transfers to digital video
302	Edit picture
303	Test screening, Legal review
304	Negative cutting, Colour correction
305	Credits, Main and ends
306	Final sound recording, Score, Songs, Voices
307	Edit sound and picture
308	Sound tracks mixed
309	Transfer digital to DVD
310	Transfer digital to film
311	Print projected to audience

0917_Production Planning

A typical production planning requires lining up in chronological order the various tasks the production team has to accomplish from the idea to the finished film on screen. A planning can be as complicated or as simple as you like. It may take up a few lines or fill dozens of sheets and computer files. It may be handled by a single person or could occupy a whole bureaucracy.

The proposed planning is basic, with the potential to adapt it to any animation technique and procedure of a particular film project. It follows the principal steps of filmmaking.

As far as the production procedure is concerned, it follows the flow chart of computer assisted animation, which is nowadays the most common technical method. Each task has a number and can therefore easily be adapted to another animation technique. Production planning is just like the production procedures, which are divided into Pre-production, Production and Post-production.

100 Pre-Production

No.	Task	1	2	3	4	5	6	7	8
101	Research, Development	■							
102	Treatment, Script		■						
103	Character and Props Design		■	■					
104	Background Design			■					
105	Script, Breakdown, Storyboard			■	■				
106	Animatic					■			
107	Portfolio, Planning, Budget						■	■	
108	Sound-Research, Voice Casting					■			
109	Recording Music, Voice Dummi						■		
110	Continuity checking						■		

200 Production

No.	Task	9	10	11	12	13	14	15	16	17	18	19	20
201	Voice Recording	■											
202	Lip sync Exposure Sheet	■											
203	Layout Background	■	■										
204	Layout Posing, Character, Exposure Sheet	■	■										
205	Background tracing on paper			■	■								
206	Animation Keys, In-Berweens on paper			■	■	■							
207	Pencil Test, Check Animation				■	■	■						
208	Animation Scan						■	■	■				
209	Animation Computer Ink and Paint						■	■	■				
210	Background Scan, Computer Paint								■				
211	Compositing of Animation-Background									■			
212	Rendering Composite										■	■	
213	Music Composition										■		
214	Music Recording											■	
215	Final Quality Check												■

300 Post-Production

No.	Task	21	22	23	24	25	26
301	Transfer to Digital Video	■					
302	Edit Picture		■				
303	Test sreening, Legal review		■				
304	Colour correction			■			
305	Credits, Main and Ends		■				
306	Final Sound recording, Scores Voices			■			
307	Final edit Sound and Picture				■		
308	Sound tracs mixed				■		
309	Tranfer Digital to DVD					■	
310	Transfer Digital to Film					■	
311	Film projected to Audience					■	

0918_Budget_Financial Planning

The budget, just like the production planning lines up the various tasks to make the film. Since the budget deals with money this is not every artist's cup of tea. Though there are a lot of excellent animation films made with a budget next to zero, the financial aspect of film making is very important in commercial film-making. It is often the very reason to make the film. Whatever film project you undertake, it is good to know and face the cost of what you are doing.

100	Pre-Production	
101	Research, Development	1.0%
102	Treatment, Script	2.0%
103	Character Design, Props Design	3.0%
104	Background or Set Design	1.0%
105	Script Breakdown, Storyboard	4.0%
106	Animatic	1.0%
107	Print Material, Portfolio, Planning Budget	1.0%
108	Sound Research, Voice Casting	1.0%
109	Recording Music, Voice Dummy	1.0%
	Total Pre-Production	**15.0%**

200	Production	
201	Voice Recording	0.5%
202	Lip sync exposure sheet	0.5%
203	Layout Background	4.0%
204	Layout-Posing, Character, Exposure Sheet	7.0%
205	Background tracing on paper	1.0%
206	Animation Keys, In-Betweens on paper	9.0%
207	Pencil test, Check animation	0.5%
208	Animation Scan	0.5%
209	Animation Computer Ink and Paint	4.0%
210	Background Scan, Computer Paint	3.0%
211	Compositing of Animation-Background	2.0%
212	Rendering Composite	1.0%
213	Sound Design, Music Composition	1.0%
214	Music Recording	0.5%
215	Final Quality Check	0.5%
	Total Production	**35.0%**

300	Post-Production	
301	Transfers to Digital Video	0.5%
302	Edit picture, Compositing, Special effects	7.0%
303	Test screening, Legal review	0.5%
304	Colour correction	0.5%
305	Credits, Main and Ends	0.5%
306	Final Sound recording, Score, Voices	1.0%
307	Final edit Sound and Pictures	2.5%
308	Sound tracks mixed	1.0%
309	Transfer Digital to DVD	0.5%
310	Transfer Digital to Film	1.0%
	Total Post-Production	**15.0%**

400	**Equipment, Material, Rental**	
401	Discs, Audio-Video-Tapes, Filmstock	1.0%
402	Art Material, Cels, Paper	1.0%
403	Video Studio, Camera, Scanner, Projector, Computer	3.0%
404	Sound Studio	3.0%
	Total Equipment, Material, Rental	**8.0%**

500	**Miscellaneous**	
501	Travelling, Accommodations, Meals	1.0%
502	Shipping, Phone, Fax, Internet	0.5%
503	Author's Rights, Text, Image, Sound	2.0%
504	Insurance, Crew, Material, Equipment	1.0%
505	Archive, Administration	0.5%
	Total Miscellaneous	**5.0%**

600	**Administration**	
601	Travelling, Accommodations, Meals	0.5%
602	Shipping, Phone, Fax, Internet	0.5%
603	Administration, Bookkeeping	1.0%
	Total Administration	**2.0%**

700	**Distribution**	
701	Travelling, Accommodations, Meals	1.0%
702	Shipping, Phone, Fax, Internet	1.0%
703	Advertisements	3.0%
704	Market, Booth, Badges	1.0%
705	Print Media, Flyers	1.0%
706	Distributor	2.0%
707	Assistant	1.0%
	Total Distribution	**10.0%**

800	**Direction and Production**	
801	Direction	5.0%
802	Assistance of direction	2.0%
803	Production	2.0%
804	Assistance of production	1.0%
	Total Direction and Production	**10.0%**
	Grand Total	**100%**

Financial Planning

All production portfolios require financial planning, and if possible a plan for distribution and activation. Before you start the project, it is good to know if you have the money to make the film and where the money will come from. Sometimes the best film idea doesn't find its way to an audience because the money aspect was not taken into account. However, even the best financial planning remains a financial fiction until the film is finished, and sometimes even beyond that...

1000	**Financial Planning**	
1001	Broadcasters_TV Stations	15.0%
1002	Cinema Distribution_Box Office	05.0%
1003	Government_Cultural Foundations	30.0%
1004	Sponsors	25.0%
1005	Co-Producer	10.0%
1006	DVD Sales_Product Merchandising	10.0%
1007	Your own resources	05.0%
	Total Financial Planning	**100.0%**

For your drawings and scraps.

1000_Production_The Tricks of the Trade

In planned animation, a good production builds on a solid pre-production. Yet the heart of every film is production. Production means going right through every single frame of the film by drawing and colouring, by animating and recording frame by frame, and then compositing every single scene with background and foreground.

Production is the hardest part of any filmmaking. It is the part where you need the perseverance, the patience and the conviction of a long distance runner. If you like to exert your blood, sweat and tears, you will love this part. In every production the animator comes to the point where the end of the tunnel cannot be seen. It's in these moments when the *Tricks of the Trade* can help you to speed up production, to make it easier, and eventually see a glimmer of light in the dark.

A frequently asked question in animation workshops is that of how long it takes to become a professional animator. Usually an animator knows when he started, but learning is a continuous process, and learning never stops. This should not discourage anybody from going into animation. The important thing is to start – and then to learn to learn... and learn... and learn... and keep learning...

It isn't so much the final result that makes the difference between a beginner and a professional animator, but the way the result is achieved. A professional animator gets quicker to the result. This is partly due to having better equipment, but also to having gained greater experience. Applying the shortcuts that lead to a quicker result comes from animating under air date pressure: if your job is due to be broadcast next week, you better hurry up!

The Tricks of the Trade are a collection of useful hints. They are not meant to be exhaustive, since animation is a business that is ever moving and technology is fast changing. Even if the basic Tricks of the Trade are still the same, the evolution from analogue to digital recording has tremendously changed the production procedure. At the end of each chapter, working for Classical Pegbar Animation or for 3D Computer Animation will be discussed.

Working every day with animation will help you discover for yourself new ways and methods to come to better and faster results. Don't forget to share your experiences with those who are starting out in this business.

In most of the animated film productions a producer and a director are involved. This couple has very often a quite different point of view about how things are going to be done. The producer's first worry is to find the money, to handle it and if possible to put some of it in his pocket. The director's priorities are more often the artistic values. He wants to make a beautiful film and hopefully be recognized as a genius in animation. Of course both would like to make a good film, fast and not too expensively.
Here they are, lost in the infernal triangle of **Quality - Cost - Time.**

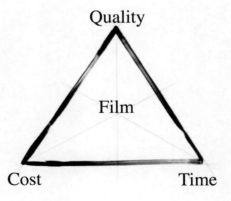

Short Time and **Good Quality**   are never **Low Cost**
Good Quality and **Low Cost**   are never **Short Time**
Low Cost and **Short Time**   are never **Good Quality**

Producer and director are bound to discuss one with each other and finally find a compromise to make the film.

1001_Layout_Posing

Layout and Posing are the steps on the way from the storyboard to animation. A solid storyboard and precise timing are the keys to successful Layout and Posing.

The model sheets of all the characters must be approved before starting the layouts. The backgrounds should be available as sketches. The layout artist will re-design, clean up, and scale the drawings in relationship to each other and bring them all to a workable size for animation. Each shot is carefully worked out considering framing and composition, camera field size, camera angles, points of view, light and shadow, perspective, foreground, overlays, match-line and props.

The layout artist has to communicate this information as clearly and dynamically as possible over to the animators and background artists. The layout artist knows the problems of the animators and he decides how a scene should be animated. The layout artist also plans the camera moves and establishes the length of holds in a shot.

Part of the layout work is also to indicate approximately the number of key drawings to be made by the animator. Use the spacing chart for these instructions. This information is then transferred to the exposure sheet.

Posing consists of indicating the most characteristic positions of the subject in time and space. Indicate first the field size and then the beginning and the end of action for each character. In more complicated scenes or for longer actions you need also to indicate intermediate positions. Each shot, scene and sequence has to be broken down into action parts that will be handled by the animator.

Example of Background
for Sequence No. 03
of the ***The Big Game*** story.

**Working for
Classical Pegbar Animation**
Layout-Posing procedure is the classical and indispensable approach for pegbar drawing animation.

**Working for
3-D Computer Animation**
A precise storyboard with indication of field size and timing for each scene doesn't need the Layout-Posing procedure,

Example of the Layout-Posing
for Sequence No. 03
of the *The Big Game* story.

Act_02_03

Act_02_07

01 The hunter and dog enter the frame

05 The hunter takes his gun and aims. The dog is highly excited.

02

06 The hunter fires.

03

07

04 They hear a strange noise and stop.

08 The dog runs off-screen.

1002_Animating_Extremes_In-Betweens

This is the heart of the whole trade. To create animations with life and personality, an animator needs skill and experience. He has to have a feeling for movements combined with an instinct for dramatic effects.

Good animation is not a straight-forward adding of one drawing to another. Timing and dynamic movements will make the drawings flow in action and create the illusion of life. In planned animation, the most expressive characteristics of an action and its extreme points are sketched first. They are sketched according to the positions indicated in the layout and exposure sheet. These drawings are called Extremes or Keys.

The In-betweens are the drawings sketched in between the Extremes and provide the flow of movement from one Extreme to another. The number of drawings needed to bridge the gap in between two Extremes depends on the speed of the movement and the distance and rate of exposure. This whole procedure is called making the Extremes and In-betweens.

The instructions of how many in-betweens and their positions are indicated on the **spacing chart**. The numbers at the beginning and the end of the chart are the extremes, while the strokes on the chart show the position and number of In-between drawings. A stroke closer to one extreme is to slow down one end of the action.

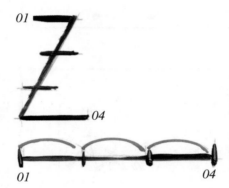 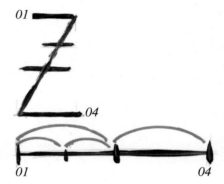

Spacing chart

Every drawing and background must be numbered according to its place in the planned animation. For multiple drawing levels, indicate the exact position of each drawing in relation to one another. Backgrounds are labeled according to the order in which they will be used. The numbered drawings and backgrounds are indicated on the exposure sheet. Numbers on key drawings are usually surrounded by a circle. The usual place to write the numbers on the animation paper is between the peg-holes.

In the example of **The Big Game**, the scene **Act_02_07** layout needs three key drawings for the hunter to get in the shooting position and seven in-betweens to fill in the space between the keys. The feet and legs will not move during this move so they can be separated from the body. The complete drawing of the hunter will therefore be on two levels. A third level is used for the dog. These levels correspond to the columns **A, B**, and **C** on the exposure sheet.

In pegbar animation, the parts involved in an action **A_01** to **A_07** and **B_01** to **B_05** are drawn on separate cels and separate levels. The remaining parts of the subject **C_01** and **Bckg 01** are "held drawings" on their own cels and level. While recording, only the repeat movements are changed and added to the "held" cel. On the screen, the animation looks like it's been redrawn for each phase.

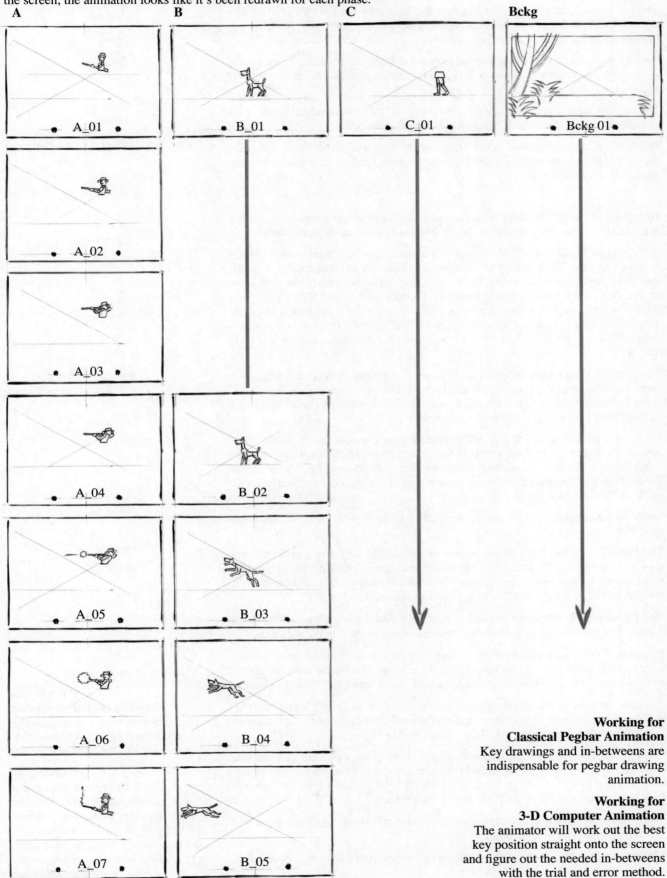

A

B

C

Bckg

A_01   B_01   C_01   Bckg 01

A_02

A_03

A_04   B_02

A_05   B_03

A_06   B_04

A_07   B_05

**Working for
Classical Pegbar Animation**
Key drawings and in-betweens are indispensable for pegbar drawing animation.

**Working for
3-D Computer Animation**
The animator will work out the best key position straight onto the screen and figure out the needed in-betweens with the trial and error method.

1003_Exposure Sheet

In the animated drawing technique, every drawing will be numbered according to its place in the planned animation. For multi-levels you must indicate the exact position of each drawing and its position on the levels. The drawings are numbered **A1 - B1 - C1 - D1** and so on, according to their proximity to the background. Backgrounds are labeled according to the order in which they will be used.

An Exposure Sheet or X-Sheet is made in order to indicate how many frames have to be exposed on each drawing or to communicate a precise edit in a computer application.

The vertical lines divide the page into columns and show the chronological order and position in time in which the drawings follow each other.

The horizontal lines represent each frame of the film and show which drawings will be combined and shot or edited at the same time. Each sheet holds 50 frames, representing two seconds.

To begin with, the **Title** of the film, as well as the name of the animator, are filled in at the top of the sheet as well as the **Sequence, Scene,** and **Sheet number.**

In the **Sound Track** column, **Action** and **Dialogue** is indicated according to their positions in time. If the action is animated to a prerecorded dialogue or piece of music, accents are written on the Exposure Sheet before you make the drawings. In this case, the Exposure Sheet becomes a kind of a vertical Bar Sheet. *(see: 1016_Dialogue_Lip Synchronised Animation)*. The dialogue is spelled out phonetically. Sound effects are also indicated in this column. In case you prefer a clear vision of time, there is a counter to indicate the minutes, seconds and picts (pictures).

The **Frames** column contains the continuous numbering of recorded frames in time. Numbering of the Exposure Sheet is cumulative for each scene. Every new scene begins at **0**. Numbers on the Exposure Sheet and numbers on the recording device frame counter must always correspond.

The columns labeled **A - B - C - D** represent four possible levels from top to bottom. **A** is on the top level and **D** is the closest to the background. In order to simplify the recording, the animator tries to work with as few levels as possible. Levels that are temporarily not in use are filled in with a clear cel and marked with an **X** on the Exposure Sheet.

In the **Bckg** (backgrounds) column the numbered backgrounds are chronologically listed.

The **Field/Truck** and **Pan** column is used to indicate the field size and the camera moves. It shows the beginning and the end of the camera truck and/or pan movement as well as how many frames it runs and the direction of it. A fieldsize three is labeled as **Fld 3.** A pan from North to South is indicated as **N - S.**

The **Recording Instruction** column is used to indicate the various functions of camera and lights, such as lens aperture, speed of exposure, filters, and so on.

In classical cel animation, an element may stay on a level without moving for a long time. Instead of using another level, the element can be cut out and pasted to the background. Cut-out pieces are indicated as **C.O.** on the Exposure Sheet.

A **Cross Dissolve** is the outgoing scene fading out as the incoming scene fades in. A Cross Dissolve over 10 frames is indicated over the numbers of frames required and shows its beginning and end. It is written as **XD 10.**

The gradual transition from black into a scene, or the gradual darkening of a scene to black, is called **Fade-In** or **Fade-Out.** The Exposure Sheet shows the beginning and end as well as the number of frames. It is written as **FI-10** for **Fade-In** over ten frames and **FO-6** for **Fade-Out** over 6 frames.

When no change is made in a given column, a vertical stroke or a continuous line is run down the page until a change is made.

The drawing number is indicated at the top and bottom of each page, even when no change is made in a given column.

**Working for
Classical Pegbar Animation**
The Exposure sheet is indispensable as a communication tool between the animator and the camera operator.

**Working for
3-D Computer Animation**
No precise Exposure sheet is needed for these procedures. An improvised X-Sheet can be used to communicate the number of frames for each scene and the kind of background and foreground used.

Exposure sheet

| | Title **Big Game** | | | | | Sq no **05** Sc no **07** | | | Sheet no **01** |

Sound Track Action Dialogue	Counter Min Sec Pict	Frames	A	B	C	D	Bckg	Truck Field	Pan	Recording Instructions
Hunter	: 01	1	A 01	B 01	C 01	X	BG 01	Fld 03	N	**Rec on film**
	: 02	2					C.O.			
Closer Look	: 03	3								**F-Stop 5.6 - 8**
	: 04	4								
Dog expecting	: 05	5								
	: 06	6						100 mm		
	: 07	7								
	: 08	8								
	: 09	9								
	: 10	1 0								
	: 11	1								**Rec Digital**
	: 12	2								
	: 13	3								**Pic Size**
	: 14	4								**720 x 576**
	: 15	5						Fld 08	S	
	: 16	6								
Ready to fire	: 17	7	A 02							**XD 10**
	: 18	8								
	: 19	9	A 03							
	: 20	2 0								
	: 21	1								
	: 22	2								
	: 23	3								
	: 24	4								
Background change	: 25	5								
	: 01	6								
	: 02	7					BG 02			
	: 03	8								
	: 04	9								
	: 05	3 0								
	: 06	1								
	: 07	2								
	: 08	3								
	: 09	4								
	: 10	5								
	: 11	6								
	: 12	7								
	: 13	8								
Fire	: 14	9	A 04							
	: 15	4 0	A 05							
Dog take off	: 16	1	A 06	B 02						
	: 17	2	A 07							
	: 18	3		B 03						
	: 19	4								
	: 20	5		B 04						
	: 21	6								
	: 22	7		B 05						
	: 23	8								
	: 24	9	A 07	X	C 01	X	BG 02			
	: 25	5 0								

Simplified Exposure Sheet

In professional animation, the exposure sheet is always established before or while the drawings are being made. However, in a short workshop you will not always have the time to explain how to properly fill in an Exposure Sheet. The participants usually make the drawings without knowing anything about an Exposure Sheet. In these situations, you may use the simplified exposure sheet. Before shooting, look through all the drawings and try to make full use of repeat movements (cycles) and holds. In standard movements, two frames are taken of each drawing.

Start by indicating the **Title** of the film or the **Name** of the participants.
Specify also the **Scene number** and the **Sheet number** if there are several of them.

In the **Drawing number** column, indicate the numbers which are on each of the individual drawings.

Next, indicate the **Numbers of drawings** and the **Rate of exposure**. If there are any repeat movements, indicate these in the **Cycles RO-RZ** column. In the column labeled **Number of cycles**, fill in how many times the cycle will be repeated. This gives a **Number of frames** for each horizontal line that will be accumulated in the **Total of frames** column.

The **Recording Instruction** column is used to indicate the various functions of the camera and lights, such as camera moves, lens aperture, speed of exposure, filters, and so on.

The Simplified Exposure sheet is filled in with the collaboration of each participant. Try to make the best use of cycle movements. Each participant should line up a total average of 250 to 500 frames.

Simplified Exposure sheet			Title **Short Cut**				Scene no **05**	Sheet no **01**
Drawing no	Numbers of drawings	Rate of exposure	Cycles RO - RZ	Numbers of cycles	Numbers of frames	Total of frames	Recording Instructions
01	01	02	-	-	100	100	**Recording on Film**
02 - 10	09	02	-	-	18	118	F-Stop 5.6 - 8 Speed 1/10 sec
11 - 16	06	02	RO	6 x	36	154	Field Size 3-8 Incident Light
17 - 30	14	01	-	-	14	168	
31	01	02	-	-	50	218	**Recording on Computer**
32 - 40	09	02	RZ	10 x	90	308	Picture Size 720 x 576
41 - 44	04	02	-	-	08	316	25 images / sec
45	01	02	-	-	20	336	
46 - 49	04	02	RO	12 x	48	384	
50	01	02	-	-	100	408	

Animaginination Robi Engler

Exposure sheet	Title					Sq no Sc no			Sheet no
Sound Track Action Counter Dialogue Min Sec Pict	Frames	A	B	C	D	Bckg	Truck Field	Pan	Recording Instructions
: 01 : 02	1 2								
: 03 : 04	3 4								
: 05 : 06	5 6								
: 07 : 08	7 8								
: 09 : 10	9 0								
: 11 : 12	1 2								
: 13 : 14	3 4								
: 15 : 16	5 6								
: 17 : 18	7 8								
: 19 : 20	9 0								
: 21 : 22	1 2								
: 23 : 24	3 4								
: 25 : 01	5 6								
: 02 : 03	7 8								
: 04 : 05	9 0								
: 06 : 07	1 2								
: 08 : 09	3 4								
: 10 : 11	5 6								
: 12 : 13	7 8								
: 14 : 15	9 0								
: 16 : 17	1 2								
: 18 : 19	3 4								
: 20 : 21	5 6								
: 22 : 23	7 8								
: 24 : 25	9 0								

Animagination Robi Engler

Simplified Exposure sheet	Title				Scene no		Sheet no
Drawing no	Numbers of drawings	Rate of exposure	Cycles RO - RZ	Numbers of cycles	Numbers of frames	Total of frames	Recording Instructions

Animagination Robi Engler

1004_Pencil Test

The usual procedure in animation is to draw in rough sketches the Extremes and the In-betweens. The rough drawings, which are still on paper, are numbered and indicated on the exposure sheet. Once the whole sequence of animation has been drawn, the next step is to look at it as a flow of movement. Before the cleaning, inking and painting procedure, these drawings are recorded on film stock or digitally with a computer program as a **Pencil Test.**

The Pencil Test is usually recorded with bottom light so that the background can be seen through the drawing paper. With digital equipment it is easy to make a pencil test. The rough pencil drawings are captured by a camera or a scanner into computer program. The drawings are recorded with the precise timing as indicated on the exposure sheet, and played back instantly in real time.

The Pencil Test is the moment of truth. The main purpose of the Pencil Test is to check the flow of action. If there are any errors, this is the best moment to change the drawings and improve them. If the test shows that the action is too slow, too fast, or out of the model sheet, then it is necessary to remake the animation and to record another pencil test.

Should the pencil test come out to full satisfaction, the drawings are ready for cleaning, tracing, and colouring.

**Working for
Classical Pegbar Animation**
Pencil Tests is indispensable for pegbar drawing animation.

**Working for
3D Computer Animation**
Pencil Tests in 3D Animation are a must and sometimes called Playblasts.

1005_Tracing_Painting

In traditional cel animation, tracing or inking means that the cleaned drawings (Cleans) are drawn onto a clear sheet of cel with pen and ink. In the photocopy procedure, the cleaned drawings on paper are transferred to cels without losing the artistic quality of the original.

The usual thickness for an Animation Cel is around 0.07mm to 0.10 mm. The size of the cel depends on the work you do. For a standard 12-field, the cels measure 270 mm by 330 mm. Cels usually come with a thin onion skin paper in between them. This paper is not removed for punching or for drawing. Handle the cel only by the edges and keep dust and grease off. Greasy spots can be removed with a few drops of rectified benzine (Lighter fuel).

Tracing is done on the front side of the cel. Since cels are fragile, *lightweight Cotton Gloves* are worn for inking and painting. The thumb and first two fingers of the glove are cut off so there is a feeling for the pen or brush. Marking pens with ink that adheres to the smooth cel surface can also be used for inking.

Painting or opaquing is done on the reverse side of the cel so the ink line will not be disturbed. The areas to paint are indicated by the inked outlines. The paint should have the consistency of a soft cream, and is applied heavily so that it spreads over the area smoothly up to the inked line. The painted part will look opaque and flat on the right side. A too thick layer of paint will leave streaks and brush marks on the front side of the cel, while a too thin layer of paint will flow over and leave transparent dots on the painted area.

Painting on cels can also be done by using grease pencils. The advantages of these pencils is that they adhere to both paper and cel, and there is no need to wait for the ink to dry. The surface, however, will not be entirely opaque or flat, but may vary from drawing to drawing, resulting in a vibrating surface when projected on the screen.

Permanent felt pens can be used to colour the cels, but they remain entirely transparent. If you don't want this transparent effect, the back of the coloured area has to be covered with white paint.

The kind of procedure, traditional or computer assisted, as well as the numbers of colours, inks, paints, pencils, or pens you will use for your animation work, is a matter of personal taste. However, it will influence the speed of production and certainly the production cost. It must be taken into consideration when planning the job.

In 2D-computer assisted production, the tracing is done by scanning the cleans into a drawing program. This technique requires a strong, consistent pencil line whose tone is as black as possible. Furthermore, all lines that delimit a surface must be closed in order to prevent the ink electronically applied from flowing all over the working area.
If your drawing style requires lines that will not be connected one to each other you may use a different layer for the painting in the computer program. The line and colour layers are merged when the painting is done.

Inking and painting with computer has become the worldwide standard in animation. The advantages, besides the lower cost, are many: no cels, no dust, no greasy spots, easy change of colours over a whole sequence, and easy colour shading and shadows.

The condition for this procedure is, however, to continue the computer assisted production line including composition and editing.

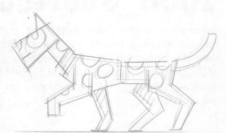

Sketch

Tracing

Painting on reverse side

Final result

Lightweight Cotton Gloves

**Working for
Classical Pegbar Animation**
The Tracing-Painting procedure is the classical and indispensable approach for classical cel animation.

**Working for
3-D Computer Animation**
Tracing-Painting in 3-D animation is the skinning, texturing and rendering procedure.

1006_Shortcuts in Animation

Economy in animation can apply to time, effort and materials. You can make all the economies you want as long as they don't show on the screen. In order to avoid the nasty cheap effects, the economies must be planned on the storyboard. Most of the proposed shortcuts can be applied to both traditional and computer-assisted animation. Most of them are even easier to make in computer program than with ink and paint on cels.

Simple Outline Figures
Use the same Model Sheet figure for a variety of characters by simply dressing them up differently.

Colours
Use colours for identification (e.g. blue for water, green for grass). Avoid fancy, time-consuming coloured surfaces. Use grease pencils on cels or soft coloured pencils for backgrounds, instead of ink and paint. In your computer program, create a personal palette for fast and easy colouring.

Repeat Movements, Cycling
Spot all the repeat movements and use them in a cycling technique, without over-using it.

01   02   03   02   01

Holds
A hold is a stationary position. For example, if the character sawing a log pauses in position 3 for a second before taking up his work again, you don't need to make 12 drawings to cover the 24 frames of that second. You can record the number of frames required on one single drawing.

Wobbling Holds
In a freestyle drawing, the lines and the colours are not steady, they move all the time. The effect is a kind of permanent wobbling. In order that a hold doesn't look like a freeze frame, you will make two or three copies of the hold picture and record them alternatively. This creates the same wobble to the hold as to the moving parts.

Background, Foreground
Elements that form a backdrop or a foreground, and don't move, can be drawn on a separate cel or computer program level.

Non-moving Parts, Held Cel
Parts of your characters which aren't moving for a while can be drawn onto a separate cel or computer program level. This is called a *Held Cel*. You can hold a certain position on one level and animate the rest of the character on the other level. You can also animate the two levels at different speeds. Keep in mind, however, that your character must look alive. A mouth that opens and shuts with a pair of rolling eyeballs is a poor bit of animation if that's all that moves.

Match-line, Mask
The match-line is used in multi-level animation to fit the moving parts on one level to the non-moving parts on the other. The match-line is usually drawn in red on the layout and will, of course, be invisible on the finished drawing.
To match the arm to the character, the match-line will show the body's limit.
A match-line is also used when a character goes behind a part of the background. A character going through a door, which is on the background can't really go behind the door frame. The body is cut off by the match-line or a mask as it enters the door, which gives the illusion of it going through.

Matchline

Panning-background
An on-the-spot walking figure, along with a panning-background, can walk for kilometres. Used with an identical take-over background, it can go along for ages!

Panning-cels
If the character has to go all the way across the screen, the repeat movements of the walk can be drawn onto the panning cel.

Multiple Shots
Use the same artwork with different field sizes, zooms or pans for variety on an otherwise simple artwork.

Reframing
The same cels or cut-out figures can be used over another background. Usually another field size is used as well. Don't forget to match figures and background sizes so they can be used for reframing in different scenes.

Reframing

Faking

This trick should not be overused, but once in a while the main action can be placed off-screen. On-screen secondary effects, like a shaking scene or dust clouds, suggest there's been an explosion. When a bomb's been lit the audience knows that an explosion is going to take place, so there's no need to animate one. Let the bomb explode off screen and the soundtrack can take care of the effects. Shake the scene on screen on a north-southeast-west compound move, violent at first, then slowing down gradually as the explosion on the sound track subsides.

Action and Background on Soundtrack

The soundtrack can, to a certain extent, replace an elaborate background by using the sounds of wind, water and birds' twitters, along with representative colours and a simple horizon line. A spring atmosphere can thus be created without drawing lots of flower blossoms and flying birds.

A 150-person symphony orchestra can be hidden in the orchestra pit, showing only the back of the conductor and a few instruments, without losing impact on the audience.

Flip-over Drawings or Cut-outs

This real work-saver is easy to apply. If you have a character moving from left to right, you can turn the drawings on cels or the cut-out figures and use them in another scene. Even though it's the same action, when flipped over with a change of field size or background it will look really different. This method is even easier to apply in computer assisted animation. Flipping individual drawings or a series of images horizontally or vertically can be done in any drawing or painting program.

Flip-over Drawings

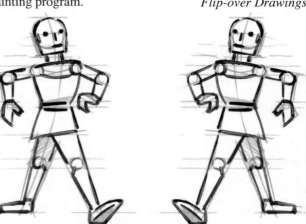

Camera and Compound Moves

Trucking-in and -out, Fades, Dissolves, Pans, Wipes, Spins, and Flips cannot, of course, replace the animation work, but they can be useful for introducing or leaving a scene, drawing attention to some detail, or creating an atmosphere. In order to avoid a strobe effect, all camera and compound moves should be made in *Ones,* even when the character is animated in *Twos.*

Photocopy

Photocopy machines have long been used in animation to help save tracing time. Although this type of work requires a special kind of machine to print on cel, even an ordinary photocopy machine can be used for interesting effects. A photo or drawing can be reproduced the number of times required. These copies can be coloured or cut out. By making copies of the copies, the details slowly disappear and the photocopies become a sort of animated artwork.

The photocopy machine can be used to reduce or enlarge and to make any number of reductions or enlargements gradually. The copies can also be coloured and cut out for use in perspective moves.

In computer-assisted animation, all the copying, resizing and framing can be done in the drawing and paint program.

**Working for
Classical Pegbar Animation**
These shortcuts are standards in animated drawing procedures.

**Working for
3-D Computer Animation**
All of these shortcuts can be used in 3-D animation, but there is a vast range of choices of other economies in all computer programs.

1007_Cycling

Cycling is a technique to save time and work, especially in pegbar animation recorded by a camera. In computer-assisted animation, cycling consists of the repetition of a series of drawings.

In fact, a lot of live movements are cyclical repetitive movements. Take, for example, walking, the flow of water or smoke, twinkling stars, turning wheels, pendulums, waving flags and nearly all mechanical movements. For all these movements, you need to draw one complete cycle of movement and then use the drawings over and over again.

There are two different kinds of repeat movements: **RO** and **RZ**.

RO-Cycle 1 2 3 4 5 6 (7 = 1)
The RO cycling method is when the movement is straight-forward and continuous. That is, when the action comes to an end, it starts all over again right from the beginning, e.g. a wheel turning or the legs of a person walking. It is important that the last drawing of the cycle leads to the first drawing of the cycle.

01   02   03   04   05   06
                                                        (07 = 01)

RZ-Shuttle 1 2 3 4 (5 = 3)
The RZ cycling is when the repetition is a to-and-fro movement. The cycle is merely a change of direction leading back to the original position. The drawings are used from the beginning to the end and back to the beginning, e.g. a ringing bell or the saw of a woodcutter.

01   02   03   04
                                    (05 = 03)

In order to achieve a directional flowing movement, the minimum number of drawings for a cyclical movement is **three**. The use of only **two** drawings would give the impression of a to-and-fro blinking movement.

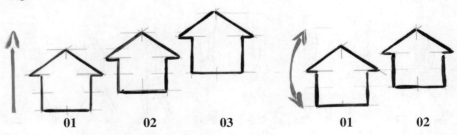

01   02   03   01   02

Some of the cyclical movements can be used with a moving background. This applies to actions in one direction, like a walking figure or a rolling car. The drawings are animated *on the spot*, which means the body remains in a stationary position and the background is moved to create the illusion that the animated subject is crossing it. The background pans in the opposite direction to the subject, to give the impression it's moving forward.

Walking Cycles

To animate a basic walk, you first draw the Key positions. The In-between draw-ings depend a lot on what kind of walk you want to animate. A cartoon-looking walk may use a 3-phase step and a realistic walk cycle uses 12 or more phases. Decide how many phases you want to use in one step, then take a walk yourself and analyse it for these positions.

You can make a limited walking cycle with 3 to 4 drawings.

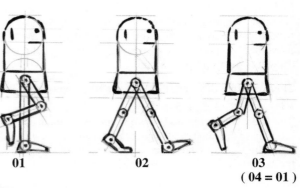

01   02   03
(04 = 01)

A semi-limited animated walking cycle, without nearside or offside leg, uses 5 to 7 drawings.

01   02   03   04   05
(06 = 01)

A walking cycle using 7 to 10 drawings is good enough for a fast walking cartoon character

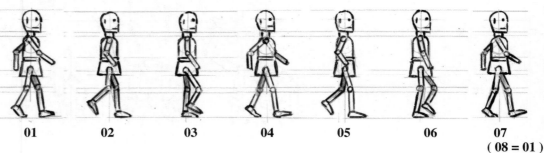

01   02   03   04   05   06   07
(08 = 01)

A fully animated walking cycle, considering left and right leg, uses 12 or more drawings.

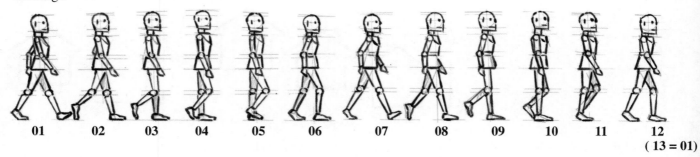

01   02   03   04   05   06   07   08   09   10   11   12
(13 = 01)

In nature, not everybody walks in the same way. There are probably as many ways of walking as people on this planet. An old person will walk slowly, a business man will hurry, a little girl will jump. Slip into the skin of your character and find the most suitable walking style for it.

Natural Phenomena Repeat Movements

Even in a live-action film, all natural phenomena are produced artificially. Neither the producer nor the actors want to wait for rainfall or the stars to glitter in the sky. While in live action films such special effects can be quite expensive, in animation this is mostly a matter of making the right drawings.

Since most natural phenomena are repeated movements, the cyclical principle can be applied to them. Don't forget that half of the phenomenon's impact is on the soundtrack!

Rain

A repeat cycle of 3 to 6 drawings is used to obtain a rain effect. In traditional animation, rain is drawn by making fine lines of white opaque ink. The lines must be parallel but not necessarily regular in distance and size. The splash of rain drops hitting the ground can be put on the same drawing. For recording by film, the lines can be drawn either on cels and used as an overlay, or on black cardboard and superimposed on a recorded scene. The superimposed technique applies especially for stop-motion animation. For computer assisted animation, the effect can be put on a separate computer program level.

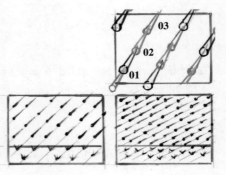

Snow

For the snow effect, apply the same principle as for rain. A three-phase RO-cycle will do it in most cases. The difference from the rain cycle is that each snow flake must be followed by another one to give the impression of a continuous, smooth movement. The snowflakes can be superimposed or recorded directly with the background on an out-of-focus level, which gives a soft appearance to the snowfall.

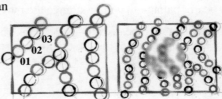

Water Drops

Ask somebody to draw a drop of water, and he will automatically make a *drop* shape. Yet in reality, a drop's form is very different. High-speed films show us how a drop *behaves* when it comes out of the tap or when the drop is hitting a surface of water. The tail of the drop doesn't really exist; but we have to draw this tail to indicate the speed, the direction, the weight and the force of the drop.

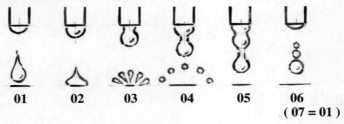

01   02   03   04   05   06
(07 = 01)

Smoke

Just like fire, smoke also comes from somewhere (cigarettes or chimneys) and goes somewhere (usually up in the air). The directional RO-repeat cycle is therefore applied. Smoke is most often translucent and the farther away it is from the source, the bigger and more diluted it becomes before it dissolves.

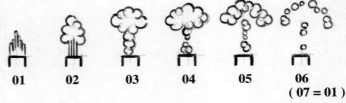

01   02   03   04   05   06
(07 = 01)

Water and Waves

For the water effect of lakes or rivers you only need to animate the highlights of the movement. A repeated RO-cycle of three drawings is enough to animate waves or moving water. A few lines of white ink or a lighter shade of the water's colour is used to indicate the movement. For moonlight or sunset on water, use the colour of the reflecting light.

The same principle is applied to indicate radio waves or any other one-directional movement.

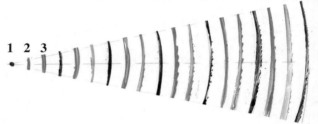

Fire and Flames

Depending on the desired effect, a candle light or a house burning, three or more drawings can be used. In cut-out animation a few flame-shaped pieces of cardboard, painted in yellow-orange are moved in a directional but accidental order.

For flames a repeated RO-cycle, 1 to 3, is used to give direction to the movement. Flames break up at the top before they start again at the bottom.

For directional waves, like smoke, the repeat movement of RO-cycle is used 1 to 3 - 1 to 3 - 1 to 3...

Waving Flags

The movement of flags or other loosely attached appendages is a wave-like movement. It's also a one-directional movement and can be expressed in an RO-cycle with 6 or more drawings.

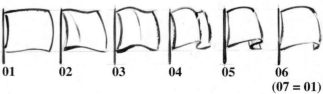

Stars and Glitters

For glittering stars or sparkling lights on shiny objects, the RO-cycle principle is used. About eight drawings with increasing and decreasing star shapes are recorded in a cycle, 1 to 8, and repeated.

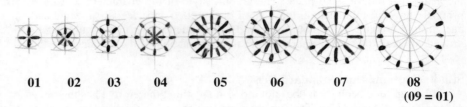

01   02   03   04   05   06   07   08
(09 = 01)

A three-phase RZ-cycle for the sparkle effect can be used to create a to-and-fro movement from 1 to 3, and repeated.

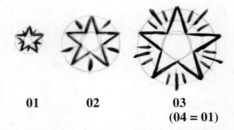

01   02   03
(04 = 01)

Random Movements

To make random movements like a restless crowd, crackling fire, or twinkling stars not to look like repeat movements, the action must be divided into parts and each part drawn on a separate sheet of paper or cel. Unlike repeat cycles, these phases are recorded in random order.

Working for
Classical Pegbar Animation
These cycling procedures are standards in classical pegbar animation.

Working for
3-D Computer Animation
There is a vast range of choices of effects in all computer programs.

1008_Background

The purpose of a background is to establish the context, to tell the audience where the action is going to take place. The graphic style of the characters will most probably have an influence on the type of background and vice versa. Style and background colours will create the mood of the scene. Use just enough background to create that atmosphere and let the imagination of the audience do the rest.

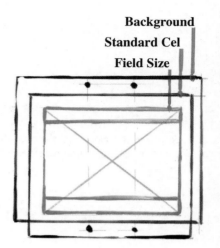

Background
Standard Cel
Field Size

Still Backgrounds and Standard Cels
A still background is one that does not move at any time; therefore it has the same proportion as a standard cel. The subject is moving around within the background.

Panning Background and Standard Cel
A panning background is used to create the illusion that the animated subject is traveling from one place to another. In reality, the background is moved by the traveling pegbar, while the subject is animated in a stationary position. This means that the body of your figure must stay in the same place and only the legs and arms are moving. In other words, your character is animated *on the spot*. The speed of the background depends on how fast or slow the subject is moving. Each move should be the length of the character's pace, or, if the character is animated in *Twos*, then each move should be half the length of the whole pace. Panning backgrounds are always recorded in *Ones*.

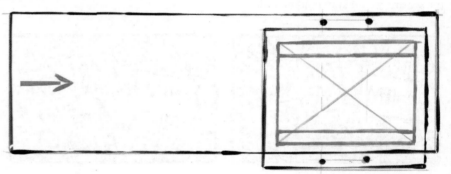

Still Backgrounds and Panning Cels
The static background is attached to the fixed pegbar and remains there throughout the action. The traveling pegbar holding the animated subject begins on one extreme off-screen position and is moved across the background to the extreme opposite position. In traditional animation, the moving cel must have the east-west dimension of three standard cels to avoid showing a cel edge.

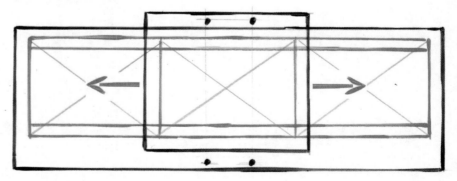

Circular Panning Background
For an endless pan, the background turns around a central point while the cel remains stationary.

Identical Take-over or Hook-up Background

A panning background can be as long as you like, but for practical reasons, it's never much longer than about one metre. If you want to make your figure walk *for hours* through the same background, you can make a **Repeat** or **Hook-up** background. This means that the end of the background is identical to its beginning, so when you come to the end of the pan you replace it with the beginning. Several backgrounds can be linked by making the end of one identical to the beginning of the next.

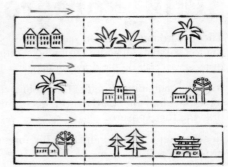

Background Deformation

When making panning backgrounds, speed and direction of the pan must be considered. Avoid straight lines which are at right angles to the direction of the move. A vertical palm tree moving on a horizontal pan is almost certain to jitter; with increased speed the palm tree must bend in the opposite direction of the pan for smooth-looking animation.

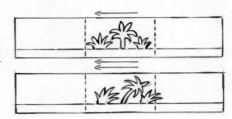

High-Speed Panning Background

A background which moves faster than about 2 cm per frame becomes a speed pan. In hold positions, vertical objects are drawn upright. By speeding up, the objects are elongated in the opposite direction of the pan, and they will blur at the edges.

A high-speed pan which is moved up 5 cm per exposure becomes a zip pan. The camera moves so quickly that the details in between the two holds are reduced to a horizontal blur. This kind of pan is used as a transition to the succeeding shot without a cut.

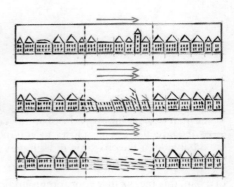

Invisible background

No doubt, this is the fastest background to make! With suitable sound effects, any kind of background can be suggested. The sound of footsteps will indicate whether the ground is soft or hard, made of stone, grass, water or sand; the sound of birds, cowbells or traffic will tell that the action takes place in the countryside or downtown.

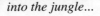

through heavy traffic...   *into the jungle...*   *to the cosy home...*

**Working for
Classical Pegbar Animation**
These procedures are standards in
classical pegbar animation.

**Working for
3-D Computer Animation**
Most of these procedures can be used
in 3-D animation.

1009_Foreground

The foreground, just as the background, is used to identify where the action is going to take place. The foreground can either be used in addition to a background, or as an overlay on the drawing paper.

In traditional animation, the foreground can be drawn on a cel and attached to the top of the drawing board. During recording the foreground must be laid over each drawing for exposure.

In computer assisted animation, the foreground is placed on a separate computer program level.

Another possibility is to cut the foreground out of stiff paper and attach it to the bottom of the drawing board. A hole must be cut in the background where the pegs are, to allow it to lie flat. This foreground must also be put over each drawing during the shooting.

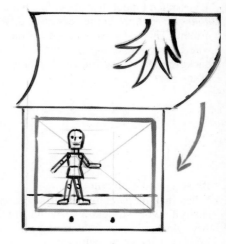

If the foreground is panning, remember that objects closer to the camera move faster than objects far away. Look at the cars rushing by while you are waiting to cross the street. The ones closer to you move faster and are bigger than those on the other side of the crossing, though they are all really moving at the same speed and have roughly the same size.

In a pan, this means that your foreground has to move faster than the background. A good rule of thumb is to move the foreground twice the speed of the background. The length of the foreground must therefore be twice the length of the background.

Foreground Cel

Background Cel

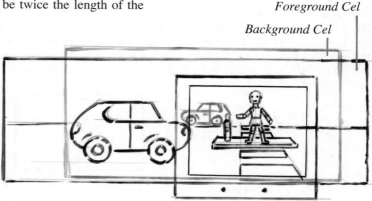

**Working for
Classical Pegbar Animation**
These procedures are standards in
classical pegbar animation

**Working for
3-D Computer Animation**
Most of these procedures can be used
in 3-D animation

1010_Multiplane

The Multiplane animation stand offers many possibilities for good effects, especially for creating the feeling of space and depth. Its most effective use is in long in or out trucks.

For traditional animation, a simple-to-make Multiplane animation stand looks somewhat like a big transparent bookshelf. The frame can easily be made out of angle iron and the levels are pieces of glass. The whole set is placed on top of the animation table. The dimensions of the multiplane depend on the size of your camera framing.

The use of levels gives a very realistic impression of 3-Dimensions. By trucking in through the levels, the objects will spread away as the camera passes over foreground to middleground and to the background.

The level on which the action takes place is called the **Focus Level;** this is usually the middleground. Focus is always on focus level. Levels should be about 20 cm apart to allow your hands room to animate objects and cut-outs or to change cels.

Lights can be attached to the multiplane itself in order to light each level. Another possibility is to fix lights to the animation stand just above the foreground. This set-up is especially useful if the multiplane is panning. The lights will remain evenly over the shooting area and the shadows of the passing objects will give a natural look to the pan.

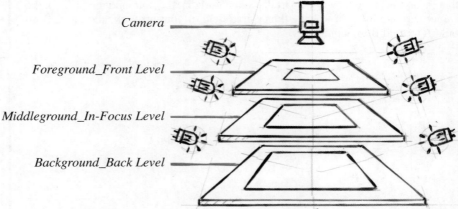

Camera

Foreground_Front Level

Middleground_In-Focus Level

Background_Back Level

If your multiplane is going to pan, the dimensions must be the length of one whole pan. For north-south moves it is advisable to turn the camera around 90°.

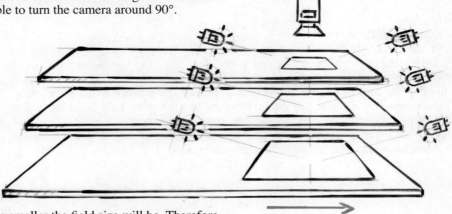

The nearer the level is to the camera, the smaller the field size will be. Therefore, objects on the foreground level seem to be bigger and move faster than the same objects on the background level. This creates the illusion of a natural-looking pan.

Objects on the fore- and middleground must be coated or painted black on the reverse side; otherwise they'll be reflected on the glass levels below. In fact, all camera and animation stand parts, as well as the ceiling, must be painted a mat black, since the glass will reflect all shiny parts like a mirror.

In planning a multiplane scene, the different levels are drawn on a sheet of paper indicating different field sizes for each level. Bigger field sizes can be used, and longer trucks can be made, if the multiplane set is used for cut-outs, since no cel size will limit the field size.

Working for Classical Pegbar Animation
These procedures are standards in classical pegbar animation.

Working for 3-D Computer Animation
These procedures can be used in 3-D animation
There is a vast choice of levels in all computer programs.

1011_Camera and Compound Moves

A compound-table top permits the artwork to move in any direction of the compass. Most of the traditional animation stands are unavailable and animators who still practice the classical technique have to find improvised solutions for camera and compound moves. However, even in digital compositing, the animator's terms for movements of camera and artwork moves remain the same.

Up and **Down**, **Forward** and **Backward** is used for camera moves, sometimes also called **Zoom-in/Zoom-out** or **Truck-in/Truck-out**. The compound moves are indicated as **West-East** for a horizontal left to right move and **South-North** for a vertical move on the artwork. Typically, a **Diagonal pan** from the left lower corner to the top right corner of the artwork would be labeled as a **SW-NE** move.

Diagonal Pan

For a diagonal pan, there must be a combined compound move horizontally and vertically at the same time and at an even speed. It's rather delicate and complicated to get a straight move.

With a single horizontal compound and a camera carriage that allows the camera to turn around on its optical axes the diagonal move can be done in one straight move.

This is how it can be done: Mount the artwork on a separate sheet of cardboard so that the axis of the pan will be parallel to the horizontal compound move. Turn the camera around in order to have the desired field of your artwork, and move from field A to field B in one move!

Traveling Off-centre

An off-centre traveling forward or backwards is made normally by trucking the camera and moving the compound table. Here is a way to make an off-centre traveling without moving the compound table:

Incline the camera and the compound table with the artwork at the same angle. The precise angle is given by the smallest and by the biggest field of the move. For the off-centre traveling, simply truck the camera up or down.

For a diagonal off-centre move, use the combination of the off-centre traveling procedure and the procedure of the diagonal pan.

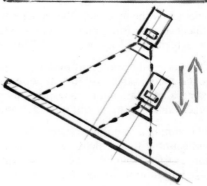

Ease-in/Ease-out

A camera or compound move made suddenly at full speed after a hold is disturbing. Movements in real life begin and end gradually. This progressive speeding up at the beginning and slowing down at the end of a move is called ease-in and ease-out. The easing can be as long or as short as required and is used in all moves: Camera truck-in and -out, Rotation, and Compound moves (east-west, north-south).

If the constant speed of a move is **5** units, you can ease-in in **4** steps: **1 2 3 4 5** is already the first of the constant speed units. For a **3**-unit constant speed, the easing could be **0.5 1 1.5 2 2.5** and **3**. Another example, for a **10**-unit constant speed the ease-in could be **2 4 6 8** and **10.**

Of course, the slower the speed-up the more extra frames you need. This has to be taken into consideration when planning the move.

For combined camera and compound moves, it is important that both moves start and end together.

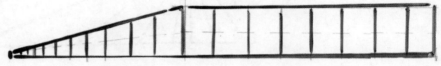

A continuous easing is when the ease-out starts as soon as the ease-in is finished.

For continuous easing an *Easing Chart* can be made. The circumference of a half circle is divided by the number of frames you want the move to be. Each point is projected onto its diameter to form a ruler with ease-in and ease-out gradations. To divide the circumference of a half circle into even parts you can use this classic and simple formula:

Length of diameter (length of the move) multiplied by $\pi = 3.14$ (PI = the Greek letter) and divided by the double number of frames required.

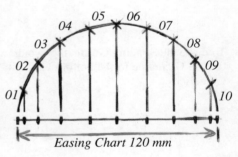
Easing Chart 120 mm

Length of the move 120 mm
Number of frames required: 10
120 x 3.14 = 376.8 : 20 = 18.84

Strobing

In a move, the more an object overlaps from one frame to another, the smoother its movement is. If there is no overlap at all, the artwork jitters because persistence of vision cannot bridge the gap between the two frames. This is called *Strobing*. To avoid the strobe effect, all camera and compound moves have to be done in *Ones*, except for the slowest which can be done in *Twos*. Contrast, shapes, and structure of the artwork play important roles. In general, a greater contrast means more risk of strobing.

To avoid strobing in fast pans, the exposure speed of a film camera can be set for a longer time, perhaps half a second. The shot is made while the table top or the camera is moved. This gives a blurred effect just as in real-life films, or a similar effect to speed lines in animation.

A side effect of strobing happens when identical objects overlap in a movement. They may appear to be stationary or create an appearance of arrested or slow motion. The classical example are the wheels of the famous stagecoach in Western films. According to the wagon speed, the wheels turn forward, appear to be stationary, or even appear to turn backwards.

**Working for
Classical Pegbar Animation**
These procedures are standards in classical pegbar animation.

**Working for
3-D Computer Animation**
Most of these procedures can be used in 3-D animation. There is a vast range of choices of other possibilities in all computer programs.

1012_Perspective_Optical Illusions

With the arrival of digital electronics, and especially virtual images, movements in perspective have become easy to make and their appearance on the screen has lost its originality, looking today like any old thing. However, the making of perspective movement by traditional hand drawings still remains something which has to be done with precision and patience.

A Spacing Guide is made in order to have an even speed of movement. The Guideline must be divided into parts which decrease in length as the object departs towards the horizon line, or increase in length as the object approaches the viewer.

Perspective in pegbar animation is planned by drawing the background with indication of a **Vanishing Point** on the horizon line.

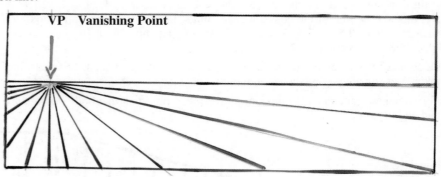

Next step is to draw the **Guide Lines** for the perspective move of the object or character. The character is drawn at the position of the beginning of the move and the position when a new walking cycle of steps will begin.

To make the **Spacing Guide,** the two drawings are linked by a diagonal line from the top Guideline to the bottom Guideline passing through the centre of the two Guidelines.

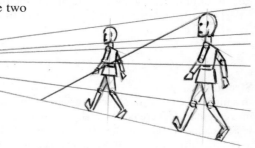

The point where the diagonal line touches the bottom line is the starting position for the next walking cycle.

This procedure is repeated until the movement comes to the desired ending point. At each crossing point of the diagonal line with the centre line, a new walking cycle starts.

The in-between drawings are made according to the feet position.

Perspective Cheat in Backgrounds

When making a background for perspective animation, there are a few things about vanishing point and horizon line you learned in art school which you'd better forget now.

Vanishing point **VP 3** is established by the projection through Vanishing Point **VP 1** and **VP 2**.

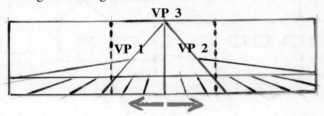

In a fast east-west pan, the middle section blurs out.

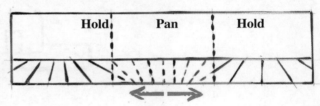

Perspective cheat is also used in a south-north pan from a down- to an up-looking shot, when the blue sky replaces the landscape for dramatic height effect.

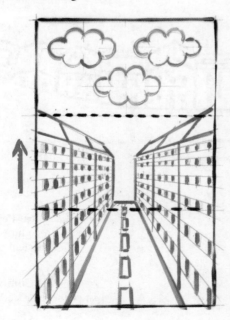

The same principle applies to a fast north-south movement, following a character falling from a roof top.

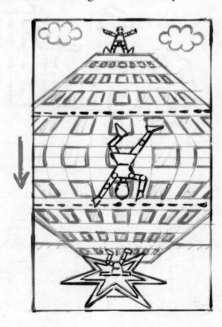

Optical Illusions

Cinema is an optical illusion by definition, since a series of static images are projected at great speed and thus create the illusion of movement. The animator uses optical illusions to create surprising effects or make complicated visual situations believable and understandable.

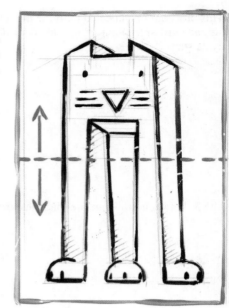

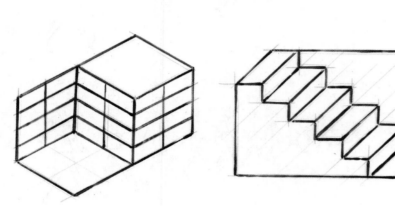

A common trick that looks funny on the artwork, but works on the screen..

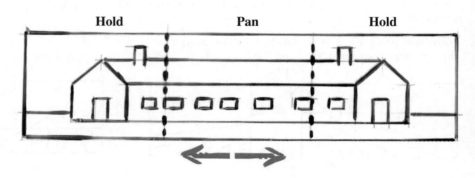

Hold   Pan   Hold

In a horizontal pan the camera angle can change from up-looking to down-looking on one single drawing.

**Working for
Classical Pegbar Animation**
These procedures are standards in
classical pegbar animation

**Working for
3D Computer Animation**
Most of these procedures can be used
in 3D animation

1013_Special Effects

In digital production, most of these effects can be done in the compositing program by using the various possibilities offered by filters, transitions and video effects. Just to name a few: Dissolves and Inverts, Page peel and Roll away, Push and Slide, Split and Swirl, Wipe and Spin, Blur and Ghost, Pinch and Spherize, Crystallize and Pointillize, Solarize and Texturize… there is no end to …izing !

This chapter is about low-cost in-camera effects, using a film camera and film stock. In-camera effects are less expensive than laboratory processes, but you run the risk of doing it all over again. Risk is part of the special effect cameraman's job, and can hardly be replaced by even the most precise tests.

In film production, some of the effects can be obtained simply by using the right light sources, filters, camera speed and position, or multi-exposure procedures. Most of these effects can be applied to plane-view and three-dimensional animation techniques. Some effects, including most of the natural phenomena effects, like rain, lightning, and explosions, have to be created differently for plane-view and three-dimensional animation.

In plane-view animation, effects are obtained with pen on paper and cels. In three-dimensional animation there are a lot of gadgets and some tinkering around to do; but with either form, there's no limit to your own fantasy and creativity. It's the very field where nothing is real or impossible!

Working for
Classical Pegbar Animation
These procedures are standards in
classical pegbar animation.

Working for
3-D Computer Animation
Most of these procedures can be used
in 3-D animation, but there is a vast
range of choices of other effects
in all computer programs.

Special Effects: Light Source

The light itself can be used for special effects, not only for three-dimensional animation but also for pegbar animation and all the other plane view animation techniques. Especially in plane view animation, light is an often neglected factor which can create mood and atmosphere.

Just about any spotlight projector with focus and with a holder for filters and masks can be used as a special light effect source. If there is no such projector available, an ordinary slide projector will do, especially as we can use the slide slot to introduce filters, masks and even slides! The slide projector can be used without the lens for a diffuse light spot or with a lens for a more or less sharp spot.

The position of the light source is also a creative factor. Top or bottom light can change the dramatic statement of the whole scene. A counter-lighting position in 3-dimensional animation has a dramatic effect throwing objects into silhouette.

Coloured light creates a day or night atmosphere and different coloured light beams are again a form of animation. The filters to *colour* the light source can be attached in front of the spotlights or introduced as transparencies into the slide projector. Heat resistant colour foils and filters can be purchased at almost any photo supply shop.

The use of black light (ultra-violet light) is a whole technique in itself. It can, however, be used along with other light sources, and adds a touch of surprising brilliance to bright colours (especially if these colours are used with a dark background).

Masks, combined with light sources, are used to reduce the surface of the light beam or to give a particular shape to it. The masks can be cut out of any heat resistant material like tin or aluminum foil. Letters or detailed images can be reproduced as slides on high contrast film thrown onto the background or the animated object by a slide projector.

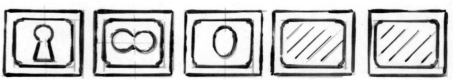

A most effective use of slide and light projection is to use it as a *back projection*. This is a low-cost way to create realistic looking backgrounds or simply to colour them. The slide is projected from the rear onto tracing paper mounted onto a wooden frame or, better, onto a special rear projection screen *available also in photo supply stores*.

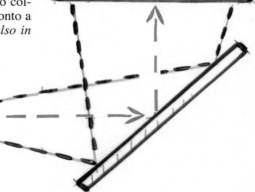

Special Effects: Filters and Lenses

Thanks to the busy manufacturers of photo and cine apparatuses, almost all the problems of special effects can be solved by some kind of filter or lens. A closer look at the different types of filters and lenses will make you conscious of the possibilities and limits. One of the dangers is the overuse of these *gadgets*. Since they are simple to use and also relatively cheap, everybody uses them. Think over the dramatic possibilities of these devices and use them only if there's a good reason to.

All these filters and special lenses are mounted in front of the camera lens. Camera and filter manufacturers supply holders in which several filters fit. Better models are able to rotate or glide.

Colour filters can be used to create an overall colour effect or atmosphere of the scene.

A contrasting blue filter brings the day-for-night effect as Hollywood knows it. Close the aperture by one or two stops for this effect.

Sunshine can be created by using a yellow filter. Don't forget that a filter will not only brighten objects of its own colour but also darken objects with complementary colours.

Pastel filters will bring a soft appearance to the picture.

Sepia filters add a nostalgic touch.

Graduated colour filters can be used to weaken a too-bright sky or water surface, or simply to graduate the whole scene.

Polarization filters are especially designed for the filmmakers. They come in pairs mounted one behind the other in a turnable holder. In a 90° crossed position there's practically no light coming through. By turning from open to closed or vice versa the light will continuously decrease or increase. That's one way to make fade-outs and fade-ins and even dissolves. But the fades and dissolves made this way are not of very good quality and should be avoided if you can do them with the shutter.

There is another range of filters which don't change the overall colour of the scene but bring, through diffraction, special light and colour effects. The inner structure of these filters breaks up the light into the colours of the spectrum. They are usually known as *Cross Screen Filters*.

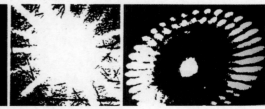

The Transparent Diffraction-Grading Filter gives a star effect to all light sources. The best effect comes from tiny but strong light sources. To create this star effect, a black cardboard can be punched with needles, strongly back lit and even superimposed over another scene. Star filters range from two to sixteen rays.

All these filters can be turned around in their holder to create genuine colour and star orgies!

Another type of filter is the diffuser. This filter brings a light, soft appearance to the whole scene without changing the sharpness. The mistmaker or fogmaker creates the misty atmosphere of a November day or the *washhouse* effect of a tropical forest. A combination of fog and green filters can be used for underwater scenes. All these filters are, of course, also available in half filters, centre spot or soft edges graduated to bring the effect to only part of the picture.

If you don't want to invest in a diffuser filter, you can simply use some petroleum jelly (i.e., Vaseline) on a piece of glass. It does the same job, and you can even give the shape you want to the diffused area.

Multiple image devices and prisms complete the arsenal of optical effect equipment. These devices will multiply and rotate your picture like a kaleidoscope or distort the scene as if you were looking through a *Ripple Glass* door.

Ripple Glass Effect

Different types of ripple glass sheets can be placed either in front of the camera lens or directly onto the artwork. The distortion effect varies according to the pattern and size of the glass and the distance from the lens. The artwork is placed on the animation table and the ripple glass between camera lens and artwork. Look through the viewfinder to ascertain the best position for the glass. Good effect comes from moving the glass to-and-fro, or rotating it. Try out different light sources; coloured light, toplight or backlight can change the whole atmosphere.

 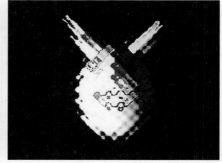

Glass Shots

A glass shot is when part of the picture composing the scene is painted onto a clear sheet of glass and placed in front of the camera. Or, instead of using paint, the picture on the glass can be a colour transparency or a collage artwork. The rest of the scene is behind the glass and the camera shoots the composite picture in one run. Although this method is mostly used in live action shooting, to save background costs, there is a way to apply it to three-dimensional animation. The important thing is that the artwork on the glass perfectly matches whatever is behind it. A match line, such as a horizon or the top of buildings, helps to align both pictures. The alignment is made by looking through the viewfinder. Artwork which forms a background on the glass shouldn't cover any elements that move behind the glass. The whole setup looks something like a vertical multiplane. For a moving glass shot, the whole plate has to be put in some gliding device and will be moved frame by frame.

For moving clouds, an identical beginning and end helps for the takeover. Focus is made in between the levels; with closed down aperture, both levels should be in focus.

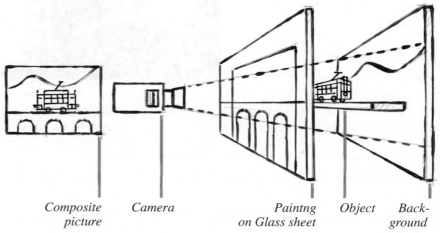

Composite   Camera   Paintng   Object   Back-
picture   on Glass sheet   ground

Special Effects: Mirror Shots

A mirror is a helpful thing to have around in a workshop. It helps for a variety of good effects, all of them fitted for low-cost production. The advantage of the mirror shot over the double exposure is that the composite picture can be seen through the viewfinder and exposed in one single shot. The disadvantage is the time-consuming set-up of the whole apparatus, and the problems of proportions and focusing of the two separate pictures.

Two different types of mirror shots are possible: The front silvered mirror shot to replace the whole image or part of it; and the two-way mirror for ghosting effects or in combination with black areas for image replacement as well.

In all cases, the mirror must be mounted to a sturdy frame, which can be tilted and pivoted in any direction. Once in place, this mirror holder must be fixed firmly. The mirror is always placed at a 45 degree position between the camera and the two sets.

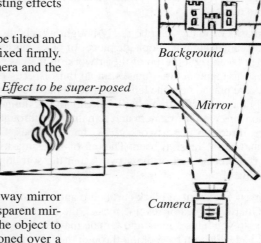

Background

Effect to be super-posed

Mirror

Camera

Composite picture

Two-Way Mirror

Rather than scratching, and thus destroying, the front mirror, a two-way mirror can be used to achieve a similar replacement effect. With the half-transparent mirror, both pictures can be seen translucently, one on top of the other. The object to be super-posed opaquely is placed on a black background and positioned over a dark area of the scene; e.g., a real fire placed into a puppet set fireplace.

The translucent ghosting effect can be achieved either with a two-way mirror or with a thin sheet of good quality glass. The result will be a half and half picture. The object to be ghosted over the scene is again placed in front of a black background.

Front-Silvered Mirror

A front-silvered mirror is used to avoid double reflections of the image, but it's fragile and has to be handled with care and cotton gloves. The mirror is versatile and can be used not only to throw light into dark corners of a set but also to shoot *around the corner*. Often in a three-dimensional set, the camera doesn't fit, but there is still enough space for a mirror.

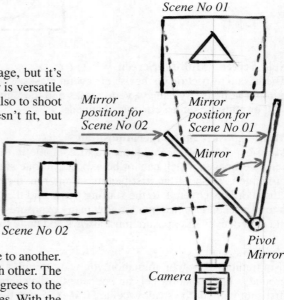

Scene No 01

Mirror position for Scene No 02

Mirror position for Scene No 01

Mirror

Scene No 02

Pivot Mirror

Camera

The same mirror can be used to make a wipe transition from one scene to another. For a wipe effect the two scenes have to be set up at 90 degrees to each other. The camera is facing the main scene and the other scene is placed at 90 degrees to the lens axis. The mirror is placed in between the camera and the two scenes. With the mirror in place, the scene is recorded at a 90 degree angle to the camera. The mirror is then pivoted around an axis outside the camera field and reveals the scene in front of the camera.

As with the glass shot, the front mirror can be used to replace part of the picture. Either part of the mirror is used to replace the image along a straight horizon line, or parts of the mirror can be scratched away to reveal the rest of the scene behind.

Special Effects: In-Camera
Mask and Mattes

There are two different uses of the masking method. The first one is to shoot the scene through a mask that cuts off part of the picture. The cut-off part of the picture remains unexposed and therefore black. Examples are the notorious keyhole or binocular-shaped mask for suggestive view shots. The other use is the reverse mask or male-female mask. In two runs, the masked off part during the first run is replaced by another scene in the second run. A familiar example is the same figure twice in the picture. Precision is necessary for cutting and placing mask and reverse mask.

The masks or mattes can be ready-bought as sets in any photo-cine supply store or they can be cut out of opaque pieces of black cardboard. The cardboard version can be placed right on top of the artwork, in the case of plane view animation, or just as the manufactured masks, in an out-of-focus position near the lens. If the masks are placed near the lens, you need a mask holder. This can be a lens hood or simply the anti-reflection board. The important thing is that it must be in a steady relationship with the camera and remain there throughout the shooting. The mask placed direct on the artwork gives sharp outlines, but demands more precision when a reverse-mask is used. The out-of-focus masks are less accurate for masking off a precise part of the artwork, but the soft edges give more leeway to the matching of the reverse mask.

The mask is cut out of black cardboard and placed over the opening of the Reflection Guard Board. For reverse masks, the shape is cut out precisely with a sharp cutter, so you have a male and female mask in one go. The exact position for one mask is decided on by looking through the viewfinder. Once in place, the mask is taped firmly to the board. The first run is made with the first mask in place. The film is rewound, with shutter closed or lens covered as usual, to the staring point. The reverse mask is placed on the shadow board so that it matches the first mask perfectly. Tape it down and remove only now the first mask. With the reverse mask in place you can shoot any artwork you want to appear within this mask. For a perfect match of both masks, the position of the camera, focus, and aperture should not be changed during the whole operation.

Split Screen / Multiple Screen

There is no restriction on the use of several masks. The frame can be split into any number of parts. By using several masks and the same number of camera runs, a split or multiple screen effect is obtained.

Multi-exposure and Superimposition

Multi-exposure is a technique used to combine in the film camera two or more separate images which cannot be exposed in one single run of the camera. The principle is to shoot the first picture in one run, then backwind the film, shutter closed or lens covered, to the starting point, and then superimpose the other picture in a second run. No matter how many exposures you make on the same film, the total density of exposure must always add up to full normal exposure.

Shadows

If in traditional pegbar animation you want to mix a shadow area with the background, a black shadow cel can be made for the character's shadow. The scene is first shot without the shadow cel at 50% exposure, then rewound and the shadow cel used over the scene to be shot again at 50%.

Clouds, Dust, Smoke, Ghosts

If the two superimposed scenes don't have to be of the same density, for clouds, dust, smoke, ghosts or the famous stream-of-thought effect, then any other proportions of exposure can be chosen. Providing the final composite picture adds up to 100% exposure.

Superimposition

Superimposition without the translucent effect is about the same as the exposure of two or more separate pictures on one film. But here each element is placed at full exposure on top of the other. Since there is no overlapping of the pictures, the composite image resembles a matted shot. It's important, however, that the areas to be used for the superimposition are black, or at least dark. If any artwork contains too many white or clear areas it is not suitable for superimposition. On the clear parts of the film, the emulsion is already burnt out and there is nothing left to be registered on. Superimposition of two equally dense pictures at full exposure has the effect of an overexposed picture. The superimposed picture will therefore always show up lighter than the background. Any parts that are not to show up in the composite picture have to be blacked out or masked off.

The Burn-in Process

Another form of superimposition is the burn-in process. Here the superimposed picture dominates and burns away whatever is behind it on the emulsion of the film stock. This method is applied for titles or for very bright elements like stars, fire, lightning, or explosions.

Camera Speed

Time is an important raw material in animation, and a camera is a *Time Machine*. Because most motion picture cameras are able to expose film at varying frame speeds, you can play around with time. The standard shooting rate in live action is 25 frames per second (FPS). Shooting at this speed reproduces normal motion with the projector running also at 25 FPS.

Shooting at lower speed (e.g. 10 FPS) produces faster motion. Shooting at higher speed (e.g. 50 FPS)-produces slower motion. In live action film production, most scenes of fighting or close ups of car crashes are sped up, to get more impact and less details. Most scenes of actors falling over cliff-tops or explosions are slowed down, to last longer and therefore be more effective.

The extreme in speeding up is when your camera takes single frames. This is called Stop-frame or Time-lapse-Cinematography. This technique is perfect to show the construction of a circus big top or the passing of the four seasons in a few minutes.

For the extremes in recording high speed, special cameras are used. To shoot 16mm full frame up to 400 FPS an intermittent camera can be used; and up to 8000 FPS special rotating prism cameras are used. The projected effect is that of a soft, floating movement, especially visible in human motions with trailing appendices.

Reverse Shooting

Some of the most common effects in animation come through reverse shooting. Think of all the objects out of order which rearrange themselves, or the paper cutouts folding or unfolding themselves.

If your camera has no reverse shooting, there is an easy trick to overcome this problem. The camera must be loaded with double perforated film stock, then fixed looking up-side-down at the artwork. The animation work is done shooting forward, scratching off or unfolding whatever has to appear or fold up in the projected film.

When the film comes back from processing, it is run upside down and tail-first through the projector. Whatever has been at the beginning will now be at the end. Using double perforated film stock in animation is a good idea anyway. You never know when your fancy invites you to see things backwards.

**Working for
Classical Pegbar Animation**
These procedures are standards in classical pegbar animation.

**Working for
3-D Computer Animation**
Most of these procedures can be used in 3-D animation, but there is a vast range of choices of other effects in all computer programs.

1014_Special Effects in Plane View Animation

For traditional animation, special effects in plane view animation have to be created with pen and paint on paper or cels. In computer assisted animation these effects can be created in one of the painting programs. The effects with repeat movements, like fire and flames, smoke and rain, are explained in the chapter on Cycling. Most of these effects, when properly painted on black cardboard, can be superimposed in double exposure over flat or three-dimensional backgrounds.

Underwater Effects
For this effect, a blue filter and a clear cel with a series of curved lines made with clear fast-drying glue is used. Let the glue dry and move the cel up and down in a wave movement near the lens in an out-of-focus position.
Another method is to use a water basin. Pour water in it, add a few aquatic plants and your goldfish, then put the whole set between camera and art-work.

Snowy Effects
Besides the snow cycle recorded frame by frame, there is a way to use a long pan cel with white dots on it. It is moved North-South at a speed and inclination which illustrate the vehemence of the snowfall. The snowflakes can be superimposed or recorded directly with the background in an out-of-focus position, giving a soft appearance to the snowfall.

Lightning
White or light-blue lightning is superimposed on the background and about three frames are overexposed. The shape of the lightning can be painted on black cardboard or cut out of it and recorded with back light.
For an even more effective impression, the background is replaced by an exact black-and-white negative replica on the overexposed frames.
The lightning effects are recorded on at least six frames of the film. Repetition can be made at desired intervals.

Explosions
Anything can explode just by increasing its shape rapidly. This becomes more expressive when the forms of the exploding object towards the end of the explosion are replaced by a star shape in white, yellow and red. A few overexposed frames and negative replica pictures will increase the effect even more. A fast zoom-out will also intensify the effect of an explosion. For after-effects you can insert a few black frames, then a cloud of dust and smoke which can disappear by making a lot of small clouds or by developing holes which become steadily bigger. Behind the clouds you can show the debris, what's left of the former scene, or even the next scene.

1015_Special Effects in Stop-Motion Animation

The key to good special effects in three-dimensional animation is a certain love for tinkering around and experimenting with all sorts of gadgets and chemicals.

Props (from the word property) are the indispensable items used by filmmakers to create most of the special effects in live action. It's the property department which keeps all the miniatures handy for model shots, ray and smoke guns, firing boxes and exploders, plastic arrows, knives and (already bloodstained) swords, frost, ice and cobwebs. Costumes, wigs, umbrellas, as well as background sets are also important requirements in filmmaking.

If you do not happen to have a property department at hand, you could have a look around in drugstores, novelty shops, photo-cine supply stores and shops for theatre and window dressing supplies. You may be surprised at how many props you will find in various stores: Plaster of Paris, Polystyrene, Liquid latex, Fibreglass and Polyester resins, or Snow and Ice for Christmas decorations, Pyrotechnic smoke pots or Smoke powder.

Firecrackers of many different types are sold in some countries around New Year's or national celebrations. That's the moment to buy the stock to last you the year.

Whether you work with ready-made props or tinker around with home-made materials, it's again the trial and error method that brings the best results. Tests can be made, but since most of these effects are shot in a continuous camera run, the control of the action and timing is much harder than in frame-by-frame plane-view animation. Some of these effects can be shot in front of a black background or in a glass-fronted black box, then superimposed.

Water and Rain
For underwater scenes, a clear glass container filled with water, which can be your aquarium, is placed between the camera and the scene and gently shaken during shooting. A fog filter and green/blue filters enhance the effect of depth or danger. Rain on a model set is done with a watering can moved to and fro above the scene. There is no need to soak the set itself, as it is usually sufficient to pour the water between the camera and the set. Counter light and out-of-focus water drops create a very realistic effect.
For rain on windows, a clear rigid sheet of acetate is positioned in front of the camera and water poured over it.

Wind and Storms
A ventilator or hair dryer replaces the wind machines used in live action films. For stormy scenes, dry leaves, bits of polystyrene granules, sawdust and water drops from the watering can are fed into the air stream. Bouncing hailstones are best imitated with shredded rice.

Lightning
Blue-coloured flashlights, along with a long exposure time bring a realistic overall lightning effect. The lightning can also be superimposed by using a black cardboard mask with the cut-out lightning shape. The mask is fixed in front of the lens with the flashlight or another strong light from behind.

Snow and Ice
Salt or sugar is the easiest available material to cover objects on a three-dimensional set for snow effect. Expanded polystyrene granules are also good, especially for falling snow. The finely shredded granules are dispensed from a container hanging above the scene. Granules falling near the lens have a realistically soft appearance. Slow-motion is a must for snowfall.
Sugar cubes, broken sheets of polystyrene or blocks of white paraffin give a realistic look to polar landscapes.
Clear, fast-drying glue makes a good substitute for icicles.

Smoke and Fog

Fog and smoke, hot springs and bewitching scenes can be created by using dry ice. In contact with lukewarm water it produces a dense white smoke. Barbecue charcoal can also be used to produce smoke. Lit and placed on a fireproof surface it glows red-hot for about thirty minutes, then a few drops of machine oil applied produce quite a bit of smoke - and smell!

To amplify the effect, fog filters or nylon stockings can be stretched over the lens. A good illusion can be created by superimposing the fog or smoke. The effect is filmed in front of a black background or a black fog-retaining box.

Fire and Flames

Hardly any of today's adventure films can avoid some sort of fire explosion. Burning cars, airplane crashes, volcanic explosions and whole towns burning are daily routines for special effects animators and the audience.

A group of little candles can be a very effective setup to imitate a small fire. The candlesticks are hidden and the flames *animated* by a stream of air. For conflagrations, forest fires, or burning landscapes, you can try sawdust with petrol poured over. Remember to close that petrol can before you light the fire! A few drops of machine oil or a plastic garbage bag helps to develop black smoke. A bit of tar on top of it creates orange flames and more dark smoke.

Fireworks manufacturers have a whole arsenal of utensils to imitate rockets or the explosions of volcanoes. Smoke powder is also available and can be added to the fire. Coloured light beams and a star filter in front of the lens brings you orgies of fire and smoke, worthy of a witches's sabbath.

A safe and simple-to-make device for a flickering flame effect is the *Flame Drum*. Ragged slots are cut into black cardboard, then the cardboard is formed into a lantern-shaped drum and hung from a line. When it is wound up (with a powerful lamp inside), then released, a flickering light is thrown from the rotating drum onto the whole background.

Flame Drum
outside   *inside*

Explosions

Explosions of houses, oil rigs, ocean steamers and cliffs are tops among the effects the audience is waiting for.

To stay on the safe side, the use of dynamite or other highly explosive materials will be left to the specialists. The secret of effective explosions is that the object to be blown up is already broken up before it takes to the air. A house can be built up in bits and pieces and stuffed with all sorts of material - from sawdust, ashes, granulated polystyrene to pre-broken furniture. Hidden behind and underneath the object is a lever on which a weight is going to fall. A firecracker and smoke powder can be set into action by the same system. Slow motion, the camera running at high speed, is a must for all good explosions.

Warning

When playing around with explosives and chemicals, a few precautions have to be strictly observed.

For chemicals:

Work only in well-ventilated areas. Avoid contact with skin. Keep all chemicals out of reach of children or domestic animals.

For explosives:

Work in the open, whenever possible. Keep them away from heat, sparks and open flames. Have a fire extinguisher and buckets of water ready. Calculate and keep a safe distance between your camera and the action. Keep explosives out of reach of children.

A last word about special effects: Don't forget that half of the effect's impact is on the soundtrack. The audience just won't believe there's a crackling fire or an explosion without an adequate sound effect. Take advantage of this great audio-visual combination. Make the best use possible of a soundtrack; it's always time-and money-saving and often less dangerous!

Working for
Classical Pegbar Animation
These procedures are standards in classical pegbar animation

Working for
3-D Computer Animation
Most of these procedures can be used in 3-D animation, but there is a vast range of choices of other effects in all computer programs.

1016_Dialogue
_Lip Synchronised Animation

The purpose of animation is not to imitate the television talking heads and their realistic lip movements. Yet there are situations when you would like to have a character to say something in a given language. The idea in dialogue and lip sync animation is to synchronise the mouth shapes of a character to the sound of his speech. To create the illusion that the character is really speaking the words on the soundtrack, not only has the mouth to be animated, but the whole face and body has to express what he is talking about.

A good approach is to study the lip movements of your own face in a mirror. Reduce what you see to a phonetic alphabet of a few basic drawings. Both the spoken words and the way you pronounce them are important. Whether you yell or whisper a word makes a lot of difference to the shape of the mouth and the whole face. Make the whole head and face fit the mouth's expression. There is no standard mouth shape for dialogue. The following drawings are **Standard Phonemic Positions for English Dialogue** and have to be adapted to each language and individual situation.

Give a number **(0-9)** to each *Phonemen* and mark these numbers according to the Dialogue Analysis in the Phonemen Numbers column of the Exposure Sheet.

English Phonemen

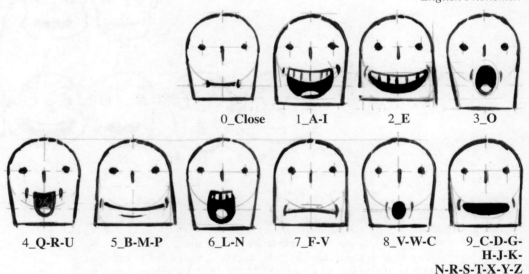

0_Close   1_A-I   2_E   3_O

4_Q-R-U   5_B-M-P   6_L-N   7_F-V   8_V-W-C   9_C-D-G-
H-J-K-
N-R-S-T-X-Y-Z

Simplified Approach

In real life, most people when speaking hardly move their lips and mouth. A too rigid precision in simulating the lip movements looks quite artificial and a simpler approach can be more efficient. Locate the closed mouth position (M-B-P-F-W-C) and the beginning and end of each word on the sound track. At these places you make the drawing no. 1. The in-between drawings are made to approximate the spoken words, by using this basic mouth-cycle.

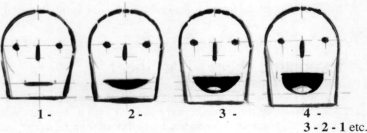

1 -   2 -   3 -   4 -
3 - 2 - 1 etc.

Lip Sync Animation: **Good Morning**

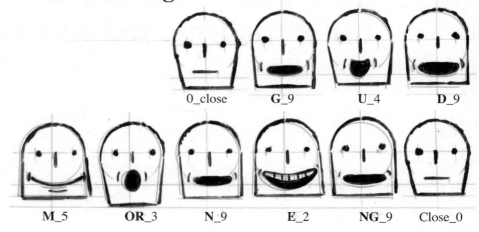

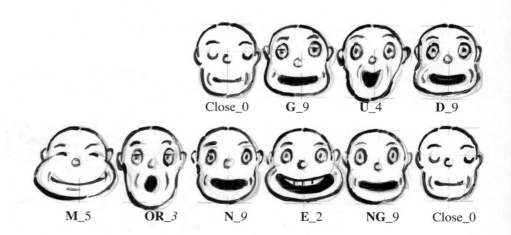

Working with film

If you work with film, the first step to a precise analysis of the dialogue is to record the voice on perforated magnetic film. The standard equipment to analyse magnetic film frame by frame is a synchroniser. If you lack this equipment you may run the magnetic film at normal projection speed through an editing table or a sound projector. Mark the beginning and end of each word on the magnetic tape. Count the frames of each word as well as the frames in between.

Working with computer

In computer assisted animation, the voice is recorded and imported as an audio file into sound or editing program. Choose a computer program with a frame-by-frame counter and set the frame rate to 25 fps. Run the soundtrack at projection speed with the program and identify the beginning and end of each word on the timeline. Count the frames of each word as well as the frames in between.

Exposure Sheet / Bar Sheet

The next step in any technique is to mark every word, according to the number of frames, on the Exposure Sheet in the **Dialogue** column. Then you return to the synchroniser/editing table or computer program to analyse every word according to the basic phonemen positions. In the **Phonemen Letters** column the words are spelled out phonetically and simplified for each frame of film. This gives you the exact place and number of frames for each **Phonemen Number** column.

Don't forget that every dialogue usually starts and ends with a closed mouth position, which is the number **0** in the **Phonemen Number** column.

Exposure sheet / Bar sheet	Title **Good Morning**				Sq no **01** / Sc no **02**	Sheet no **01**

Dialogue	Phonemen Letters	Frames	Phonemen Numbers	Dialogue	Phonemen Letters	Frames	Phonemen Numbers
	Close	1 2	**0**			1 2	
		3 4				3 4	
		5 6				5 6	
Good	**G**	7 8	**9**			7 8	
		9 **1**0				9 0	
	U	1 2	**4**			1 2	
		3 4				3 4	
	D	5 6	**9**			5 6	
		7 8				7 8	
Morning	**M**	9 **2**0	**5**			9 0	
	OR	1 2	**3**			1 2	
		3 4				3 4	
	N	5 6	**9**			5 6	
	E	7 8	**2**			7 8	
		9 **3**0				9 0	
	NG	1 2	**9**			1 2	
		3 4				3 4	
	Close	5 6	**0**			5 6	
		7 8				7 8	
		9 **4**0				9 0	
		1 **4**2				1 2	
		3 4				3 4	
		5 6				5 6	
		7 8				7 8	
		9 **5**0				9 0	

Animagination Robi Engler

Exposure sheet Bar sheet	Title				Dialogue	Sq no Sc no	Sheet no	
Dialogue	Phonemen Letters	Frames	Phonemen Numbers		Dialogue	Phonemen Letters	Frames	Phonemen Numbers
		1 2					1 2	
		3 4					3 4	
		5 6					5 6	
		7 8					7 8	
		9 0					9 0	
		1 2					1 2	
		3 4					3 4	
		5 6					5 6	
		7 8					7 8	
		9 0					9 0	
		1 2					1 2	
		3 4					3 4	
		5 6					5 6	
		7 8					7 8	
		9 0					9 0	
		1 2					1 2	
		3 4					3 4	
		5 6					5 6	
		7 8					7 8	
		9 0					9 0	
		1 2					1 2	
		3 4					3 4	
		5 6					5 6	
		7 8					7 8	
		9 0					9 0	

Animagination Robi Engler

1017_Animated Technical Diagrams

There is a fundamental difference between book and film diagrams. The book diagram is often an illustration of the text and can be looked at as long as one needs to. The film diagram stands on its own and has to be understood during the projection time. A commentary may help to carry the message over to the audience, but there should be as little speech as possible. The message should be entirely transposed into visual animated language.

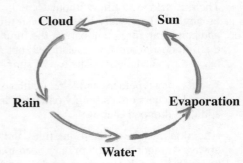

Technical animation is most often used in the field of training, educational, medical and industrial films. In these fields, animation can show action in a better perspective than in live action films. Think of the functioning of a gasoline engine, a gun, or part of the human body. Animation makes action literally transparent and shows the relevant information only.

Most mechanical, natural and human movements are repeat actions; e.g. engine working, electrical circuit, water and blood circulation, digestion, etc. Cycling is therefore the appropriate principle for most technical diagrams.

To create technical diagrams in traditional film animation such as flow charts, statistics and organigrams, the use of transparencies is most effective. The complete diagram is reproduced on high contrast film and lit from beneath. Black masks are used to cover or uncover the different elements. The best result is achieved if the successive apparition is synchronised to a given soundtrack. Superimposition and multi-exposure techniques add variety and flexibility to technical diagrams, since they can be superimposed on just about any coloured background or existing document.

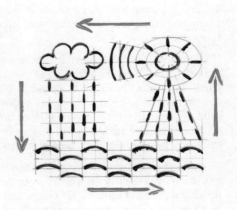

The scratch-off technique is another common method of diagram animation. The complete diagram is drawn on a cel with paint, then scratched off bit by bit and recorded, either in reverse, to make the diagram appear, or in forward to make it disappear. Add a little soap to the paint so it will not crack or peel.

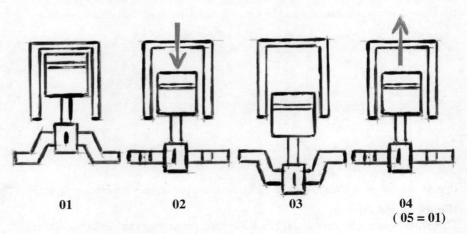

01   02   03   04
                                (05 = 01)

Cut-out bits and pieces can also be added or taken off any prepared diagram. The objects may be cut-outs of paper and any other material or ready-made adhesive rub-offs.

Working with an analysed soundtrack helps you get the timing right. It also means the animation will fit the message.

In computer-assisted animation, diagrams are created in any kind of drawing program. The animation can be done using compositing or editing program, where masks on separate levels are moved to cover and uncover the different elements. Most computer programs also offers a great number of transitions and special effects to animate the diagrams.

1018_Letters and Figures

There is seldom a film without some kind of letters and figures for title, credits or captions. Especially in educational films, letters and numbers are widely used and can be an important part of the film's visuals. When planning titles, not only the film design must be considered, but remember that titles are usually made to be read by an audience. The use of simple letters increases the legibility of titles.

Avoid fancy typefaces and letters with serifs, as they tend to recede into the background. Letters on a strongly patterned background can be made more legible by adding a dropped shadow.

Attention must be given to the titles and background contrast. Bright colours are always stronger than dull or dark ones. On a dark background, white letters appear bigger than black ones do on a clear background, even if they have precisely the same size. Bright letters on a dark background are easier to read and less tiring for the viewer's eyes.

Titles can be handmade and recorded with film or video, or they can be created in a computer program. Most programs offers an infinite number of fonts and transition effects.

If you decide that your titles are not just any titles and that you are bored with the old title cards, here are a few ideas to stimulate your imagination:
Chalk on a blackboard or a sidewalk. Paint on car windows and shot from the interior while the car moves. Spray-paint on brick walls, carved in clay, drawn in sand or snow. Lipstick on your girl- or boyfriend's back, toothpaste or razor foam on the bathroom mirror, cornflakes or ice cubes on the kitchen table, or cut-out titles on a laundry line recorded in motion.

Titles can be written on a piece of glass or a cel, so the background can be seen behind them. Fix the title in front of your camera so the background can move while the title remains stationary. Of course, all titles can be animated: you can spin, flip or wipe them. They can appear or disappear letter by letter. When recording on film, use the reverse shooting technique discussed in the special effects section.

If your taste is more classical, here are some basic techniques for producing titles.

Handwritten Letters
This work, made with pencil and brush, demands craftsmanship and a knowledge of calligraphy and composition.

Cut-out Letters
A low-cost way to produce good-looking titles is to create cut-out letters and to use them over and over. Letters may be cut out of cardboard, plastic, felt or any other *cutable* material. Printed letters can also be cut out of newspapers and magazines.

Stenciled Letters

Stenciled letters come in a limited variety of typefaces. They are economical because they can be used countless times, with nearly all colours, opaque or transparent, and on all kinds of surfaces, even on three-dimensional objects such as bottles, curtains and balloons.

Typewritten Letters

If you use a typewriter to produce your titles, you'll need a photographic enlargement of the original or a camera with macro focusing capability.

Animagination
Films d'animation

Typeset Letters

This lettering looks professional. A home computer can be used to type and print the documents to be recorded with film or video.

Stamped Letters

This technique is similar to the stenciled letter method and can be used over and over on almost any surface. An alphabet of rubber letters is used to print one letter after another.

Scratch-off Letters

The scratch-off technique is used to make a title appear or disappear. The title can be handwritten with brush and paint on a clear cel or a glass plate. Mix a little soap into the paint so it will not crack off when you gradually scratch the line off. Use a soft wooden ice-cream stick for scratching so you will not damage the cel. To make the title appear, use the reverse shooting technique.

31-97

Photocomposition Letters

A way to produce professional looking titles is to use photocomposition. A fully electronic machine is handled like a typewriter, but letters are produced in excellent quality on a high contrast film. The letters can be transparent on opaque black film or black on clear film. The best result is achieved by using a high contrast negative of the titles and recording with lighting from underneath. Coloured titles are produced by placing a coloured transparent behind the film, then filming both together.

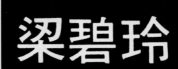

Superimposition / Burn-in Process

The multi-run technique is a system often used in professional title making. The background is photographed during the first run of the camera. The film is then rewound in the camera, with the shutter closed or lens covered, to the starting point. In the second run, the titles are superimposed. As long as the title is white, it can be actually burned into the film emulsion. White exposure on film emulsion burns out what was there in the first place.

The double exposure technique is also used to keep the title in a constant position and size, while there is a pan or a zoom on the background. Conversely, the background can be in a fixed position and the title can be animated.

1019_Television Applications

Animation intended for broadcasting over television requires a different treatment than films conceived for theatrical release.

Screen Size

The television screen does not reproduce the entire area of a given frame of film; it cuts off a certain percentage all the way around the perimeter. This is called the television *cut-off*.

The dimension of a 16mm frame is 7.5 mm to 10.3 mm. The proportion of the so-called standard aspect ratio is therefore 1:1.39, which comes to a rough 3:4.

The aspect ratio for 35 mm film is 1:1.30 for silent film, 1:1.33 for academy format and 1:1.85, 1:1.75 or 1:1.66 for wide screen, which comes to anything in between 3:4 and 3:5.

The traditional standard television screen is more quadratic, cutting off more on the right and left side of the film frame than on the bottom and top. There is a distortion-free area in the middle of the screen where all significant action should take place and where all titles, subtitles and credits should appear. To see immediately what will be transmitted on the screen, you may use a television-field mask which can be put over the artwork.

The proportion of a television screen, however, is about 4:5.
In terms of pixels this represents a proportion of 576:720 pixels.

Standard TV Screen
720 x 576   5 : 4

Television transmitted area
Television safe action area
Television safe title area 4:5

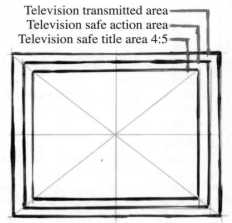

The proportion of the new standard for High Definition Television is 16:9, which comes to a rough 5:3.
In terms of pixels this represents a proportion of 1920:1080 pixels.

High DefinitionTV Screen
1920 x 1080   16 : 9

Television transmitted area
Television safe action area
Television safe title area 4:5

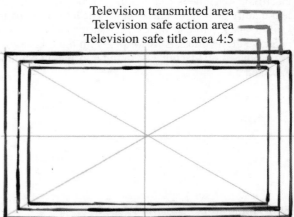

Safety Area for Titles

Letters on the television screen are meant to be read by the audience. To avoid illegibility there should never be more than 25 capital letters or 30 lower case letters in one line. Try to keep each title under 6 words. If it's longer, make two out of it or use a roll title.

aaaaaaaaaaaaaaaaaaaaaaaaaaaaaa

01 02 03 04 05 06 07 08 09 10 11 12 13 14 15 16 17 18 19 20 21 22 23 24 25 26 27 28 2ç

AAAAAAAAAAAAAAAAAAAAAAAA

01 02 03 04 05 06 07 08 09 10 11 12 13 14 15 16 17 18 19 20 21 22 23 24

Colours

The choice of colours must, of course, be left to each animator's taste. It is part of the creative freedom. The following hints are not meant to affect the choice of colours, but rather the use of them.

Colours are not merely used for decoration but to draw attention. Good visual impact can come from a pure black-and-white artwork with just one colour to underline the main interest. The use of colour should be carefully thought over and applied in a meaningful way.

Bright colours are used for main actions. Incidental animation and backgrounds can be done in monochrome colours. In visual communication, colours are used for identification: green for plants, brown for earth, blue for water and air. Do not change the colour coding during the film

Grey Scale

Television and film also have different distortions of the grey scale. Television requires a narrower spectrum of greys. Ten different grey shades, including black and white, are sufficient. Low-contrast images reproduce better on television and computer screens than high-contrast works. Pure black and white may produce *bloom*, a halo that forms around extreme values.

Proportions

Television audiences are less attentive and they must understand quickly. Moreover, television and computer screens are smaller than movie screens. On a television screen, the facial expression of character with realistic proportions is difficult to read. If facial expression is a priority, the size of the head of a character can take half of its body.

Silhouettes Test

For television applications, extreme positions of an action should be readable even in silhouette. When you opaque the whole drawing you should still be able to see what the figure is doing. The silhouette test is the key to this understanding and it is a *must* for television and whenever the message has to be punched across clearly and unmistakably.

For your own drawings and scraps.

1100_Post-Production_Added Value

Post-production is the last step in the production line. In a well-prepared and planned animation production, this part should be a piece of cake. The more you prepare in pre-production and the better you work during production, the less you have to worry about in post-production.

However, in digital filmmaking, post-production has become more and more important within the whole production procedure. In some cases, the post-production part has become just as important as the production part itself. This shift from production to post-production as the most important step means that many things that had usually been done in the production part will now be done in post-production. Naturally, there is also a budget shift. The production part, which in classical cel animation took up to 50% of the budget, recedes to under 35% in digital production, and the post-production part gets the money *saved* from the production part.

Digital post-production also requires different kinds of artists. All those who used to work in film labs, processing film stock, cutting and splicing negative film, making prints and optical soundtracks, are now in front of a computer screen, or have retired!

Digital filmmaking needs human resources familiar with computer hardware and software. In today's animation studios, these engineers and technician are passionate young people born long after the disappearance of the mechanical and optical recording to film stock.

Music Copyright

Post-production is also closely associated with sound design and sound creation. Remember that music in written or recorded form is copyright protected. Whether you show your film in festivals, on the internet, or use any other form of public distribution, you are not allowed to use any protected material without the written permission of the copyright holder. Without a release stating that you have the permission to use the music, the distribution of your film will be impossible.

To avoid copyright problems, it is much easier to create your own soundtrack. If you are not a musician yourself, composers and musicians will be happy to create an original soundtrack for you! So take your soundtrack into your own hands, creating sounds to fit your own needs. It's fun, and there are no royalties to pay; in fact, you or your composer will be the one to collect the royalties!

Here are the four indispensable steps of post-production.

01_Picture Editing / Compositing

Editing should be easy if the storyboard and the animatic were done carefully. Picture editing means taking all the scenes and sequences and putting them together in chronological order, according to the Animatic.

Major editing problems, factual errors, lack of continuity, or lack of clear thinking, can never be solved at the editing table. In most cases, this means re-shooting the scenes and sequences - or in the worst case, you are back to scriptwriting and storyboarding

In **Film production**, this is done with a film splicer on an editing table. The effects, like fade-in, fade-out, and dissolves, are indicated on the work print and executed by the film laboratory.

In **Digital production,** not only are the pictures edited, but a lot of effects are also made during this stage of production. This is done with editing/compositing software by using the various possibilities offered by filters, transitions and visual effects.

02_Sound Editing / Compositing

Sound design is usually closely associated with post-production. However, in a correct production procedure, the sound research and design is done in pre-production. The final soundtrack that will accompany the film requires the editing of sound effects, music, and voices to match the images.

There are many ways to match sound and image. Sound can be created by looking at the visuals and then adding to the final pictures. Sound can be pre-recorded and the visuals then animated to the soundtrack. Some animators prefer a sort of in between situation where the picture first inspires the musician for a sound layout. This sound then inspires the filmmaker for the visuals. The final music is made at the end to fully match the mood and beat of the film.

In **Film production**, this is done on a film editing table using perforated sound tape.

In **Digital production** one of the various editing/compositing software programs can be used. These programs usually propose an unlimited library of ready to use sound effects. It is the animator who decides if he will use this *clip-art sound* or work with a composer and create an original soundtrack.

03_Screening / Evaluation

A lot of energy, hope, and money, goes into a film production. During the whole production procedure you have been collecting, selecting, and evaluating your ideas and visuals. Your concept has been exposed and approved by a lot of people, maybe even including some film commissions. The first screening with an audience is, however, always something special. It is the *moment of truth*. Whatever the reaction and comments of the audience, for the filmmaker it is a great moment to learn. In the dark of the screening room, you will feel what parts of the original idea get across to the audience and what gets lost along the way. It is also the moment you will reload your batteries for a new project. The end of one film is the beginning of the next one.

04_Distribution / Promotion

Some animators like to do everything themselves: from the film idea to distribution. More and more animators, however, consider that the distribution and promotion of their films is not really their job. At this point, the least a filmmaker can do is to show the film, with his presence, in as many places as possible and to enter the film in festivals that showcase animated films.

As a matter of fact, it is not easy to successfully distribute a short animated film. One of the major handicaps is that most of animated films are short and so don't fit into theatrical release format.

In animated Hollywood feature film productions, the budget for promotion and distribution is nearly double the cost of production. This is not really what happens in the world of individual animated filmmaking. Despite these budget problems, every film should have a distributor to take care of your baby and - hopefully - make a lot of money!

1101_Sound Design_Sound Track

Sound is certainly an essential raw material for any animated film. A good sense for music helps the animator to find solutions for timing and rhythm. Sound design is the strategy to control the soundtrack; the sound effects, music, and voices. An audience watching a film receives the sound track in this order: **First** sound effects, **Second** music, and **Third** voices.

First: Sound Effects

Sound effects underline the action and they are usually added to the final picture. They correspond to visual exaggeration - the cartoon effect. Impossible situations are reinforced with sound effects. Sound effects are used punctually to reinforce and accentuate the film's action, and to help to get the message across. Sound effects can suggest an off-screen action. The main action, for instance, a battle or an accident, takes place off-screen. On the screen, we see already the next scene, or secondary effects, like a cloud of dust or objects flying across the screen. In this case, the sound reinforces the secondary effects and underlines the main action, which is off-screen.

Second: Music

Music is a good medium to transport thoughts and emotions. Music creates the mood of a film. Emotions and memories are carried more by sound and smell than by visuals. The sound of a music box can bring you straight back to childhood. The sound of an accordion makes you long for or brings memories of love. The sound of a flute and waves brings peace to your heart. The sound of hard rock and techno gets you into an urban ambiance. Folk music carries the audience to a particular country or culture.

Synchronised music is music to which the film action has been made by analysing the sound track. The action follows the beat of the music, like dancers in a ballet.

Post-synchronised music is made to accompany the film's action and to create a mood. Music can be used to illustrate the sound of wind, machines or stampeding elephants. It can be an emotional sound floor over the whole film or a short punctuation.

Wild track is the name of a sound, often a combination of sound effects, with music and voices. The sounds are matched more or less to the action, but not necessarily synchronised.

Contrapuntal sound is sound having rhythm, meaning, and direction running counter the picture.

Third: Voices

Lip-sync dialogue spoken by a character is a pre-recorded voice track that is analysed so that the drawings will fit the lip movement of the character precisely. In lip-sync dialogue, the animated character actually speaks the words of an actor. To make the content believable, the character has to express the content with facial expressions and body language.

Commentary or voice-off should not be used so much to explain the film's action as to give supplementary information and a new dimension to the film. Voice-off works to provide comments and guide you through the film. Contrapuntal voice-off can add a new and entirely different dimension to the visuals.

The voice of *Claude Pieplu* in the *Shadoks* has dramatically influenced this television series and not to forget the masterful interpretation of *Peter Ustinov* for *Prince John* and *King Richard* in *Walt Disney's* feature film *Robin Hood*.

It is not an exaggeration to say that half of the film's impact comes from the soundtrack. Sound draws, just like a spotlight, the attention of the audience to a particular part of the screen. Sound can be used to describe and replace, to some extent, a whole invisible background.

1102_Visual Scores_Sound Patterns

Animators like to look at their work as visual music or musical pictures. Ever since the very first animated film productions, it was clear that there was a strong relationship between sound and animation. Animation mirrors the nature of musical expression. The soundtrack is the backbone and the structure of time.

Animation and sound share many common elements. Animation and music have a basic mathematical foundation. They both move forward and at a given speed. They both disappear from our visual and audio perception when the film or the tape stops running. Tempo is related to visual beat, while sound effects correspond to visual exaggeration and orchestration relates to the overall mood. Music patterns are like visual repetitions and rhythm. Repetition in music is like cycling in animation. Just as the composer controls the music note by note, the animator controls the visuals frame by frame.

Charles Blanc-Gatti, the *painter of sounds*, made the animated film *Chromophony* in 1939. In the title sequence we can read the following:
*Chromophony is devoted to the bringing together of sounds and colours. For a long time, poets, musicians, and painters had a presentiment of a relationship between sound and colour. Physicists have told us that both have a common basis: vibrations. Today, through the radio, we can **hear** music; tomorrow, by means of television, we shall **see** music.*

In the film *Chromophony*, Charles Blanc-Gatti transposed the music of *The Entry of the Gladiators* by Czech composer **Julius Ernest Wilhelm Fucik** (1897) into an animated musical picture.

Charles Blanc-Gatti was not only a *painter of sound* but also an *animator of sounds*.

Fucik's music gives the structure for colours and shapes, and also the structure of time. Charles Blanc-Gatti has carefully analysed the soundtrack and made the visuals match perfectly with the soundtrack.

Time is one of the raw materials the animator has to deal with. Time is something abstract, invisible to our eyes, and we need some support to get our hands on the invisible. Sound and music are strong structures for time. Sound can be used to make drawings in time or to visualize the timing. Music helps the animator to find solutions for problems of timing and rhythm. Music can be *timed down* to make a movement breakdown or a visual score, very much like a musical score.

Dramatic Intensity

Time

Music generates ideas and movement. An idea can be born straight from the sound-track, without passing through written words. Take any piece of music, close your eyes, listen to it intensely, and you will see pictures. Shapes, forms and colours will come to your mind. You will make your own interior cinema. Take a brush, ink, and a long sheet of paper, listen over and over again to the music, and then draw what you see in your mind. Take another brush with another colour. Listen to the same music and draw on top of it again what you see and feel. Make the same exercise with your eyes closed. The result is a visual score, a musical pattern, a structure for the passing of time, perhaps similar to the soundtrack waveform in the timeline of a computer editing software, or to an optical soundtrack on a film. By applying a timeline to these inspirational drawings you will have a structure of time.

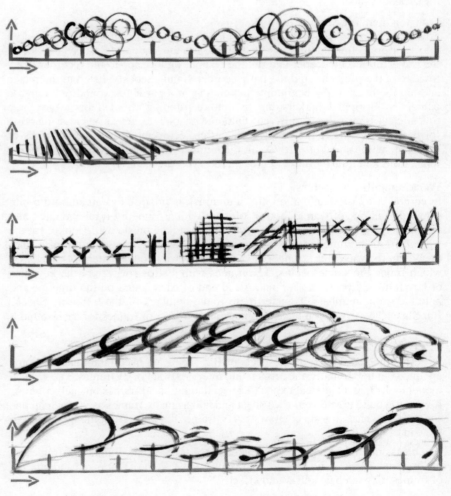

1103_Animating to Sound
_Analysing Sound Track

Animating to pre-recorded sound is a must for lip-sync animation, in order to match the mouth positions with the recorded words. As a matter of fact, it is much easier to match a picture to the sound than the reverse. The same method is used when the visuals have to fit the sound perfectly, as for animated songs, or simply if the music is the principal element of the film.

To analyse a piece of music you should listen to it several times to get a feeling for the mood and beat of the part you would like to animate. You will have to listen to the soundtrack over and over again to discover the *heartbeat* of the track, the important sound effects, the turning points of the music, and the beginning and ending of voices.

If the music is composed especially for your film, you may ask the composer to give you the score. This *written music* sheets gives you a precise idea of what happens - invisibly - on the tape.

Working with Film
Depending on your technical equipment, there are several ways to analyse a soundtrack. The working procedure is identical to analysing a dialogue for lip-sync animation *(see Chapter 1016_Dialogue_Lip-Synchonised Animation)*

Perforated Sound Tape
The recorded sound can be transferred to perforated sound tape. Run this tape through an editing table or synchroniser and mark with a coloured grease pencil or a permanent marker the beat of the music or the beginning and ending of a particular sound straight on the tape. Repeat this with different coloured pencils to get an average timing. The spots noted are the keynotes or key frames. Now count the frames between the spots on the perforated tape and transfer these figures on the exposure sheet.

Quarter-inch Tape and Mini-disk
To analyse a sound from a quarter-inch tape or a mini-disk, put a roll of film leader into your projector and hit the beat straight onto the leader. Make a sync mark on the projector and the leader and put the clapper on the tape to the recorder head. Switch on the projector and the tape recorder simultaneously, listen to the music and tap the beat, or the beginning and ending of a particular sound, with grease pencils or felt-tipped markers directly onto the running film. Do this two or three times, each time using a different coloured marker to get an average marking for every sound. Take the film out of the projector and locate the positions of dialogue, actions, and effects. Count the number of frames between the different indications and transfer these figures on the exposure sheet.

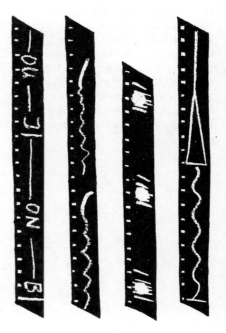

Working with Computers
In computer assisted animation, the soundtrack is imported as an audio file into sound or editing software. Choose software with a frame by frame counter, and set the frame rate to 25 fps. Listen several times to the music while looking at the waveform in the timeline. The waveform is the visual representation of sound; the bigger the wave, the stronger the sound. This way you can identify exactly on which frame the sound occurs. The frames with a strong wave are the keynotes or key frames. Locate the beginning and end of each sound on the timeline and note the frame numbers. Transfer these frame numbers on the Exposure Sheet / Bar Sheet. This gives you the exact place and number of frames for each sound.

Exposure Sheet or Bar Sheet
Different models for Exposure sheets or Bar sheets are used in animation. Some are lined out horizontally and broken into intervals of 24 or 25 frames. The vertical model looks like a classical exposure sheet and holds 50 frames on each column. It is up to you to create your own sheet and add as many frames as you can on one sheet. In any case, the sheet shows every frame of sound, from the beginning to the end of the film.

The beats and effects have to be transfered according to the number of frames on the exposure sheet in the beat column. This gives you the exact place and number of frames for each beat and sound effect.

Exposure sheet Bar sheet	Title	**JOURNEY**			Sq no **03** Sc no **07**		Sheet no **01**	
Music Description	Frames	Beat	Music Description	Frames	Beat	Music Description	Frames	Beat
	1 2			1 2			1 2	
DRUM	3 4			3 4			3 4	
	5 6			5 6			5 6	
CYMBAL	7 8			7 8			7 8	
	9 **1**0			9 0			9 0	
	1 2			1 2			1 2	
	3 4			3 4			3 4	
	5 6			5 6			5 6	
DRUM	7 8			7 8			7 8	
	9 **2**0			9 0			9 0	
KEEP BEAT	1 2			1 2			1 2	
	3 4			3 4			3 4	
	5 6			5 6			5 6	
FADE OUT	7 8			7 8			7 8	
	9 **3**0			9 0			9 0	
	1 2			1 2			1 2	
CYMBAL	3 4			3 4			3 4	
	5 6			5 6			5 6	
	7 8			7 8			7 8	
	9 **4**0			9 0			9 0	
	1 2			1 2			1 2	
DRUM	3 4			3 4			3 4	
	5 6			5 6			5 6	
	7 8			7 8			7 8	
	9 **5**0			9 0			9 0	

Animagination Robi Engler

Exposure sheet Bar sheet	Title			Sq no Sc no	Sheet no

Music Description	Frames	Beat	Music Description	Frames	Beat	Music Description	Frames	Beat
	1 2			1 2			1 2	
	3 4			3 4			3 4	
	5 6			5 6			5 6	
	7 8			7 8			7 8	
	9 0			9 0			9 0	
	1 2			1 2			1 2	
	3 4			3 4			3 4	
	5 6			5 6			5 6	
	7 8			7 8			7 8	
	9 0			9 0			9 0	
	1 2			1 2			1 2	
	3 4			3 4			3 4	
	5 6			5 6			5 6	
	7 8			7 8			7 8	
	9 0			9 0			9 0	
	1 2			1 2			1 2	
	3 4			3 4			3 4	
	5 6			5 6			5 6	
	7 8			7 8			7 8	
	9 0			9 0			9 0	
	1 2			1 2			1 2	
	3 4			3 4			3 4	
	5 6			5 6			5 6	
	7 8			7 8			7 8	
	9 0			9 0			9 0	

1104_Post-Synchronisation_Dubbing

In animated filmmaking, there are two ways to match sound and images. One way is to match the picture to the pre-recorded soundtrack by analysing the soundtrack and creating the visuals according to this analysis.

The other one is to add sound to the finished film by post-synchronisation. This is done by recording the effects, music, or voices while watching the animation play. This method has been used ever since sound film was invented.

Synchronised music and sound effects give more impact to any animated film. In continuous recording with video or film, the sound is generally synchronised with the picture because the recording is done simultaneously. In animation, however the sound is usually recorded separately and synchronised to the picture with the help of editing facilities.

Dubbing
This is the term for the post-synchronisation of lip-sync dialogue. The basic conditions for dubbing are to have the film with the original lip-sync recording and the written text of the language in which the dubbing will be made. The actor watches the film and speaks the new version over the original one. Usually the actor makes two or three takes to be in accordance with the original. The sound engineer adjusts the final take to precisely match the lip movement.

Working with Film
For animation recorded with film, the finished film needs to be projected and the sound is recorded on magnetic tape. The magnetic support can be of perforated magnetic film, a quarter inch tape *6.3 mm* or a mini-disk.
In order to synchronize sound and picture, the sound has to be recorded with a co-ordinated starting point. Every film has at its beginning a visual universal counting leader. On the last frame of this countdown there is a short and sharp sound *one thousand hertz*. This is the clapper or synchronisation point for image and sound. For sound recording while watching the film, the projector or the editing table has to be isolated from the recording room, in order not to record the noise of the film running through the machines. Several takes are made and numbered, until you feel you have a good recording. The good takes are selected and the best one is edited into the film.

Working with Computer
In computer assisted animation, the sound recording procedure is quite similar to working with film, yet technically much easier to synchronize sound and images. The picture file is imported into one of the editing programs and a microphone is connected to the computer. In the program you choose audio capture and the sound is recorded through the microphone while you watch the picture. Several takes are made, and after selection, the best one is imported and edited using the same program.

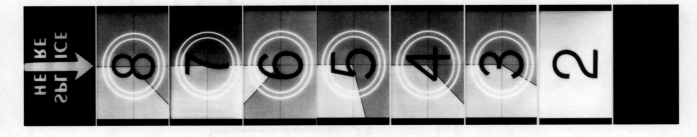

1105_Creating and Recording Sound Effects

The better you hear, the more you see is what a good friend and sound engineer told me. It's true. The clearer things are on the soundtrack, the better the visuals will be accepted. Creating sound effects for the film might be just that little boost the visuals need to be understood by the audience.

Most of the sound effects can be found on CD-samplers or on sound software. It is your choice to create and record music and sound effects yourself instead of using existing recorded sounds. If you are short on ideas, just listen to the late *Spike Jones* (1912-1965) and his *City Slickers* orchestra!

In filmmaking, the sound effects are usually the last thing that is done, and time for sound effect recording is often limited. Work has to be organized and the roles of each musician clearly defined.

Don't forget that there is not only an instrumental but also a vocal approach possible. Even if not everybody has the voice of *Maria Callas*, your mouth and nose can create genuine sound effects. High pitched soprano or deep bass sounds are wonderful to create all the BRRR-CRACCLOMP-CLICK-CLICK-TWANG-WHOOP-WHAPETY-WHAPETY-WHAPETY WHAP-BANG-BANG-BOING-BOOM-SPLASH-NYAHH-NYAHH…

Before recording, make an inventory of all sound instruments available, and get familiar with the possibilities of each one. This inventory of sound makes you conscious of the aspects of each instrument, as well as the possibilities of the musicians.

The recorded pieces can be played back at different speeds; slowed down or speeded up, with echo or reverberation, or played in reverse to find out the different possibilities and limits of the technical equipment.

See what you can do with the recording system itself, playing nearer or farther away from the microphone. Record on separate tracks and play back both tracks at one time.

The general mood and atmosphere of the sounds to be made must be discussed and a "dry run" can be made beforehand. The instruments must be placed according to their force and importance nearer or farther from the microphone. The position of the microphone in recording sound effects is most important and can play a creative part in the recording. Before the sound starts, an announcement must be made on the tape in order to come clear on the editing table, including the *Name of the scene* and the *Number of the take*. Example: *Scene Two, Take Two....*

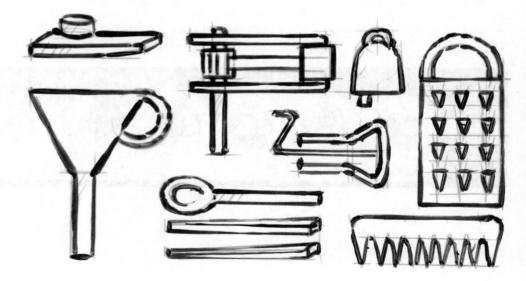

Recording and Synchronisation of Sound Effects.

Post-synchronisation is when the sound is added to the finished film, which is done by recording the effects, music, or voices while watching the animation play. The film and tape are run and all parts concerning that scene are recorded. The sound is then played back, synced with the picture. A second take or a third and fourth are made until the result is satisfactory. The good takes are noted and only these are transferred to perforated sound tape or imported into editing software.

A sound effect instrument is just about anything producing some sort of sound. This starts, of course, with the mouth and the hands. A lot of good sound instruments can be found among kitchen utensils: spoons, forks, graters, coffee mills, etc. Another good and cheap source of sound effect instruments is a children's toy shop: drums, rattles, bells, xylophones, mouth drums, flutes, horns, etc. In music shops you may find items like mouth harps and bird callers.

In addition to instruments, a number of sounds can be produced by playing around with the tape recorder itself. Try out old takes by playing them backwards, speeding them up, or slowing them down.

This list of the following sound effects and how to make them is, of course, far from complete. Every animator has his own tricks and the same sound can be made in more than one way. The important thing is to get started, and then everybody will surely find a whole collection of rubbish that can hardly be used for anything else but sound effects. A good collection of sound effect instruments can be cheap or cost you a small fortune, according to which flea market or antique shop you choose for your purchases. Anyway, it's fun to collect and play around with, creating just that unusual bit of sound nobody could do like you.

Effect

Material needed

Rain
Pour water out of a watering can into a water basin.

Watering can, Water basin

Heavy Rain
In addition to the above, pour lentils or dry rice into a cardboard cover or box.

Lentils, Rice, Cardboard

Tropical Rain
Put an effervescent tablet *for example: Alka Seltzer* in a glass of water. Record it with the microphone very close. Replay at lower speed.

Effervescent tablet

Ocean, Waves
Put lentils or rice in a cardboard box lid and balance the lid from side to side in the rhythm of waves.

Rice, Cardboard box

Thunder
Shake a thin sheet of metal copper or brass in a jerky movement according to the thunder strikes. Record twice the speed or play back half the speed.

Sheet of thin metal

Wind
Hold your hands in the form of a shell in front of your mouth and blow.

Your own Hands

Explosion or Earthquake
Blow air into a paper bag and burst it with your hands. Keep rubbing the paper after the burst. Replay about four times slower for explosion and about eight times slower for earthquakes.

Paper bag

Fire
Crinkle a plastic bag or piece of cellophane near the microphone. In addition you can crack a wooden matchbox between your fingers near the mic.

Cellophane, wooden Matchbox

Gunshot, Cannon Shot, Dynamite or Explosion
Hold one end of a wooden ruler flat on a hard surface, pull it up at the other end and let it snap down at high speed. Record twice the speed or play back half the speed for a cannon shot and four or eight times slower for a dynamite explosion.

Wooden Ruler

Sound of Horses
Take two half shells of a coconut and strike one to another in the rhythm of a horse's steps. The sound of the nostrils is made by breathing near, but not into, the microphone. For hooves on pebbles simply hit a pile of gravel or rice with the coconuts.

Two half shells of coconut
Pile of gravel or rice

For the sound of hooves on grass, use a carpet to hit on. If no coconuts are available you can replace them with two empty yoghurt cups.

Carpet
Coconut or empty Yoghurt cups

For the sound of galloping horses, sit down on a chair and strike alternatively your chest and your knees with the palms of your hands in the rhythm of a horse's gallop.

Your own Hands and Body

Rowing a Boat
Move the water in a bucket with the palms of your hands in the rhythm of paddles touching the water. Somebody else moves an old hinge to-and-fro in the same rhythm.

Water bucket, old Hinge

Diving or Swimming
Hit the water surface with one half of a coconut shell.

Water basin, half shells of Coconut

Heartbeat
Take your handkerchief and pull it, holding two corners, with sharp strokes near the microphone at the rhythm of heartbeats. There are 70 heartbeats every minute which makes one beat every 21 frames.

Handkerchief

Birds Flying
Shake a big handkerchief, folded in a triangle, near the microphone.

Handkerchief

Birds or Mice
Turn a cork on a wet glass surface. Different bird callers can also be found in toy shops, music shops or sports shops specialising in hunting equipment.

Cork and glass surface

Cricket or Locust
Snap the small teeth of a comb with your fingernails near the microphone.

Comb with small teeth

Frog
Snap the broad teeth of a comb with your fingernails and play it back half speed.

Comb with broad teeth

Human Steps
Hold a chopstick or a wooden ruler in the middle between your fingers and strike alternately one end or the other on different surfaces, according to the step desired.

Chopstick or Wooden ruler

Another method is simply to sit on a chair and record your own footsteps marking time on different surfaces. Use a pair of old shoes with leather soles to get the right *tapping* effect.

Pair of old shoes with leather soles

For human steps in a forest or on leaves, step on a bunch of magnetic tape or a pile of plastic bags.

Bunch of magnetic tape or
pile of plastic bags

For steps on gravel walk on lentils or rice in a cardboard box. For steps in mud, put the gravel in a basin and add some water.

Cardboard with rice, Water basin

For steps in snow or sand, squeeze a linen bag filled with starch to the rhythm of steps. If you can't find starch, use one of those moist absorbing bags you can find in most optical instrument packing.

Bag filled with starch

1106_Editing_Compositing _Image and Sound

Animated films are made in the heads of the animators and not on the editing table. If the visual concept is carefully worked into storyboard and layout, the editing should not be a big problem. But even then, editing is a job on its own and needs some skill and equipment.

Working with Film

If you happen to have a professional editing table, the whole job is a piece of cake. If not, the basic equipment includes a film viewer for looking at the picture, two pairs of rewinders for holding the reels of the film, and a splicer for joining whatever you cut. There are two different splicer types. One uses glue and the other adhesive tape. The tape model is usually used for editing work prints. Make sure to put the adhesive tape on both sides of the film, if you want it to run smoothly through the projector. The glue model is used by the lab to edit the negative cutting.

The first step in editing is viewing the film. Have a quiet look at the whole film and judge the work. Then make a rough cut by joining all the scenes in the right order. Continue by removing the unnecessary scenes. Keep them however - you never know if you'll change your mind.

Editing sound and image needs more equipment and skill. If you have a editing table with picture and soundtracks, you are well-equipped for the job. If not, what you need, in addition to the viewer, is a synchroniser with a sound head and amplifier. A sound splicer, or a pair of anti-magnetic scissors, and special sound splicing tape is also required.

The film and the perforated sound tape are run through the synchroniser. A start mark is made at the beginning, and the sound and picture are then edited to match each other.

When sound and image are synced from beginning to end, both are sent to the laboratory, where for the 16mm format there are two possibilities: COMMAG or COMOPT prints. With the first method the perforated soundtrack is transferred to the magnetic strip of film and you receive a sync COMMAG print. For COMOPT prints, an optical image of the soundtrack is made on clear film and printed on the edge of the film. For 35mm prints there is no choice: only COMOPT is available.

Working with Computers

In computer assisted animation, pictures and sound files have to be imported into an editing/compositing program. The files have to be formatted in order to be accepted by a particular program. Picture files usually comes in PICT and JPEG format and editing programs normally accept AIFF or WAV sound files.

In digital production, this is done in a compositing program by using the various possibilities offered by filters, transitions, and visual effects. Just to name a few: dissolves and inverts, pushes and slides, wipes and spins, blurs and ghost crystallising and pointillising, solarising and texturising... there's no limit to ...isings !

For your own drawings and scraps.

1200_Teaching and Learning Animation

You always teach what you would like to learn, and in the way you would have liked to learn it. Without doubt, this is the driving motor for every teacher. Without this motivation, teaching would be boring and the students would turn their back to the subject.

When I was first asked to teach animation, I didn't really know how and where to start. All I knew was how I learned myself - that is, by doing it, by making mistakes, and by doing it again. I still believe in this trial-and-error method.

This is why I like the fast and direct animation techniques and recording with computer programs. Only when the student can see his drawings or cut-out pieces flicker over the screen does the learning process begin. Before that, it is all myth and black magic.

I have been interested in animation ever since I was a kid. But simply watching films and reading books did not make animation any easier to learn. I became a graphic artist, and only after knocking around in advertising agencies for ten years did I feel that old stirring again. I then started to paint on old film stock and move around bits of paper in front of a borrowed camera. Only after these experiences, I decided to take animation classes in art school and start a new professional life from scratch.

Today, animation has entered most of the art schools. There is an international association for teaching animation and animation classes and workshops are offered just about anywhere from Universities to Vacation camps. Tomorrow, animation will enter Primary schools and Kindergartens, and this is where future animators will be born!

1201_Teaching Animation in School: Why ?

by Nicole Salomon

Learning to Read and Write Images and Sounds

Our epoch is the age of images: comic strips, advertisements, television, movies, video games, virtual reality… submerge and fascinate the younger generations.

Moving images are champions in the land of consumption, but little has been done to prepare the primary consumer - the children - for this flood of images. Nobody prepared them to face, judge, appreciate, use, and master the images to which they are exposed.

The apprenticeship in traditional reading and writing happens at school; the understanding and creation of images has to be learned at school as well.

In the avalanche of images discharged daily by television, animated cartoons are best known to children. Cartoons are part of animated films, a special cinematographic technique creating movies frame by frame. Being entertainment and art at the same time, this kind of cinema is so unknown that it has been classified once and for all as movies for kids. This classification has allowed the genre to produce childish, stupid, and aesthetically poor films in great quantities.

Reading Animation

Now, there are animated films that are pure masterpieces of art. It is urgent that young people get to know these films and learn to appreciate an art that is contemporary to them. They have to know how to *read* these films.

Writing Animation

Animated films are also a marvelous medium of expression, using forms, rhythm, time, and movement all at the same time. It is urgent that young people learn to *write* animation, to express what they feel at an age when they have not yet mastered the written and spoken language of adults.

The animated film, basically non-verbal, is a privileged form of communication. At times when everybody talks about getting people closer to each other and national frontiers are falling, it is important to communicate directly without the handicap of a language barrier.

Initiation

Initiating schoolchildren to animated filmmaking means to make them understand the phenomenon of retina persistence and make them feel all the magic of the cinema by demystifying it, because it is based upon an optical illusion. It is also an opportunity to make them discover and construct the optical toys of pre-cinema: folioscope and phenakistiscope – the *pioneers* of real cinema.

From this point on, which is also an initiation to the phenomenon of cinema in general, the class could go into scriptwriting, storyboarding, and the making of a short animated film.

Whatever will be the animation technique, you will have to tell a story, to have imagination, and to exercise the oral and written expression according to the age of the audience. Next, you will have to visualize the script's content, which is the moment to concentrate; chattering and gossiping is no good for visual expressions. You will have to concentrate on the essential elements and find symbolic and expressive pictures to visualize the content. It is a privileged moment when youngsters can draw on their world of images and become conscious about the meaning of what they see.

Another important moment is the choice of the animation technique. Here, the advice of a professional animator is most welcome. You will have to choose the technique that best fits your project and the age of the participants.

Whether it is animated drawings, clay, cut-outs, silhouettes, or puppets, each technique requires some manual work. It is in this handy-craft part where the creativity of the children explodes. It is the creative use of scissors, glue, tape, and rags that makes animated filmmaking so appreciated by children.

The technical and financial barriers you will meet when you go into real-life filmmaking are a lot smaller when you work with the frame by frame technique. Most of the equipment can be made out of scrap materials.

Arithmetic

Arithmetic plays an important role in animated filmmaking. Starting with the fundamental twenty-four frames per second, you will have to figure out the time and space for each image. You will have to make calculations, use a chronometer, and finally measure the abyss that separates the time it takes to make the film and the time you see the illusion of it on the screen - a phenomenon which will always astonish beginners…

Group Work

The making of an animated film is a multidisciplinary activity and is therefore a group work. Every participant is not only responsible for an individual part of the film, but also for the group part. The challenge is to make the best film, not to be better than the other participants. There is no competition, but rather a motivation to create a group work without any good or bad notes.

Recording the Images

The recording of the images with film or computer is an important step in the production procedure. The young animators will learn to handle the cinematographic technology, and in a practical way to overcome the fear of technical equipment.

First Screening

After recording comes the screening. It is an unforgettable moment for everyone to watch for the first time the artwork they created become alive. It is pure emotion, as there is no comparison whatsoever with the most perfectly written exercise, and no comparison with the most beautiful drawing on a sheet of paper.

Sound Recording

Sound recording is a moment of both research and amusement. At this stage, the participants will understand the importance of sound in animated filmmaking. Bringing sound to the images is more than just adding value; the successful mixture of sound and images is the heart of any animated film.

Projection and Presentation

The final satisfaction comes when the film is projected to a public – parents, friends – who will react to the film and make the filmmakers conscious about the power of communication in animated films.

Just Do It…

Hopefully, there will be some teachers who are ready to initiate themselves to the frame by frame technique and share the adventure of animated filmmaking with their students. They will experience the richness and the pedagogical prolongation of this *modern activity*. Teachers should not hesitate to ask for collaboration with professional animators in order that the pedagogical experience will go along with another important moment: contact with artists.

Nicole Salomon
Co-Founder of the AAA Workshop
in Annecy, France

Co-Founder of the International
Animated Film Festival
in Annecy, France

Honorary General Secretary of ASIFA
International Association of
Animated Films

1202_Workshop Philosophy

There is a saying: *Tell me and I will forget, show me and I will remember, let me do it and I will understand.*

This holds true for particants of animation workshops, to develop their skills and competences. In animation workshops, participants surely learn to animate, but the principal goal of those films is not so much the result but the making of it. The participants have to master the subject before they can make the film and will learn to express themselves in a creative and non-verbal way.

One of the aims of a workshop is to offer a basic knowledge of how to make animated films. This is why the use of fast, direct animation techniques such as cut-out, clay, and drawing-on-paper animation should be privileged.

The participants are encouraged and given every chance to express themselves creatively; they alone decide on the content and graphic style of their film work.

The idea of an *Animation Workshop* rather than an *Animation Cours*e comes from a certain philosophy as to what positive group work entails. It also takes into consideration the time necessary to install the technical equipment and to get all the participants started on their projects. Of course, much depends on the system your workshop has to fit into, but if you have a choice, it should be planned for several consecutive hours, days or weeks.

Today's major difficulty in organising workshops at public schools is not so much technical or financial; it's to find time slots in the busy curriculum of the students. Today, students - from primary school to university - are very, very busy. The lessons are short and their planning is overloaded with *must* activities like mathematics and languages. To make room for these *musts*, cuts are made in the visuals arts and music. Math and languages are privileged because our schools have to prepare kids for the competition they will face after their years in school. Every pedagogue knows that this policy is leading our society straight into the wall. Today's administrators responsible for education forget that deep knowledge and success in life requires more intelligence than intellect.

Whatever the duration of the workshop, participants should not be disturbed by professional or private affairs. It's a good idea to move the participants out of their daily context and make the workshop somewhere on a *lonely island*. It is significant that all good training centres are away from production areas, and most often in the countryside. There are no office hours, and arrangements can be made for those who want to work longer into the evening.

The workshop requires every participant to handle the different stages of production. The result of every workshop is always a short animated film. It's not so much the final result as the practical work involved in making a film that is important. It is only through *doing* that participants learn the production procedures involved in animated filmmaking.

1203_Workshop Organization

Participants' Who's Who
In a workshop where participants don't know each other beforehand, the best way to start is with a *Who's Who*. Each person will tell why he or she came to the animation workshop (and not to the yoga course next door). After this, there is a visit to the workshop. The technical equipment is, of course, already set up and the basic materials are ready.

Introductory Film Screening
At this point, the teacher could show one of his personal films, because the participants would surely like to know who is the person in front of them. Next comes a film or two which will encourage and stimulate the participants, even if the film is far beyond what the participants will ever achieve during the workshop.

Synopsis of Animation Techniques
A film showing examples of the different techniques saves a lot of time and answers many of the FAQ's (Frequent Asked Questions) in a non-verbal way. The projection of the synoptic chart of all the animation techniques will open the eyes and minds of participants to the incredible variety of animation techniques.

Brainstorming the Subject
The first activity for participants is to brainstorm the subject of the film they are going to make. Participants who work on their own ideas are more motivated. Brainstorming can be done by the group or individually.

Collecting Ideas
Participants write or draw their ideas on paper or on the black or white board. This activity should not take more than one hour. After a first table round-up, take a break and let the ideas come *down to earth*.

Selecting Ideas
At this point, the expressed ideas have to be discussed and finally selected. The one who is responsible for the workshop should not hesitate to strongly support the idea which seems the best one to be realized under the given conditions.

Storyboarding
This is the moment when participants will get real hands-on experience and can prove their ability to visualize ideas. Drawing ability is not the foremost problem. Storyboard drawings can be quite rough. What we need are communicative drawings, especially for a project which is not made in the animated drawing technique. The important thing is to show the content and the continuity of the film. Preparation of the storyboards takes quite some time. Allow for this time, for it is at this stage that all the factual errors, lack of continuity, and lack of clear thinking should be discovered and corrected.

Time Factor
Special care must be taken that every participant has time to finish whatever he or she plans on the storyboard. Rather than let beginners go into a feature length film with three main characters, twenty secondary characters and a few animals, tell them to choose something simple like a dancer with a repeat movement or the morphing of forms and shapes.

Creation of Artwork
Once the storyboard is accepted, the participants will create the artwork. For those who go into animated drawings, they will have to prepare the drawing board with pegs and indication of field sizes, punch all the paper and cels, and then start the long process of drawing. After finishing and checking the key drawings, the inbetweens can be made. If there is time for colouration, it can be done; but it does not matter if there is no colour. The important thing is to make the drawings move.

For those who are doing direct animation techniques, such as clay or powder animation, they will have to make the objects they want to animate, create the background, set up the lights, and choose the camera angle and framing.

Recording the Images
Recording of direct animation starts right after the objects and the set are ready. Since the creative animation work happens in front of the camera, the recording time will last much longer than for pegbar animation.

When the drawings for the pegbar animation are finished, they are checked and an exposure sheet is established taking advantage of cyclic movements as much as possible. The drawing board is then brought over to the animation stand for recording. If you are recording with film, the exposed film stock should be taken to the lab directly after shooting. It is important that the participants see the result as soon as possible.

First Screening
Working with film requires some time for the film to be processed in the film laboratory. When the processed film comes back from the lab, there is an exciting and anxious moment for the participants - and the teacher - when they see for the first time the life they have blown into the objects and drawings. It's also the moment to discover whether or not everything worked on the technical side. Was the shutter open? Was the aperture right? Did the lab do a good job? You can never be grateful enough to people working in the laboratory for doing their job professionally.

If any of the above elements - and there are many more - failed, you should go through the previous chapters again. An animator must be ready for re-recording a thousand times. Let's hope the first shooting is the good one; there is a saying that when you shoot twice you're bound to shoot three times or more!

No such problems – but many more others – come up when the recording is made into computer program. If everything has been fine-tuned, the result can be seen right away, and you can save your anxiety for the next computer set-up.

Editing
If detailed planning has been carefully done in pre-production, the editing of an animated film is usually a piece of cake. A few adjustments may still be necessary - deleting a few frames here and there, or speeding up an action.

Sound Effects
When editing is completed, one can enjoy adding the music and sound effects. There are no rigid rules on how to use sound effects, but remember that the soundtrack contributes to about 50% of the impact of an animated film. Effects and music can be taken from special records, but it's more fun to use homemade sounds which make the participants more aware of the creative role of the soundtrack.

Discussion_Information
Parallel to the practical work, there can be a half-hour lecture every day related to the actual work in progress and to the basic principles of animation.

Exercises: Homework
If the workshop lasts for a few weeks, there will be enough time to give exercises as homework. It also helps to check if the basic principles discussed have been understood. On the following day, the exercises are corrected and discussed.

Film Screening
A good idea is to screen a selection of animated films at the end of the day or on a particular evening of the week. Animated films are a culture of their own, so it's fun to run an *Animated Cinema Club* during the workshop. It is important for future animators to know what is going on in the world of animation.

If your schedule is too tight for film screenings, forget about it. If you have to choose between making your own films or looking at films made by others, the choice is easy...

Books on Animation
Some books on film animation should be made available. They are displayed in the workshop, and participants are encouraged to read them. They can be taken home for bedtime reading or for the weekend.
This manual can be given to the participants page by page, according to the information they need during their works in progress.

Screening of Finished Films_Evaluation

As soon as a film is finished, it is screened in front of all the participants of the workshop. It's a good idea to invite all the people who were involved in the making of the film for this *Happening*. Technicians, administrators, secretaries, typists and the people from the laboratory. They are all interested in seeing what came out of the bits and pieces they have seen at the various production stages. Don't forget to bring friends, moms and dads, and other family members; this makes an audience to react to the film, which has more learning impact on the filmmaker than criticism or praise from a teacher.

After the Workshop...

Hopefully, the participants will be associated with projects that require them to make full use of their newly acquired skills. Workshop participants should be encouraged to teach their knowledge to others.

1204_Workshop Schedules

Here are a few examples of how a workshop can be organized. The examples are schematic because every workshop requires a specific programme taking into account the number of participants, the equipment available, and the overall purpose of the undertaking. The following schedules are meant for basic courses, with participants who are not at all, or only little, acquainted with animation.

Workshops in Six Sessions

This is what you can do when a rigid system obliges you to split up the workshop into separate sessions, afternoons or evening classes:

First Session: Afternoon or Evening

Contact: Participants' *Who's Who*, Presentation of workshop programme and animation techniques used during the workshop, Visit to technical installation, Formation of groups (if any).

Practical work: Brainstorming of film content, script, storyboarding (partly as homework for the next meeting).

Second Session: Afternoon or Evening

Lecture: Information and discussion on basic principles:
0601_Time and Space = Timing, 0602_Guidelines and Spacing Guide
Practical work: Discussion and adaptation of the storyboard,
        Pegbar animation: creation of character and background design,
        Direct animation: creation of character, background or set design.

Third Session: Afternoon or Evening

Lecture: Information and discussion on basic principles:
0603_ Extremes and In-Betweens, 0604_ Rate of Exposure and Action Speed
Practical work: Pegbar animation: Animated drawings.
        Direct animation: Start recording

Fourth Session: Afternoon or Evening

Lecture: Information and discussion of basic principles:
0605_Dynamic Movement, 0606_Action Lines, Strong Poses, Silhouette Test
Practical work: Pegbar animation: Start Recording,
        Direct animation: Continue recording,
Creation and recording of title and credits (it's important for beginners to see their name on the screen)
If you are recording with film, the exposed film stock is taken straight to the laboratory for processing.
In digital production there will be one day more for creating and recording, since there is no waiting for the film to be processed; the results can be seen immediately after each take.

Fifth Session: Afternoon or Evening

Lecture: Information and discussion of basic principles:
0607-Follow-Through and Overlap, 0608_Anticipation, Stretch and Squash
Practical work: Screening of processed film, Editing of the film, Creating and recording of music and sound effects, Editing of sound effects. This editing can also be made by the teacher in between the fifth and the sixth session, since there is not much creative work involved here.
If you are working with film, the lab will make a print with a magnetic sound strip. The sound is transferred with the help of a film projector to the magnetic sound strip.
In digital production, the recording and editing of sound and images is made using computer program

Sixth Session: Afternoon or Evening

Practical work: Screening of finished films with friends and family, Discussion and evaluation of the whole workshop, Screening of animated films made by other animators.

Fix a date for the next workshop !

Weekend Workshop

If the workshop can be organized for a weekend, you probably won't have more actual hours than you had for the six-session course, but the consecutive hours count double. The work of the group will be more efficient because they have the time to get to know each other. Meals can be taken in common and this helps a lot to create a group spirit. After the weekend, one evening during the following week should be reserved for making sound effects and editing and another evening for the screening of the finished film.

Here is how a weekend schedule could look:

Friday Evening
Contact: Participants *Who's Who,* Presentation of weekend programme and animation techniques used during the workshop, Visit to the technical installation, Formation of groups (if any).
Practical work: Brainstorming of content and scenario. Storyboarding can be given as homework for the inevitable sleepless night.

Saturday Morning
Lecture: Information and discussion of basic principles,
0601_Time and Space = Spacing, 0602_Guidelines and Spacing Guide, 0603_ Extremes and In-Betweens , 0604_Rate of Exposure and Action Speed
Practical work: Discussion and adaptation of the storyboard
         Pegbar animation: creation of characters and background design
         Direct animation: creation of characters, background or set

Saturday Afternoon and Evening
Practical work: Pegbar animation: Animated drawings,
         Direct animation: Start recording

Sunday Morning
Lecture: Information and discussion of basic principles:
0605_Dynamic Movement, 0906_Action Lines, Strong Poses and the Silhouette Test, 0607_Follow-Through and Overlapping, 0608_Anticipation, Stretch and Squash
Practical work: Pegbar animation: Start recording,
         Direct animation: Continue recording.

Sunday Afternoon and Evening
Practical work: Pegbar animation: Start recording,
         Direct animation: Continue recording
Creation and recording of title and credits (it's important for beginners to see their name on the screen)
When recording on film, the exposed film stock is taken directly to the laboratory for processing on Monday morning.
Since there is not much creative work involved in the picture editing, this can also be done by the teacher as soon as the film is back from the lab.
In digital production, there will be a half day more for creating and recording, since there is no waiting for the film to be processed; the results can be seen immediately after each take.

An Evening during the Following Week
Practical work: Screening of processed and edited films, creation and recording of sound effects. If you are working with film, the lab will make a print with a magnetic sound strip. The sound is transferred with the help of a film projector to the magnetic sound strip.
In digital production, the recording and editing of sound and images is made using computer program.

Another Evening a Week Later
Practical work: Screening of finished films (make them public). Discussion and evaluation of the whole workshop. Screening of animated films made by other animators.

Fix a date for the next workshop!

One Week Workshop

Just in case some miracle should make it possible to run an animation workshop for a whole week, here is how you can fill up what will be likely the shortest week of your life.

Monday

Contact: Participants' *Who's Who*, Presentation of the week's programme, Visit to the technical installation, Information and discussion on all the animation techniques which could be made during the workshop, Formation of groups (if any).
Practical work: Brainstorming of content, scenarios, storyboarding, Choice of the animation techniques for this workshop

Tuesday

Lecture: Information and discussion of basic principles:
0601_Time and Space = Timing, 0602_Guidelines and Spacing Guide.
Practical work: Discussion and adaptation of storyboards,
          Pegbar animation: Creation of drawings,
          Direct animation: Creation of characters, backgrounds and sets

Wednesday

Lecture: Information and discussion of basic principles:
0603_ Extremes and In-Betweens, 0604_ Rate of Exposure and Action Speed.
Practical work: Pegbar animation: Creation of drawings,
          Direct animation: Recording of direct animation.

Thursday

Lecture: Information and discussion of basic principles:
0605_Dynamic Movement, 0606_Action Line, Strong Poses, and the Silhouette Test.
Practical work: Pegbar animation: Start Recording,
          Direct animation: Continue recording.
Creation and recording of title and credits (it's important for beginners to see their name on the screen).

If you are recording on film, the exposed film stock is taken straight to the laboratory for processing.
Since there is not much creative work involved in the picture editing, this can also be done by the teacher as soon as the film is back from the lab.

In digital production, there will be one day more for creating and recording, since there is no waiting for the film to be processed; the result can be seen immediately after each take.

Friday

Lecture: Information and discussion of basic principles:
0607-Follow-Through and Overlap, 0608_Anticipation, Stretch, and Squash.
Practical work: Screening processed film, Picture editing, Creation and recording sound effects, Sound editing and mixing of sound tracks.
If you are working with film, the lab will make a print with a magnetic sound strip. The sound is transferred with the help of a film projector to the magnetic sound strip.
In digital production, the recording and editing of sound and images is made in computer program.

Friday Evening or Saturday

Practical work: Screening of finished films (make them public). Discussion and evaluation of the whole workshop. Screening of animated films made by other animators.

Fix a date for the next workshop!

1205_Workshop Preparation_Check List

It is important that right from the beginning of the workshop the technical installation is ready and tested. The proper functioning of all equipment is the responsibility of the teaching animator. This means:
Work only with a equipment you know perfectly well
All the recording devices are tested
A stand-by camera or a stand-by computer is available
A stock of light bulbs is ready
Material according to the basic tools list for each technique is at hand

Go through this checklist before the participants arrive.

Checklist of Equipment for Recording on Film

01_Animation tables are set up

02_Lights are installed

03_Field size is indicated on the background or set

04_Cameras are in a fixed position and loaded with film stock

05_Focus is checked and indicated

06_Aperture is checked and indicated

07_Shutter is open and blocked

08_Camera and film tests have been made under these exact conditions

If you are working on film, you should know the film lab and its terms of delivery. If necessary, special arrangements have to be made with the lab in order to have the processed film back the following day.

Checklist of Equipment for Digital Recording on Computer Program

01_Animation tables are set up

02_Lights are installed

03_Field size is indicated on the background or set

04_Cameras are in fixed position and connected to the computers

05_Focus is checked and and put to manual

06_Aperture is checked and put to manual

07_Recording program test has been made under these exact conditions

08_Transfer to editing program is tested

Working with Filmstock
During the Workshop, it is important to go through the checklist once in a while and make sure there is still enough film stock in the camera. Many animators have already exposed carefully the pressure plate of their film camera frame by frame!

Working with a Computer
When recording to computer program make sure to save your work after each scene and make back-ups at the end of the recording.

Equipment for Recording on Film

Image recording
Film camera
Super-8, 16mm, 35mm Film stock
Exposure meter

Animation stand / Tripod
Shadow board
Lights
Spare bulbs
Cables, Multiple sockets

Sound recording
Audio recorder
Headphones
Microphone
Cables and jacks
Sound samples with author's right
FMA freemusicarchive.org

Editing image and sound
Film viewer
Film splicer
Picture and sound leader
Cables and jacks

Projection, image and sound
Film projector
Speakers, cables

Graphic and animation material
Animation board
Glass plates for multi-plane
Lightbox
Office puncher
Masking tape
White drawing paper, 50-60gsm
Tracing paper
Colour paper
Scissors
Cutter
Pencils
Felt pens
Colour pencils

Selection of animated films
Player for Mini-DV, DVD

Equipment for Recording on Computer Program

Image recording
DV camcorder
Computer
Program with stop-motion capture
External Hard disk 120 G
DC cables
Firewire or USB cable

Animation stand / Tripod
Shadow board
Lights
Spare bulbs
Cables, Multiple sockets

Sound recording
Audio recorder
Headphones
Microphone
Cables and jacks
Sound samples with author's right
FMA freemusicarchive.org

Editing image and sound
Computer
Program for editing sound and image
DVD-R, CD-R disks
DVD burner
Mini DV cassettes
Cables and jacks

Projection, image and sound
Video projector / Video monitor
Speakers, cables
DVD player

Graphic and animation material
Animation board
Glass plates for multi-plane
Lightbox
Office puncher
Masking tape
White drawing paper, 50-60gsm
Tracing paper
Colour paper
Scissors
Cutter
Pencils
Felt pens
Colour pencils

Selection of animated films
Player for Mini-DV, DVD

1206_Group Work and Individual Work

This chapter is not about how to set up a production line for the animation industry, but it's an attempt at finding ways of working as a group and achieving a homogeneous result.

Although a personal film is basically an individual endeavour, working together can be stimulating for every animator.

Positive experiences have not only been made during workshops, but also in daily practice. The successful TV serial *What if I had... What if I could...* was made by three independent animators. Thanks to a common plot, the different stories, animation techniques, and styles fit together to produce an enviable result.

Conceptions of Group Films
These are a few examples of principles to obtain a homogeneous result by a group of participants:

01_Relay Principle

02_Common Background Principle

03_Common Object Principle

04_Common Plot Principle

05_Common Soundtrack Principle

06_Common Tools Principle

07_Stories-In-The-Story Principle

01_Relay Principle
Animated Drawings: Pegbar Animation
This is a method to link individual scenes when the pegbar animation technique is used. An example is the metamorphosis of faces one into the other. Every animator draws his or her own portrait and makes a copy of it. The animators then keep their drawings and give a copy to the person sitting next to them. The last participant gives the copy to the first participant. Now everybody has two drawings: his or her own portrait and the one from his or her neighbor.

Participant_01   Participant_02   Participant_03

Participant_04   Participant_05   Participant_X

The next step is to link the two drawings by making a - hopefully funny - transition from one portrait to the other. The minimum of required in-between drawings is nine.

While recording the drawings, attention must be given that the last drawing of each participant's scene is identical with the first one of the following participant's scene. It is understood that this principle works also with any other two identical drawings than faces.

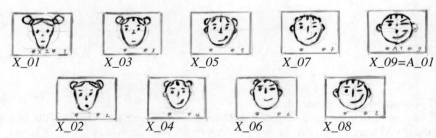

X_01   X_03   X_05   X_07   X_09=A_01

X_02   X_04   X_06   X_08

Direct Animation: Under-the-Camera Animation
The relay principle can also be applied to direct animation techniques. To give clay or powder animation a certain continuity, each person takes over the situation left by the previous animator. The projected film looks very much like a *Exquisite Cadaver* (Surrealists term used for mix and match surprise artwork).

02_Common Background Principle

For cut-out animation or animated objects, a common background can be used to link the different scenes. Each participant animates individual objects in front of the common background.

03_Common Object Principle

The idea is to animate the same object but in different styles and techniques. Think of a simple object, like a milk bottle or a pair of scissors. Look what each animator can make out of it: one animating the real object, the other using drawings of it, another in cut-out or collage, or using powder or clay.

04_Common Plot Principle

The framework for a group project can be a simple but strong subject like fire, water, loneliness, love, happiness, or fear. Every participant treats the same subject from a personal point of view, in an individual style and animation technique. The film will be like opening doors into the same room, but furnished differently.

05_Common Soundtrack Principle

A good soundtrack can also provide a backdrop for a group project. The sound can either be created and recorded by the group, or an existing soundtrack can be used. The soundtrack is analysed and part of it is given to each participant, who works in his or her own style and animation technique. If the soundtrack is strong enough, it will help to achieve a homogeneous result for the whole film.

It makes things even easier if you animate a song. The lyrics of the song are cut into pieces according to the number of participants. The lyrics give the content and the music gives the timing of the film. **Attention**: make sure you can handle the author's copyright of music and lyrics.

07_Common Tools Principle

Whatever principle you use, give the same tools to every participant. This is a must if you want to achieve a homogeneous result with the whole group. You can try to go still further and *limit* the participants to the same kind of pencils, the same kind of cardboard, the same kind of clay, and even the same range of colours.

The participants' first reaction to these restrictions is usually revolt. It is only during working that they discover the stimulating effects of these restrictions, and they will soon forget that they are *limited*.

07_The Stories-In-The-Story Principle

The advantage of this principle is that a group film is achieved and yet every animator can express him or herself individually.

It allows a group of animators to make a film jointly without the rigid division of labour as encountered in the animation industry. Each animator is free to create their own individual story as long as it fits into the group story which provides the backbone of the story. Without the group story, the whole film would become nothing more than small, unrelated sequences, and in fact the difference in style and content of each individual story is usually such that it cannot be understood without the framework of the group story.

The Group Story

The first activity for the group is to brainstorm a story into which individual stories can fit. An example could be a theatre with a curtain: at each rising and falling an individual story starts and ends. Take a TV set: at each change of programme, another individual story begins. Take a picture book: at each turn of the page, there's another story; take an art gallery: each painting has its own story to tell; take an elevator: at each floor the door opens to another story.

A direct animation technique is always used to create the group story and the individual stories are always done in pegbar animation. This permits every participant to learn two different techniques. Furthermore the camera can be used for the direct animation technique while the creative work for pegbar animation is done on the drawing board, away from the camera. Each participant creates a segment of the group story which, after editing, immediately precedes his or her own individual story. The action in the group story happens at the same time and at the same place or at places which can easily be related.

All parts of the group story employ the same animation technique (cut-outs, clay, animated objects, powder, etc.) Once the group film background and characters are prepared, one participant after the other animates one part of the group story while the others are busy drawing their individual stories.

The Individual Stories

Knowing the plot of the group story, each person can fit their own story into whatever story directly precedes it. The action of the individual stories does not necessarily happen in the same place as that of the group story. On the contrary, they all happen in different places. The best result is achieved by setting individual stories in another context, especially since the animation technique is different.

For the individual stories, the pegbar animation technique is always used for the reasons mentioned above, and to help beginners understand and apply the basic principles of animation. This work with pencils and pegbar happens during the shooting of the group story. By the time the direct animation shooting is finished, one of the participant's pegbar animation will be ready for shooting.

The title and credits are made by a participant who has finished his own work. When the film comes back from processing, the editing is done so that every participant's individual film follows their own part of the group film.

Group Story   Individual Story

Group Story   Individual Story

There are, of course, other possibilities or conceptions for group work. Try to invent a new one with the participants. Maybe they don't feel at all like going into a group project and prefer to make individual bits and pieces and leave it at that. However, group work, and particularly the *Stories-In-The-Story Principle*, usually have a stimulating influence on the participants, especially on beginners.

Robi Engler, knows what he is talking about.
He has conducted all sorts of workshops for all sorts of participants, young and old, students and teachers.

The first edition of this book became for me, and for many collaborators of our workshop, a genuine Bible.

Robi Engler, with this precious book, has enlarged and prolonged the world of animation lovers.

This book is made to be studied and re-studied, and be thought over.

Robi Engler sait de quoi il parle,

lui qui a conduit tant d'ateliers —

en direction de tant de publics:

jeunes et adultes, élèves et enseignants

Cet ouvrage est devenu

pour moi et pour de nombreux

collaborateurs de notre Atelier

une véritable Bible.

Robi Engler, avec ce livre précieux,

a su élargir et prolonger le monde

des amoureux, ~~fous~~ du cinéma d'animation.

Un ouvrage, qu'on lit qu'on relit

et sur lequel on réfléchit.

Nicole Salomon